SOMETHING CHANGED

BEN DOBSON

SOMETHING CHANGED

BEEFY, BOADICEA, BRIXTON, BUNTING AND HOW CRICKET HELPED CHANGE THE NATION

pitch

First published by Pitch Publishing, 2025
1

Pitch Publishing
9 Donnington Park,
85 Birdham Road,
Chichester, West Sussex,
PO20 7AJ

www.pitchpublishing.co.uk
info@pitchpublishing.co.uk

A CIP catalogue record is available for this book
from the British Library.

ISBN 978 1 83680 162 7

Typesetting and origination by Pitch Publishing

MIX
Paper | Supporting responsible forestry
FSC™ C016779

Printed and bound on FSC® certified paper in line with
our continuing commitment to ethical business practices,
sustainability and the environment.

Printed and bound in India by Replika Press Pvt. Ltd.

Contents

'The country needed a lift at that time and along came cricket and 1981 and everything changed … it changed my life – and it changed England.'

Ian Botham

By the same author

CHASING RAINBOWS

From Innocence to Purgatory and Redemption as a Compulsive Sports Fan

'A very funny book – I laughed out loud – and very relatable ... Sport can be a strange and frustrating mistress'

Stuart Broad MBE,
ex-Nottinghamshire & England

'Chasing Rainbows ... something we all do. A great read, still smiling'

Neil Fairbrother,
ex-Lancashire and England

TOO GOOD TO BE FORGOTTEN

Three Wise Men From Football's Golden Era

'A loving – and overdue – celebration of three giants of English management'

Jonathan Northcroft,
Chief Football Writer, The Sunday Times

'At last, a football book with its facts right which I can read from cover to cover'

Steve Williams,
ex-Southampton, Arsenal and England

'Ben Dobson has put together an absorbing narrative'

Eric Brown,
Sports Journalists' Association

'Dobson encapsulates the essence of an unforgettable decade. His meticulous research and storytelling prowess make *Too Good To Be Forgotten* a must-read for football enthusiasts, history buffs, and anyone seeking inspiration from extraordinary lives.'

Matt Riley,
goodreads

TAKING THE POSITIVES

A Year of Ben Stokes and England Cricket's Brave New World

'A great diary-based account of a year as a cricket fan. Honest and funny, Ben has a clever style mixing his own love of the game with the ups and downs of a cricket fan.'

Amazon Reviews

For Brian Lyndon, who inspired and

nurtured my love of history

and

for Dad, who did the same for my love

of cricket, the finest of all games.

Acknowledgements

'Some details in life may look insignificant but appear to be vital leitmotifs in a person's life ... People regularly walk down the memory lane of their early youth. The paper boats of their childhood are recurrently floating on the waves of their mind and bring back the mood and the spirit of the days.'

Erik Pervernagie, painter and writer
Paper Boats Forever

A BOOK covering such a broad timescale, not just of sport but of its wider social setting, required significant research and I am indebted to the vast amount of literature I was able to reference and the detail available to me through the archives of the remarkable British Library. A day spent in its phenomenal newsroom in the company of its unfailingly knowledgeable and helpful curators is one to be cherished. The memory lane of my early youth was revisited every time.

Thanks are also due to the various historians and authors who have been there before me and whose work offered valuable insights. Some tomes I return to more than once in the course of the book but I believe with good reason. I make no apology, other than to the man himself, for my dedication to Simon Barnes's *The Meaning of Sport* – it is something of a bible to me and so full of sense and empathy that it is impossible to ignore. I urge you to read it. The incomparable

John Arlott, primarily for cricket, and Duncan Sandbrook, on modern history, are two more favourite mentors.

Finally, a thank you to my publishers at Pitch for their ongoing belief and support. Without their expertise and enthusiasm this would never have made it to the bookshelves.

Frontispiece

Sunday, 2 August 1981

IT'S A broiling hot afternoon. The summer so far, the year so far, in fact the decade so far, don't seem to have offered up many days like this and a beleaguered British public is taking to the gardens, pools and barbecues of the land to soak it in. Some 20,000 of them are packed into Birmingham's Edgbaston cricket ground soaking up the same thing and more; England are about to take the most improbable series lead in Ashes history on the back of a one-man force of nature.

'He's bagged five wickets, he's grabbed a stump!' The exclamation and tone of the perpetually lugubrious commentator Jim Laker are as close to exultant as he's ever likely to get. Extraordinary events beget extraordinary reactions. In this moment Ian Botham, one arm raised to the heavens, the other wielding that stump as a ceremonial sword, seems the embodiment of something approaching a national rebirth and is bringing to a triumphant end a week which will, in time, be seen as the epicentre of a year like no other. Six days previously, in the gloom of the continually dank weather the summer has so far delivered, a young man had become the first and last civilian fatality of the riots which have punctuated the spring and summer across Britain's cities. Twenty four hours later, the bunting and a large swathe of the population had come out to seek some relief, some hope, blind or otherwise, in a display of patriotism absent since the sunny days of the Silver Jubilee four years previously, seizing on a royal wedding as a chance to change the mood. The morning after, England had

begun the fourth Test in Birmingham and now, in glorious heat and sunshine at last, four days on they have secured their second preposterous comeback victory in three weeks to lead the Ashes series. The pomp and circumstance of the wedding, rather than subsiding, are entering their second phase with Edgbaston now a riot of a different hue to those of Brixton, Moss Side or Toxteth – one of Union flags and their peculiarly British sartorial equivalent less visible at Westminster Abbey – the same flag reprised in a pair of shorts. The mood is moving from depression to hope, from national self-deprecation to pride and belief. It feels long overdue.

Prologue

'Cricket, more than any other game, is one of nostalgias.'

John Arlott

ASKING MYSELF at the end what this book is about I realised it is essentially about relationships and how they intertwine. It is about the relationship between our country's sport and the wider culture and society in which it exists, the relationship between mood and reality – how the former, whether it be determined by such national obsessions as the weather, musical and artistic genres or sport, so often presages the latter – and the relationship between the two most iconic British individuals of the timespan it covers, Margaret Thatcher and Ian Botham – not a direct relationship but one of a striking synergy of beliefs, character and fortunes. It is also about opportunities and outcomes – both had opportunities laid before them which influenced their journeys as many of us do; not all of us have the drive and ability to turn those opportunities into life-changing achievements in the way these two central characters were to do. To a degree, it is also about the relationship between the times of 50 years ago and those of today.

Finally, it is about how these elements contributed during the 1970s and 80s to a period of perhaps the most significant change in our country's fundamental character and future direction since the industrial revolution, world wars notwithstanding. And at its heart reside the 12 months of 1981 – the supreme example of the influence of national mood, and that created by the nation's sport, on the sort of change which shapes destiny. It was one of the most remarkable years of the 20th century in every aspect highlighted above, in culture and in politics, littered with seminal, dichotomous events and sliding-doors moments. Its mid-point was a clearly identifiable moment in time in which mood, and much else thereafter, began to shift. It was, too, a momentous year in the history of the game of cricket, that curious British institution, specifically in the form of the England cricket team, the legendary Ashes series it seemingly lost and then won, and the feats of one man which rescued him from the darkest depths to the status of national hero.

Context is everything. At the times when sport seems to matter more than simply in its results, what is happening all around it is of the utmost relevance. This is a book which explores one of the most obvious examples of such a corollary between sport and its society – perhaps, in England at least, the most pronounced in the history of the century. The sport of 1981 in this country – specifically the cricket – is the common thread in this story. There is also a narrative in how the paths of Thatcher and Botham would shadow each other in an almost fanciful way – until the facts of the matter are studied it could be considered the stuff of fiction. Here, therefore, it was the intention to revisit some of the most thrilling and transformational cricket ever played, placing it in the context of what came before and what came after. As an inveterate nostalgist who sees the years in which I grew up as some of the most compelling and metamorphic in our recent history, I found the whole thing fascinating. I hope you might too.

Yes, as one of those sport obsessives who lets that aspect of life dictate rather too much of their own mood, I may be biased. But sport matters – end of story. Or rather beginning of story, otherwise I've just written the most pointless book in history.

PART ONE:

SOMETHING CHANGED

Something Changed

'There are rare moments in history when one man or woman can, almost alone, shape a nation. Now is such a moment.'

Old Moore's Almanack
December 1980

'A profound change came over Britain in the early 1980s'.

Andy Beckett
Promised You a Miracle

'There is a temptation to portray change as inevitable and its advocates as merely those who are best able to articulate it. Yet change, be it political, economic, social or cultural, is put in motion by specific decisions.'

Graham Stewart,
Bang! A History of Britain in the 1980s

CHANGE IS 'put in motion by specific decisions' yes, but also by specific events and specific individuals. In 1981, with a consequence for the rest of the decade and the future direction of Britain, things were put in motion by two particular dictators of change, Ian Botham and Margaret Thatcher – an unlikely combination at first glance but a powerful one on closer examination. What changed first in this singular year within a transformational decade was a national mindset. Both these personalities were clear in their own minds that this was the key to a brighter future and was the thing above all others that they wanted to influence. Graham Stewart contends that, by the end of their careers at the end of the decade 'Britain was no longer a country gripped by a mindset of terminal retreat but was capable of overcoming difficult odds.' Retreat was not a word in the vocabulary of Botham or Thatcher and that new mindset had its source in their own heads before it could be assimilated by their publics. 1981 was a year in which change was anywhere and everywhere and the mood swung from the desperate to the euphoric.

In assessing both the importance of this specific year and the roles of the two gunslingers within it, it is necessary to consider a broader timescale to place it in its proper context and explain its relevance – where it came from and what it left behind, hence the span of this book. The transformation between an inclination to self-deprecation bordering on shame, fatalism or nihilism and a restored pride in the country was a definitive feature of Britain through the 1970s and 80s when the change of communal mood presaged more significant evolution. Some of it happened in the course of a few weeks, some was only to become visible over time. Its chief architects, Botham and Thatcher, would demonstrate by example over the course of their careers that difficult odds were there to be overcome – even those as apparently unassailable as 500-1 against. But 1981 was where it really happened, when something changed.

Lessons From The Past

At the mid-point of the decade, a discredited Conservative government seen by many, including some of its own members as too centrist, too wedded to consensus, hounded by increasingly challenging industrial relations and lacking inspirational leadership, has been ousted in favour of a Labour administration many felt could do little worse. But it begins to dawn that a left-leaning socialist government is perhaps not as in tune with the innate nature of the British electorate after all as rather more radical policies start to bite and the unions are bought off at a price of increasing inflation, economic woes and currency crises. The opposition has elected a new leader to address what it perceives has cost them the election, with a turn to the political right deemed the only way back into the public's affection. A third, minority party is playing a role which confuses the landscape and both the traditional parties. The media is bringing dire warnings of very dark and dangerous days ahead; the country has lost faith in the future and some are even questioning people's right to have a pride in their homeland. The nation's sporting fortunes are one hope of a little relief from the incessant negativity and we continue to pin our faith on England and watch in large numbers in a triumph of hope over expectation.

Is this 2025? It certainly could be. In fact, in this case the portrait is of Britain 50 years earlier, at the start of 1975. As this book neared its completion and its journey to the publisher, the headlines in the newspapers could have come straight from that era. The ever-understated *Daily Mail* front page screams 'UK FACES CRISIS LIKE THE 1970s, REEVES WARNED'; in the *Daily Telegraph,* the editorial subtitled 'We may all be paying the price of the Reeves Premium for a long time' argues that the chancellor's income from punitive and previously camouflaged tax rises in the recent budget, rather than going to the public services the voters would have anticipated are in fact being swallowed up in the increasing payments required to service a national debt which is out of control; the new Conservative leader Kemi Badenoch's interview is headed 'Unions have taken back control in Labour's Britain.'

In his book on the Thatcher era *No Such Thing As Society,* the historian Andy McSmith considers what shifts in public mood and thinking paved the way for both Margaret Thatcher's arrival at 10 Downing Street in May 1979 and the inauguration of Ronald Reagan in January 1981, and allowed them to sustain and dominate the 80s. 'Some saw a sickness in Western democracies … in which individual liberty was being sacrificed to an obsession with social justice.' Does that sound familiar? It may be that we are not far from just the same adjustment today as a stasis and resignation seeps into the public and political consciousness. A close ally of prime minister Keir Starmer, reports the *Daily Telegraph*, has warned 'lots of people are not saying "something must be done" but "nothing can be done"'. That was Britain's mood in the 1970s to a tee. At such times, those for whom 'nothing can be done' is anathema step up. Enter Thatcher and Botham and 1981.

So I found another strand to my narrative before I was done. Although this book is indeed about change and a significant time in the nation's social history, it also has relevance in the here and now – all this has been a reminder that for all the inevitability of change there is also nothing new under the sun. The mirrors of 50 years ago are all around us. What we don't know today is how the addressing of the perceived crisis will play out over the next ten years – how the wheel will be turned. But in what follows perhaps there will be a hint of a lesson from history for our society today.

Sport and Society

'All things are about sport. Or perhaps sport is about all things.'

Simon Barnes
The Meaning of Sport

ALBERT CAMUS, writer and goalkeeper, insisted 'what I most surely know in the long run about morality and the obligations of men, I owe to sport'. And if that's good enough for Albert I suppose it should be good enough for the rest of us.

In the post-war Britain of 1948 people were in need of an escape, a distraction. The relief and celebrations of VE Day in 1945, the Victory Parade of 1946 and the marriage of Princess Elizabeth and Phillip Mountbatten the following year had been replaced by something less palatable: reality. The privations of rationing and the cost of recovery at home accompanied the independence of India which heralded the gradual break-up of an empire and, to some, the end of Britain as they had always known it. The country wrapped itself in sport, and with television still an option available to only a small percentage they flocked to see it live. As would be the case with the return of sport after COVID-19 the following century, the attraction at the time was less in partisanship, though victories would have been welcomed, but simply in the fact that sport was there at all. London's second hosting of an Olympic Games that summer was a resounding success (and an embryonic attempt at the sort of television outside broadcast which would shortly change sport's consumption forever). Huge crowds followed not just domestic football matches (the 83,260 who attended the Manchester United v Arsenal match at Maine Road on 17 January remains the highest-ever attendance at a top-flight football match in England to this day) but greeted Don Bradman's all-conquering Australian cricketers on the first Ashes tour of England for ten years. The Australians were welcomed with great fanfare across the country, with the record for the largest Test crowd in England broken three times in three Tests – attendance records which still stand. To today's generation of cricket followers, the idea of 32,000 people attending a county tour match would beggar belief but that was the recorded number who watched Essex host Bradman's side by the sea at Southend. It was a day which captured the vicissitudes of cricket perfectly, especially for an Englishman. That first day would be the only time on the tour that the Australians were bowled out by the opposition within a day; the issue being that by that time they had scored the small matter of 721 runs. Such were the trials of following English sides against their oldest cricketing foe, and so they were to remain.

For the next five years sport played a huge role in the lives of a people seeking happy release, culminating in the nirvana of the summer of 1953, the Matthews Cup Final at Wembley at its beginning, the coronation of a new Queen a month later and the national celebrations climaxing in the recapture of the Ashes at the Oval after a record period of 18 years and 362 days at its end. Britain was back. Reality was to bite yet again before the end of the year when the Hungarian footballers came to Wembley in November to introduce the English audience to the idea that they might not be in the vanguard of everything after all – sporting and otherwise – in thrashing the home team 6-3. But what the royal wedding and the Ashes had demonstrated that summer was that, more so than in 1948, the television age was upon us and the consumption of major events would be changed for all time. Whereas during the pre- and immediate post-war years sport was hugely attended as an entertainment, shared by those who were *there*, going forward these sporting and cultural moments would become a genuinely national experience shared by the country as one. A great event is something that unites practically everyone. Sport is one of the few things that can truly unite a nation and so it was to prove in 1981. Along with this new notion of shared experience would come an increased capacity to influence mood and the future as never before. It would take another royal wedding and another Ashes to give that phenomenon its most manifest expression.

The summer of 1953 was to be the last for some time in which cricket played such a part in the uplift of the nation's mood. The 50s and 60s might have been a relatively successful period in terms of the national team's results, but the cricket itself was often uninspiring and it never connected in the same way until its mirror image of royal pomp, national renewal and Ashes heroism 28 years later.

That's not to say that Test cricket in that time didn't continue to impact Britain's society. The West Indies' first series victory in England came in 1950, just two summers after the Empire Windrush had landed at Tilbury docks, bringing the first wave of Caribbean immigrants to Britain. The win held a far greater resonance for that diaspora and the people they had left behind than could be gleaned from the simple fact of a 3-1 scoreline. Their countrymen were to lose only one series in the adopted homeland in the next half a century, something that was, over 50 years, to challenge perceptions, change attitudes and contribute in no small part to assimilation. The subsequent victories in 1963 and 1966, adorned by the athletic grace and brilliance of the world's finest ever all-round cricketer, Garfield Sobers, again had a social relevance beyond the scorecards. The former came the year after Jamaica and Trinidad achieved their independence;

the latter acted as an additional celebration for Barbados and Guyana as they too gained their own autonomy that year. The colonists were no longer the masters.

If the 50s and 60s were the decades when Britain 'welcomed' a large number of West Indians into its society, the 70s saw a sharp increase in an Asian immigrant population, spiked particularly by the 27,000 refugees the 'mother country' re-homed on their expulsion from Uganda by its dictator Idi Amin in 1972. A majority of that number were of Indian origin. The challenges of acceptance against a backdrop of suspicion and prejudice were no easier for them than they had been for those from the Caribbean. One thing historical colonialism had given both, however, was a love of cricket which was a part of their identity. India's first-ever series victory in England in 1971 made the same statement for them as had been the case for the West Indians. It was one of ability, of pride and of togetherness and another example of sport's unarguable impact upon a society and the peoples who populate it. Headingley 1981 would make this point again and, considering the state of the country that year, just in time. Bob Willis, the fast bowler who clinched the win which began the redemption remembered that after that game 'friends were telling me that the effect on morale in factories, pubs and offices was astonishing – that incalculable psychological thing …'

It's what sport can do.

How might we define society – particularly when this era's most influential political and social force once famously suggested that no such thing exists? In truth, the assertion Margaret Thatcher made in her *Woman's Hour* radio interview in 1987 is too often taken at face value, discarding the wider context of the conversation. It was an expression of the strong conviction, which would determine her political strategy throughout the 1980s, that it was incumbent on each individual to take responsibility for their route in life rather than to recline on an overblown state. Those who had ambition and were willing to work hard to realise it were her kind of people. In this she had a firm disciple in the country's highest-profile sportsman. Ian Botham had built his career on just such principles, proving that the supposedly elitist national sport of cricket was no insurmountable bastion of privilege to a talented blue-collar aspirant determined to conquer it. So, here I'm considering society in the sense of a community – some form of shared experience and mood common to a large percentage of the nation. The historian Alwyn W. Turner certainly saw it that way, writing of British sport in the early 80s that it was 'something of a brief golden age of sporting achievement, being the one area of public life that offered relief from the gloom … and in terms of sporting inspiration little could rival the performance of the England cricket team in the 1981 Ashes series.' This is the fundamental thread of what follows.

Some might question the depiction of a national rebirth in 1981. After all, Margaret Thatcher was still officially, so the polls advised us, the most unpopular prime minister of the century well into December that year, and plenty of the people living under her premiership felt no direct or immediate sense of an upturn in their lives, so can a pop music renaissance, a wedding and a cricket match be seen as anything more than brief moments in time – oases in a desert yet to be crossed – rather than indicators of lasting change? Moreover, some might consider it glib to credit a sporting moment with a role in one of the country's most significant periods of social evolution. But it is far from fanciful, or an indulgence of the lifelong sports follower, to suggest that sport and society are inextricably linked. As Roger Domenghetti suggested in his book on the impact of sport on 1980s Britain, *Everybody Wants To Rule The World,* the deep connections between sport and the rest of society tend to go unrecognised or ignored, but it doesn't mean they don't exist. John Arlott, the acknowledged doyen of cricket's chroniclers, was more than a just cricket man. A poet and a raconteur, he had an unerring eye which made him a hugely perceptive social commentator possessed of an enviable facility for the right words, whether with the pen or the microphone. Arlott was insistent that sport is bound to change in tandem with the society in which it exists and, in doing so, reflect it. Coming from such a reliable source, I take this as my justification for marrying the cricketing story of the year – and the years before and after – with the politics and culture of those times. In fact, this was one year when a sport – cricket – and the deeds of one of its purveyors, not only reflected but actually *influenced* society and its redefinition in the years ahead. This is where 1981, and specifically Botham's Ashes, stand out and it is no force-fit to consider cricket and Botham as prime movers within a wider story of the development of the country.

If this has any danger of an overplay, I return to the summation of the role of sport within society offered by another personal favourite writer, Simon Barnes. In one sentence he captures the truth of it: 'sport is everything and nothing … a waste of time and something which can enrich all who come into contact with it', his implication being that apparently trivial or not, it still plays a role in our lives more than that of just an idle pastime. Barnes also alludes to the fickle nature of those who follow sport, suggesting we don't see our heroes plain and we prefer to oscillate between undue hope and undue despair. Never more so than in 1981, both in sport and in society, was such a contention so starkly illustrated. Either way, Barnes has no doubt that 'sport is part of the rhythm of national life '. He recalled the British public's embracing of the London Olympics in 2012 'surfing the wave of rising hope as a shared thing, a common experience'. This, too, was the tale of 1981.

And what is sport's attraction anyway? At its heart it is surely about conflict, about stories and about characters as much as it is about results. In other words, we consume sport in much the same way as we consume politics. Barnes sees in humans 'a species of fabulists. We live for the tale, for the revelation of character'. The revelation of some old-school English character was desperately needed in 1981 and in Botham and Thatcher the country found exactly that. The English are often aware of a diffidence within themselves – a sense of embarrassment and apology. That neither Botham nor Thatcher evinced any such traits made them what they were.

The former England cricketer Ed Smith wrote in *What Sport Tells Us About Life* that neither history nor sport is an exact science because both involve human beings and we are unique. People don't agree about the past and don't agree about the weighting of causes and the decisive moments. This is why in a study such as this, when it comes to sport and history most arguments are not about what happened, but what *mattered*. That can inform how that knowledge might help influence responses to the challenges ahead. Whilst this text may not appear in Starmer or Badenoch's red boxes any time soon, this would suggest it might offer them some useful insights.

There is another reason why sport influenced the nation even more at the start of the 80s than it does today – the communal experience of its consumption, particularly via the television. In 1981 the country still existed on a ration of three channels. The limited space for sport (my father was driven to distraction each time the horse racing interrupted the flow of a Test match on the BBC) and the lack of competition for the rights to broadcast them meant that the bigger events were true moments in time, often drawing in those with a limited interest in the sport itself, and the more successful sports people became figures of national recognition. Today we are a more disparate society, particularly in the way we consume culture and experience events. Rapid and rabid developments in technology have actually made us more alone as individuals than ever before. Now, you probably have to be a fan of a particular sport to pay much attention and even then, as I can confirm personally, much of it washes over you given its ubiquitousness. In the early 80s, cricket, even with its irritating televisual interruptions, garnered considerably more live broadcast time than any other game with the natural consequence being a higher national profile. Therefore, as Domenghetti pointed out, 'it was just the right time for Botham to take on the role of leading man'. Thatcher herself may have been divorced from the television for most of her life, but the country over which she presided in the 80s was not – therefore it, and the sport which dominated its schedules, *did* matter to her indirectly whether she realised it or not.

Whilst today those who reach a level of recognition transcending their sport tend to do so for other reasons than simply performances on the pitch, back then sporting deeds alone could elevate some to the consciousness of even the sports-ambivalent or agnostic. Admittedly, before the decade was out Botham's status as the country's highest-profile sportsman also owed something to some colourful extra-curricular exploits, but his fame and popularity came initially from the hope that he might be the man to bring joy and resuscitation to one of our national sports. This is why, although it could be argued some of the achievements of Ben Stokes today stand comparison with those of Botham, he would be seen as an icon of his sport not, as was Botham in the 80s, a true cultural one. Come 1981 there *was* a change in mood and perception which would ultimately find its outcome in a very different nation and the society in which sport existed meant it played its part in this as almost never before.

A Very British Insanity

'Cricket is uniquely bound up with English identity in all its complexity and subtlety. The story of English cricket, to some extent, is also the story of England itself.'

Ed Smith
What Sport Tells Us About Life

MAKING A case for sport as an influencer upon our wider world is one thing; for some, arguing that cricket might be that sport is altogether more tenuous. Yet many of the finest writers on this beautiful game have suggested over the years that cricket, for England and the English in particular, is not simply a game but an institution which reflects the character of our society and evolves in concert with it over time. Arlott insisted that cricket always developed as the world also changed, at times almost out of recognition. In a farewell piece written for *Wisden Cricket Monthly* in November 1980, he expanded the point. 'Always there is some degree of change as the game falls into step with the community that supports it. While seeming to stand still, cricket is perpetually in motion. That is its charm – the illusion of permanence within a pattern of development.' Sometimes that can also be the story of everyday life and that community to which he refers.

Even if the game is indeed closely linked to its wider environment, it might be suggested that few of the working-class demographic most obviously affected by the economic downturn of the late 70s and early 80s really cared a jot about cricket. But sometimes it is wise to challenge preconceptions. Arlott once referred to cricket as 'that particularly British form of insanity' and so it is. Cricket is not only intrinsically linked to a sense of Britishness but something wedded to the nation's psyche. It is not the exclusive preserve of the privileged few. In truth, cricket has always crossed the class divide – more so than its exaggerated image of cucumber sandwiches and batsmen in cravats sometimes suggests. For every Douglas Jardine, Ted Dexter, Colin Ingleby-McKenzie or Mike Brearley, there has been a Harold Larwood, a Colin Milburn, a David Steele or a Ben Stokes. Or indeed, an Ian Botham. For every Eton and Oxford man there has been one from a state school background, or someone pulled straight out of the mines. This is true of the game's supporter base too. There is certainly a connection between cricket and the British middle to upper classes – visit the Harris Garden at Lord's and the salmon pink trousers and *Fortnum*'s hampers may still overwhelm you. There is also something of a connection between the MCC membership and the traditional old-school Conservative party demographic. J.B. Priestley once painted a picture of the MCC members as complacent, overweight males in the terminal stages of alcoholic poisoning. That might be a little over-the-top for the grandees in her party but post-war Toryism prior to Thatcher was a club for gentlemen, or those who aspired to be gentlemen. Enoch Powell gave them a different name – that of 'Athenian oligarchs'. In cricket, this has often portrayed a group confident in their own superiority and an assumption that they alone know what the game should stand for, displaying indignation at anything they believe to be beyond the pale. Botham's father-in-law Gerry Waller saw them as 'those pompous jackasses, there by privilege rather than on merit', which was an articulation of what most irritated Botham and Thatcher about their respective establishments. (In 2023, in the aftermath of the controversial dismissal of Jonny Bairstow in an Ashes Test at Lord's which led to unprecedented physical altercations in the Long Room, the *Daily Telegraph* captured this in a spoof letter to itself purporting to be about the need to uphold the 'spirit of cricket'. Penned by Sir Herbert Gusset, The Old Scoring Box, Great Stokes, near Bazball-on-the-Naze, it spouted the outrage that he and his fellow MCC member Sir Simon Redtrouser felt at the incident. Perfect.) But the Western Terrace at Headingley or the Hollis Stand at Edgbaston are rather different experiences and the Barmy Army, whose support all over the world is so treasured by the players themselves, is hardly made up of the alumni of our public schools. One of the reasons Botham appealed to the masses and was to become one of the faces of the decade was his own working-class hinterland.

So, to suggest cricket didn't connect in any way with the majority of the British public would be a fallacy. In fact, 1981 was the year in which the comprehensive schoolboy Botham made cricket more working-class relevant than ever before. People may struggle today to appreciate how a cricketer could so bestride the nation's consciousness, but as the sportswriter and broadcaster Pat Murphy wrote late in the 80s, 'outside the members of the royal family, Ian Botham must have the best-known face in Britain. In the last decade no politician [Thatcher being an exception] or public entertainer has been in the public eye so consistently'. This was a cricketer for pity's sake. Botham's rather surreal development into an icon of British life in the decade was also aided by the absence of any comparable contribution to rejuvenation from the country's international footballers. The desperate matches they often played out at the start of the decade actually helped to elevate Botham. It also helped that Botham was wont to reserve some of his most stirring deeds for Ashes battles. If cricket was important in the country's perception of itself, contests between England and Australia took that to new heights. Dennis

Lillee and Rodney Marsh were two of the most formidable competitors in Ashes history, the ultimate Australians who were players and characters with whom Botham chimed. So ingrained was their picture of what an Englishman looked like and stood for that they were convinced Botham should have been born Australian and respected him as such. They agreed that all they really cared about throughout their Test careers was England and the need to put down the colonials and prick their pomposity. The Ashes were what mattered to both sides and to both countries. These contests were a matter of national standing. Botham believed in this, hence his heightened pleasure when he made a difference. His former team-mate turned implacable enemy, Peter Roebuck, felt that a national sporting team was a reflection of the nation itself and perhaps this is why we're so desperate for success when times are tough.

With the national football team failing to provide any such succour in 1981 and their followers dragging Britain's name through the mud across the cities of Europe, the moment was ripe for cricket to take the stage. There was little doubt, as people who had never before shown the slightest interest were pressing their noses against the windows of Radio Rentals and Rumbelows in city centres all over the country, that cricket had become a genuine and important strand of the nation's story. On the BBC's news and current affairs programme *Nationwide* at the end of the Headingley Test, the presenter Sue Cook, nobody's idea of an archetypal member of the Barmy Army, announced, 'Well even I'm excited and cricket usually bores me silly.' The other reason that cricket was best placed to reflect the oscillating nature of that summer lies in the nature of a Test match series. Few other sports have the protracted timescale, the number of variables and the capacity for a long and fluctuating narrative. David Gower played for England that summer and looking back he admitted he had forgotten that there was indeed a political backdrop to it with 'the country in low dudgeon'. He was clear that for them to have lost to Australia would have added to the general mood of depression, whereas Headingley and the subsequent wins were 'enough to raise the spirits of at least its cricket-loving public'. The country came almost to a standstill as the story played out, with trading suspended on the stock exchange and, as the *Daily Telegraph* pointed out, 'housewives who had not the slightest interest in cricket stopped their housework to switch on' (which is admittedly an image very much of its time). Whether it is stretching the point to see one as the source of the other, it was a fact that as victory neared, the FTSE index rallied on the markets. The full appreciation of that backdrop and the impact of the cricket on the country's self-perception took time to sink in for more than just Gower. A book rushed out that autumn to take advantage of the Botham-mania, *The Incredible Tests*, makes no mention at all of a possible broader social context, but the *From the Ashes* DVD which revisited it with the benefit of considerable hindsight 30 years later didn't fail to allude to it. Sometimes the recognition of true value takes time. As the cricket writer David Frith looked back on the events and conclusion of the Headingley 1981 Test match he wrote:

> 'While everyone drew fresh breath, groundsman Keith Boyce dug up a piece of the pitch to send to the Soil Research Centre for analysis. A portion should have been consigned to the Department of Information as a symbol and reminder of the fighting spirit which not only won a fabulous Test match but can win much larger social and economic battles.'

There is also a proof in history here. Cricket's symbiotic relationship with the nation and its fortunes and its mood over many years has often been most pronounced at times of greatest need and that marriage has not always been exclusive to Britain. Simon Barnes considers the 1983 World Cup victory the second most significant moment in Indian history after independence, leading to greater prosperity and the shedding of the image of subservience. Cricket had changed a nation by altering its self-perception. Where cricket matters, it matters. Another of the greatest writers on the game, Neville Cardus, frequently painted pictures of cricket in its wider context. He recalled the Ashes series of 1948 and being brought to tears by the sight of Keith Miller and Denis Compton lifting the hearts of 'a pale-faced, dowdy crowd existing on rations' in the sombre years following the Second World War. 'There were no rations in an innings by Compton.' In 1977 England enjoyed a relative stroll to Ashes victory in the sunny summer of the Silver Jubilee but England's cricket in general through the first half of the 70s, prior to the arrival of I.T. Botham, was reflective of a more general downbeat mood and a record of ongoing underachievement. After an epic Ashes victory in Australia was secured in February 1971, a collection of underwhelming results would follow in quick succession. A record run of 26 Tests without defeat was abruptly halted by India that summer as they won both a Test match and a series in England for the first time.

The next summer England were held to a drawn series at home by an Australian touring side of comparatively ordinary quality, prior to a series defeat in India over the winter. There followed a draw in Pakistan, a brief respite at home to New Zealand, a thrashing at home by the West Indies and a draw in the Caribbean. Three Test wins out of six in the home summer of 1974 presaged the traumatic 5-1 hammering at the hands of the Australians that winter and a home defeat by the same opposition six months later. By the time the West Indies dealt out their lesson in 1976 England's cricket-following public had the same sense of weary resignation as the rest of the nation. England's place in the world order had slipped, seemingly without the prospect of rescue, its cricketing journey in step with all else around it. In a letter to *The Times* at the time Air

Chief Marshal Sir Christopher Foxley-Norris, who may sound like a character from *The Fall and Rise of Reginald Perrin* or president-elect of MCC but was nonetheless entitled to his view, bemoaned that 'on the playing fields of the world we appear to have become the perennial losers'.

Cricket continued to echo the pattern of good and bad as Britain headed into the 1990s on the back of another decade of boom and bust – or bust, boom and bust. We had seen it all before. If many had become used to this cycle as the way of British politics and our social experience, it continued to find a pretty good metaphor in the England cricket team. But during the 1980s that metaphor came as much from an individual as it did from the team. There have been, and always will be, plenty of outstanding world-class cricketers for us to enjoy. But there are only a few who give the game something more on and off the field – those who can take a game and change it, bending it to their will in the most critical of moments not just once but again and again; those who have you feeling that nothing is impossible and no game is lost; those who truly entertain and capture the interest of an audience which extends beyond the game's cognoscenti; those who can lift a nation. Pat Murphy said of the 1981 summer, 'Botham was the hero of the land, cogent proof of the value of sport of a society dogged at that time by the spectre of unemployment and rising tension in the inner cities. Just as Denis Compton delighted many in the immediate years of post-war austerity, so it was with Botham in 1981.' Simon Barnes refers to W.G. Grace as 'a symbol of all-conquering British rightness' at the end of the Victorian age, so the impact of certain cricketers on our self-perception started early. Compton had been another example, all style, elegance and, we liked to think, British dash, in regaining the Ashes after 18 years as the coronation year attempted to mark the end of austerity and the beginning of a new era of post-war hope and opportunity – something Botham and a royal wedding were to replicate. Barnes insists that you can't contemplate British social history without such figures. A societal impact was not something exclusive to *English* cricketers either. We saw Vivian Richards offering a lead to the Windrush generation seeking respect, equality and a place in British society and standing up for his people in the 70s and 80s and Imran Khan building a pride and identity in the nascent nation of Pakistan, often at odds with itself and others, and bringing it global success and recognition. Now Botham was to make his own impact. 'English cricket at its best celebrates the breadth and colour of the country it reflects, represents, and at times *inspires*,' wrote Ed Smith. So it would be with Ian Botham and his cricket in 1981, restoring the pride of a nation after years of economic, industrial decline and winters of discontent, at the centre of a year of riots and disintegrating communities. In the view of the social historian Dominic Sandbrook, starting at Headingley Botham became the greatest patriotic icon of the age. In a society such as ours sport does indeed have an influence on mood and, at times, a communal sense of well-being. And it can diminish or restore that thing called national pride.

The Pride of a Nation

WHETHER OR not it is wise have a pride in one's nation today appears to be a matter of personal opinion. For some, a pride in Britishness however that be defined is an important part of their lives and make-up. For others, it is a matter of supreme indifference. Recent years have seen an increasing attack on British history and culture, an erosion or renunciation of Britishness, emanating from a view that these are fundamentally flawed constructs flooded with examples of shameful historical behaviour and a negative impact on the wider world. Depending on your point of view this is either wokeism and virtue-signalling, or a justified and necessary position of contrition. In 2023 the Archbishop of York, Stephen Cottrell, called for 'a vision of what it means to be English as part of the United Kingdom' and, against a background of apparent flagellation of the English by their own metropolitan elite, suggested that the average English person's 'heartfelt cry to be heard is often disregarded, wilfully misunderstood or patronised as being backwardly xenophobic'. An English notion of national pride is complex, but such a pride, especially at times when it becomes a communal experience, plays a fundamental role in the spirit and the prosperity of the country and should not be something necessitating a defence.

Writer Stephen Fry offers a personal opinion that 'patriotism is loving one's country; nationalism is hating everyone else's country'. In the 1970s and 80s there was valid concern about the growth of the latter within English society, often borne out by those following the national football team. 'The British Disease' was a phrase borrowed (rather unfairly for supporters from Scotland and Wales, although they did at times display a sporting hatred of England itself) from its initial usage as a depiction of the country's industrial strife in the 1970s, to describe those who got their kicks from rampaging around Europe following both their club sides and national team, wreaking violent havoc and through their self-stated nationalism bringing shame upon the rest of us. If England's cricket was, by the mid-70s, in tune with the pervading sense of decline, its football team took decline in its stride and dialled it up to humiliation. The world champions of the 60s and favourites but quarter-final losers at the 1970 World Cup managed to navigate the entire decade from that point on without qualifying for a single World Cup or European Championship finals tournament. The national shock of the elimination by Poland at Wembley in 1973 further depressed those who were used to taking refuge in sport from the realities of life. The regression from world champions to serial failures over ten years was seen as symptomatic of a wider sense of self-loathing pervading Britain as its people became resigned to economic decline and, at best, second-class status within the world. For a nation which only three decades previously had played a first-hand role in saving the world from tyranny and had once introduced to that world such life-changing innovations as the industrial revolution, such a decline painted a picture of national disgrace.

The flag-waving, street-partying pomp of VE Day was one fleeting moment of undiluted patriotism which few derided. It was not to sustain, however, in the reality of the aftermath of the war and its impact on a decade of shortages and struggle ahead. Notwithstanding the joyous moment when England lifted the World Cup in 1966, the Silver Jubilee of 1977 was the next time such a national celebration was shared around the country. But again, within a year Britain was heading for gloom – this time the Winter of Discontent, then recession and the dignity-sapping plague of mass unemployment. The third post-war excuse to get the flags out was to arrive midway through 1981. The wedding of Prince Charles and Lady Diana Spencer is therefore one of the moments in time most relevant to the coming narrative. *One* of the moments, but only one amidst a rainfall of other events and related characters that swept through the year, for better or for worse depending on one's opinion and political persuasion.

In his history of Thatcher's years in office, *Rejoice, Rejoice!*, the historian Alwyn W. Turner highlights what drove Thatcher's vision and what, with help from Botham, 1981 was to deliver: 'To counter the British self-disparagement of the 70s, a new sense of patriotism was to be encouraged … a reborn pride in the nation.' In the end the year would indeed bring a rebirth of patriotic populism which would be the spark that ignited the changes ahead and would endure for much of the decade.

In the Mood

*'If we can create the right national mood,
ideas will flourish.'*

Margaret Thatcher
Speech to the Conservative Party summer school, 1979

IN *RISE Up and Salute the Sun*, the American author Suzy Kassem wrote that 'transformations are part of life. We are constantly being changed by things changing around us. Nobody can control the environment, the economy, luck or the moods of others … Positions change. Dispositions change. Experiences change. Opportunities and attitudes change'.

Margaret Thatcher may well have agreed with a lot of that, but not the idea that nobody could control it; on the contrary, it was her fundamental mission to do that very thing. The economy was of course to play a major part, but she firmly believed that changing dispositions and attitudes, particularly those she found in Britain when she came to power, was the critical first step. It was all about changing the mood.

Change is a certainty, but a bringer of uncertainty. It can be immediate and obvious or more imperceptible, a slower burn. It can arrive in the form of a specific moment or it can evolve over time, gathering momentum through a myriad of the apparently insignificant. For an individual, the birth of a child or the passing of someone close can change life in an instant. From a communal or societal perspective, at the moment the Hiroshima bomb was dropped or in the instant that the Twin Towers collapsed onto the streets of New York

City it was clear the world was going to be a very different place in the future. Change can be concrete and factual – perhaps a piece of government policy such as a bill allowing people to purchase their own council houses and immediately offering them a new vision of their future. But change can also be more subtle, its true significance only identifiable with hindsight. It can evolve existentially in the form of mood. A more ethereal mutation in mood can ultimately instigate a change in reality, for the two are inextricably linked. This is something both Thatcher and Botham understood and why they both saw such importance in positive mindsets – both in living their own ambitions and encouraging those of others.

An Emeritus Professor of Psychology at Dundee University, Trevor Harley, has studied mood extensively and identifies it as a temporary state which is distinguished from a person's personality. He also insists that the study of how various elements affect our mood is not easy as an empirical science since individuals react differently to different stimuli. It may be that what has an influence is more placebo effect than scientific fact – the things that affect mood may be truisms that we believe because we are told they are so. But an effect is still an effect and Harley acknowledges that the factors that can play a part in this are numerous and eclectic even if some are barely recognised as having done so – but recognising them is important if one accepts that reality is often born of perception. The transformation in communal mood which remains the hallmark of 1981 was rooted in several clearly identifiable elements: its politics and economics certainly, but also its music and culture, its weather and its sport.

The relationship between mood and reality is also a mutualistic one. The economic conditions of a particular time have an obvious impact in affecting people's living standards and, in more turbulent and prolonged periods of upheaval, the positivity or otherwise of their vision of, and hopes for, the future. But you don't have to be Chief Advisor to the

Treasury to understand that little things such as confidence have a bearing on future reality in the capitalist model of economics. There was no economic reason behind the life-affecting downturns of Black Monday or the 2008 banking crisis. It is, we're told, the nervousness of the bond markets where these things originate; it is a loss of faith in the future, an atrophy of belief rather than anything real. Optimism and pessimism may be justified or misplaced, but the triumph of one over the other often dictates the direction of travel. So if politics and culture impact mood, so mood in return has a marked effect on them.

Alongside the more immediately recognisable impact of politics, the cultural atmosphere – the creativity and expression found in, say, the 1960s – is just as important a contributor to the national frame of mind in the optimism or sobriety of the music and the arts which pervade our daily life. Even the weather, not least through its vagaries in Britain, can heavily influence mood. How many of us recall with greatest affection those summers when the sun shone and enticed us into a more gregarious state of mind, regardless of the realities of life at the time? For me, those of 1975, '76 and '77 are examples which sway my memories of youth, creating an artificially rosy glow of nostalgia. Sport, also ingrained in our culture, acts in much the same way, affecting us perhaps more than we are ready to acknowledge. Not everyone lives a life in which sport is a core influence upon their mood, but enough of us do to make it relevant to our shared view of our own nation and how much of a spring is added to our step, day-to-day, for however fleeting a moment. Following the fortunes of our sporting favourites can release those neurotransmitters dopamine and serotonin which directly affect our level of contentment. In his analysis of British social history since 1975 *From Anger to Apathy* the historian Mark Garrett goes as far as to suggest that the England football team's defeat in the World Cup quarter-final in 1970 as reigning world champions was 'a blow which with hindsight seemed to have begun the prolonged slide in British morale'. The record of England's cricket team seemed to shadow the mood in a similar way. Since regaining the Ashes in 1953 in a celebratory, patriotic summer and through the decade of the 60s as England came to rule the football world, they won more than twice as many Tests as they lost. After the Ashes win of 1970/71 until the series of Botham's arrival seven years later they declined to a losing record. Garrett alluded to this as well, with specific reference to 1975. 'The poor performance of the English cricketers undoubtedly added to the sense of national malaise.' Sport matters. And sport has a surreal tendency to mirror the mood of the times.

'And if it hasn't turned the match upside down, it's certainly turned the character of the match upside down ...'

The words with which Christopher Martin-Jenkins greeted Ian Botham's century at Headingley – at the epicentre of this story in July 1981 – were perhaps more insightful and apposite than we, and he himself, appreciated at the time. They were uttered not at the moment when cricket's most famous comeback was complete, the match won and the Ashes revived but, as they suggest, at a point where such an outcome still seemed fanciful. But they encapsulated something else apparent in that instant – that Botham's innings and the manner of it had given England, it's team and it's public, an afternoon of hope, something of which to feel proud and the possibility of a rescue rope to grasp. In short, it had changed the mood. For Botham and Headingley, read the country itself ... if the year of 1981 didn't turn the *country* upside down, it certainly turned the *character* of the country upside down.

In his autobiographical novel *Min Kamp,* the Norwegian author Karl Ove Knausgaard suggested 'mood ... is everywhere but nothing in itself, more like a colour in which thoughts are thought, a colour through which the world is seen'. If so, the colour of 1981 would change like its weather over the course of the year from grey to blue in a marked change of mood, through an unprecedented 12 months of change in all of these disparate and yet connected elements. In almost every respect, it was to be a year like no other.

A Year Like No Other

'All moments are poised between past and future; there are always reminders of the world yesterday and glimpses of the world tomorrow. But there are some moments when the contrast is especially sharp.'

Dominic Sandbrook
Who Dares Wins

WHY 1981? Because it was just such a year poised between past and future in which the contrasts were not only sharp but came along in a dizzying multitude. Seminal moments were everywhere. The capture of the Yorkshire Ripper at the same time as the mourning of John Lennon; IRA hunger strikes and funerals and one of the weddings of the century; inner-city riots followed by communal street parties; the first UK diagnosis of a new disease called Acquired Immune Deficiency Syndrome – a source of social fear, ignorance and much intolerance that lasted the decade – and the arrival of IBM's first personal computer leading another society-changing phenomenon; in popular music, the break-up of The Specials and the arrival of the New Romantics, a goodbye to Two Tone and the music of social commentary and hello to hedonism and commercial ambition; the patriotic nostalgia of a British Oscar winning-film and critically acclaimed television drama and success in the song contests of Europe but shame and violence in its football stadiums and towns; goodbye to Tom Baker's Doctor

Who and hello to Del Boy; the weather joining the narrative, eerily shadowing the dark times and lighting up the good; records for the hottest, coldest, wettest and snowiest days and months; records for Coe and Ovett; farewell to the century's greatest sporting icon and to the darling of Wimbledon and hello to the Superbrat; the first new major political party since the formation of the Labour Party in the opening year of the century, whilst that party was simultaneously pulling itself apart; the most contentious budget in history which might have been the death of the government but would prevail against all expectation and dissention; the miserable cricketing stories of Barbados and Lord's and the exultation in Leeds and Birmingham. Above all, the darkest days and the revivals of two transformative individuals. The contrasts were various and fascinating, existing and evolving in tandem throughout the year, one reflecting the other.

Weather With You

NOTORIOUSLY CAPRICIOUS in any year, the British weather through that of 1981 was some of the most interesting and dramatic of the 20th century. Weather's contribution to mood is enhanced when you live in an environment so at the mercy of its vicissitudes. This is an area of particular focus for Professor Harley who addressed it in detail in *The Psychology of Weather.* He calls the study 'psycho-meteorology' and it gives credibility to the suggestion that 1981's weather and its close association to other events played its part in the change to come. 1980 may have been a drab, wet summer, but the first half of 1981 was the coldest and darkest for a decade. Harley refers to correlations as opposed to causations – in other words there may be a degree of coincidence in the influence weather can have on mood but it is no less real regardless. He also keeps records and analysis of the British weather by year and considers 1981 'an outstanding year' within the century – outstanding in this context not meaning unremittingly enjoyable but virtually unrivalled in its extremes and contrasts. In '81, those extremes and contrasts reflected in many ways – not least at Lord's, Headingley and Edgbaston and in the fortunes of Ian Botham and English cricket – a sport for which the weather is so important.

For the British, the weather is embedded in our psyche in the same way as the cricket. Harley notes that few natural phenomena impact on so many of us with such variation. 'The weather … can affect us in many ways. It can even affect who we elect as our leaders and our government.' Others poke fun at this British conversational obsession but there is a reason for it – that moment early on a summer's morning when the curtains are drawn back to reveal whether an azure-blue sky or an inability to see your hands in front of your face and a temperature more akin to January determines the potential of the day ahead. In '81 these two opposing possibilities were nothing out of the ordinary in themselves; what was extraordinary was the way the lows and highs that appeared on the television maps of Bill Giles and Michael Fish would run alongside the unhappy and the happy events of the year in a surreal concordance. The drabbest of early summers hung over the ongoing recession and the first two unsuccessful Tests of an Ashes series conspicuous in their lack of drama or entertainment. Then as England took the Ashes by the throat, the royal wedding had bunting and patriotism back in fashion for the first time since the hot summer of the Jubilee, and the recession was declared officially over, so the sun came out and the temperatures soared as summer seemed to have somehow rescued itself and the public at the last. Heavy snowfall in February had stood out against the images of England's cricketers in the islands of the Caribbean and was followed by the second wettest March of the century to sit alongside the most controversial and most pessimistic government budget of the century. The first half of April was the warmest for 20 years, accompanying not just the first of the Brixton riots but also the arrival of the Australian cricketers, a British Eurovision success and the most uplifting Grand National victory in living memory, whilst the second half was the coldest of the century with large areas of the country blanketed in more snow as unemployment was announced as having hit two and a half million. The miserable cold continued into early May, a gloom enhanced by the unrelentingly downbeat news of economic woes and the death of IRA hunger striker Bobby Sands. The 'cold and dull' June gave England's defeat in the first Test an additional sense of melancholy whilst the violent thunderstorms of the first half of July were the soundtrack to the nadir of captain Botham's form and his resignation at Lord's, the Moss Side and Toxteth riots and the serendipitous arrival of The Specials' 'Ghost Town' at the top of the charts. The cricket and the weather continued their tango as the conclusion of matters at Headingley preceded the emergence of hot sun in time for patriotic celebrations at St Paul's Cathedral and Edgbaston alike. The sun remained, for the most part, until the Ashes were safely home and the hunger strikes and riots also consigned to history. An astonishing 105 tornadoes across the country in November and the coldest, snowiest December of the century were a fitting end to one of the most dramatic years of our times.

Weather and the mood and fortunes of the country woven together: a coincidence perhaps, but also historical fact. The then BBC news reporter, John Sergeant, remembered of the first half of 1981 that 'the overall political situation was so severe with a deep recession and inflation over ten per cent that it was weirdly appropriate that the weather that came with that was so awful'. Harley concludes in his study that although the effects of weather on mood 'are quite small, which shouldn't surprise us as at any one time it is just one of many things afflicting us', they are real. So it was in 1981 when those 'many things' coalesced in an unprecedented fashion.

The British Are Coming

'Even Mrs Thatcher experienced culture's ability to shape people's deepest thoughts.'

Andy Beckett
Promised You a Miracle

CULTURAL INFLUENCES are often at the heart of sense of social positivity or gloom. The Roaring Twenties, the Swinging Sixties, the Britpop and, if I have to say it, Cool Britannia of the mid-90s – these were feel-good periods even if they were inevitably fleeting, followed respectively by the Great Depression, the sick man of Europe days of three-day weeks, devaluation and the Winter of Discontent, and the financial implosion of the mid-2000s. They were also times in which the British public wore a renewed pride in its own nation and position in the world. When The Beatles, The Dave Clark Five and Herman's Hermits were at the heart of the British invasion of the US in the 60s, the titles themselves, 'She Loves You', 'Glad All Over', 'I'm Into Something Good', were dripping with optimism. Although Britpop didn't cross the Atlantic in quite the same way, many saw parallels with the London of the 60s which spread around the nation's major cities, with Union Jacks the most consistently visible manifestation of its personality. Music would play its part in the story of 1981, and film would join the party too and reprise the conquering bands of the 60s in colonising the notoriously inward-looking American market.

That Birmingham (and its Test match highlighted at the start of this book) should be one location of England cricket's contribution to a change of atmosphere feels apt given the role the city played in mirroring the early '80s through its cultural expression. The West Midlands had been the driving force in the Two Tone movement in which the music of working-class bands from the area, often formed of black and white members in concert, gave their own stark commentary on the country in which we lived, reflecting the times through their output. In doing so they captured, in 1980 and the first half of 1981, the sense of hopelessness pervading the country's youth in particular, articulating the 'no future' vision more credibly than John Lydon and the Sex Pistols had done whilst offering an alternative to another period of national celebration in 1977. The music writer Jay McDowell suggested 'the idea of finishing school and being thrown into the mess that was England in 1975 made Lydon feel hopeless', and his railing against it was seen as an attempt to shock (which succeeded) more than the message of solidarity with the working class which was at its core. The Two Tone of 1980–81 seemed more genuine. Whilst the genre's most celebrated single originated in Coventry in the form of The Specials' astonishing 'Ghost Town' in July '81, an unintended but felicitous soundtrack accompaniment to the summer's inner-city riots, two bands who became the second city's most successful of the decade would bellwether and chronicle the times recently past and the times to come just as appropriately. That same July, the apparent nihilism and the no-longer-latent sense of anger at, and distrust of, Margaret Thatcher and the early days of her government, were uncompromisingly articulated in UB40's polemic single 'One In Ten'. At the same time, Duran Duran reached the UK top ten for the first time with 'Girls On Film'. If artistically there is no contest between the two (a subjective view), the transmutation between the political protest of one and the commercial hedonism of the other was both stark and relevant. Hindsight confers a symbolism on the arrival of Duran Duran into the space left by the acrimonious split of The Specials that same month in the moment of their greatest creation. They were a very different proposition, in the vanguard of the New Romantic movement which rejected any idea of political and social commentary in favour of decadence and having a damn good time – the coming pre-eminent force in pop culture alongside Adam and his ants, bringing any number of similar artists along with them and soon to be categorised by The Guardian's Michael Hann as 'Thatcherism on vinyl'.

The weariness of the serious pretention of the 70s music press in the form of such bumptious titles as the *New Musical Express* saw another change towards glossy optimism in the media which followed the new pop culture. *Smash Hits* was a colour magazine which took itself far less seriously than the previously dominant broadsheets and was the perfect accompaniment and helping hand to the new breed of ambitious pop bands. Launched in 1978, that it was offering the coming generation more of what it wanted than the old-school music papers was evidenced in a circulation in 1981 heading towards a million copies a week. People wanted optimism and an alternative to the pomposity and negativity of the previous music literature. If the NME was the right vehicle for the 70s, here was the one which would perfectly reflect the new mood of the 80s. On 1 August 1981, it would be followed by another of the year's transformational arrivals – that of MTV.

In his book *Promised You a Miracle* Andy Beckett noted this change to a soundtrack for the coming Thatcher era: 'The raw styles of the 1970s gave way to a new glossiness and careerism.' Under the chapter title of 'Secret Thatcherites', Beckett saw at its top table the self-professed staunchly left-wing Gary Kemp of Spandau Ballet and that 'whether Kemp and his fellow troubadours liked it or not, their careers – both their manner and their success – were as Thatcherite as they come'. Music artists in Britain were no longer afraid to say they wanted to be rich. In fact Kemp, whatever his politics, was perfectly aware of, and comfortable with, what the new movement reflected. 'It highlighted a cult of self – a powerful philosophy which would exemplify the coming decade.' Indeed it would, though by its midpoint plenty would be ready to substitute the word 'self' with 'greed'. It was to be the era when artists became businessmen. Many, such as Culture Club's Jon Moss, turned openly Conservative, and even those who didn't were more than happy to benefit from the world of increased commercialism in the same way as Ian Botham was to go through a similar evolution in the field of sport. If UB40 had captured the mood and concerns of the country prior to this climactic month, Simon Le Bon and his cohorts were ushering in the future by its close. The release of their second album, *Rio,* in May 1982, even more dandy, glossy and commercially successful than their first effort, meant its consumption would begin in tandem with victory for Thatcher in the Falklands and make a perfect standard-bearer for the unashamed ambition and excess which would characterise the decade from then on. It was, said the music critic Simon Reynolds, 'as if the floodgates had opened to irrigate the charts with a rejuvenating gush of colour, exuberance and optimism'. From pessimism to optimism. July 1981 – the moment of change.

There were plenty of signs of what was to come in the words of those driving that change. When interviewed by Paul Morley for the *NME* music paper at the end of 1980, the frontman of another new band associated with a fresh outlook and ambition, ABC's Martin Fry, talked of 'a sign of the new optimism', as if that was something he was anticipating as he looked ahead to 1981. Fry's stated wish to move on from 'the dreary attitude' was echoed in the recollections of the time by a member of a band perhaps considered less transformative, but Cheryl Baker's Bucks Fizz were to be the embodiment of the fresh attitude from the moment they briefly reintroduced at least some element of success to the country in April, with victory in the Eurovision Song Contest at a time when it was still something of a national event. (Perhaps an indication of how desperate things were.) 'We'd come out of this kind of negativity of the 70s and it was a very angry time. We were just looking forward to something bright and colourful.' By the start of 1982 the family-friendly band were at number one again with the preposterously glitzy video for 'The Land of Make Believe'. Further removed from 'Ghost Town' this could not be but, make believe or not, it seemed to confirm people were ready for a land of optimism rather than negativity. Perhaps a realisation was growing that happiness, justified or otherwise, would be a more agreeable state than anger, as Duran Duran keyboard player Nick Rhodes indicated in 1981. 'Having a good time is what it's all about these days … it's time entertainers got back to entertaining.' Perhaps Botham was a Duran Duran disciple too – he would most certainly have agreed. Or perhaps he had shared a beer with Gary Kemp, who put his message simply: 'We're just saying … "make the best of yourself".' Although undoubtedly nostalgic in its fashion and look, the new genre was driven by a new breed of ambitious, opportunistic young men and women with a determination to shape their own futures rather than bemoan their fate. The music journalist Beverley Glick met Duran Duran for their first-ever major press interview in 1980 and remembers the band members as the most ambitious teenagers she had ever met. Similarly Gary Kemp was interviewed by Betty Page for *Sounds* late in 1980 and already seemed on-message with the Thatcherite philosophy despite what would later transpire were very different politics. In an article titled 'Spandau Ballet – A Manifesto for the 80's', Kemp suggested, 'I'd like people to make the most of themselves rather than the least of themselves … if you haven't got anything, you should make the most of yourself and your appearance. If that's all you've got, make the most of it, beat everyone at it.' He claimed of the New Romantic movement that 'the whole scene attracts people who want to achieve something, in any direction, whether it's art or whether it's money. It's ambition'. And it wasn't just those fronting the bands who were displaying the 'new optimism' by their actions. In 1981 the producer Pete Waterman's business was setting out on the path that was to make him one of the dominant forces in the music business in the 80s. He was another ambitious music entrepreneur determined to make his own way. His philosophy, fighting through the year's worst weather to ensure he got to the places required to keep the business alive, was 'if that guy didn't make it, I made it'. It was Ian Botham incarnate. Waterman, talking of the December snow which would bring the country to a halt, highlighted the way in which the determiners of mood interlinked. 'In some way, the weather probably changed the music industry [in 1981].' With little else to occupy them, Britain's youth were buying records in their droves, making these new bands in the process. Perhaps it is little surprise that as the movement developed through 1981 its most successful proponents would become the totem the era of one Margaret Thatcher. Historian Dylan Jones wrote a detailed chronicle of Britain in the 80s and concluded that after the apathy and resignation of the 70s when the words 'stagnation' and 'collapse' filled the air, this decade talked of 'growth' and was 'crowded with a generation devoted to self-empowerment and social change'. In this, Margaret Thatcher and Ian Botham had undoubtedly shown the way.

Even such an icon of the 70s as David Bowie, noted for his idiosyncratic innovation more than his adoption of existing trends, gave his blessing to what was happening in the new musical genre and the creativity behind it. He had given it a significant lead in the summer of 1980 with the futuristic, some might say incomprehensible, video for his number one hit 'Ashes to Ashes'. His phrase used to describe what he, and they, were trying to articulate. 'Nostalgia for the future', is perhaps the perfect summation of the place the country found itself come 1981. Another might be the sentence uttered by Robert Elms, a friend and associate of Gary Kemp, in depicting the Blitz nightclub which was the home territory of the New Romantics. 'A creative environment where individualism was stressed and change was vital' could almost have been words created for the opening pages of a Thatcher manifesto.

But the British creative renaissance and fondness for nostalgia was not confined to this musical evolution, the zeitgeist was also being captured in film and television in the same moment. 1981 gave the nation a dose of what it proved it wanted via *Chariots of Fire* in the cinemas and a production of Evelyn Waugh's *Brideshead Revisited* on the small screen, both of which took advantage of and stoked that desire for a revival in patriotism – an excuse to make a pride in Britain fashionable and acceptable once more and for *Chariots'* screenwriter Colin Welland to coin one of the more memorable soundbites of the 80s when announcing to both the Academy and the US at large on accepting an Oscar early in 1982 that, in the world of the arts at least, 'The British are coming!' Over-exuberant or not, the exultation encapsulated the public's sense that by the end of '81, the country was fighting back – a sense that was enhanced by a similar renaissance in British sport.

The Changing Of The Guard

'The year 1981 was as vintage a period for sport as it was for street parties, bunting and cup cakes'.

Daily Mail Online

1981'S THEME of change was all-pervasive in the sports which the nation continued to follow in huge numbers. The 20th century's most recognisable sporting figure, Muhammad Ali, finally took his leave from boxing, though not our consciousness, with his final defeat confirming his last fight had arrived several years too late for everyone's comfort. Thus the sportsman with the highest-ever global profile and the greatest icon of the sporting century departed the scene. The passing of batons was everywhere. The British summer institution that is Wimbledon had been annexed by the taciturn, ice-cool and unfailingly polite Swede Björn Borg as his personal fiefdom for the previous five years. He was adored by his audience who deemed such personal and professional traits to be in keeping with their vision of the world they had created in SW19 and there appeared no reason this state of affairs might change anytime soon. That July, however, a reason appeared in the form of the young, brash and voluble challenger John McEnroe. In two summer weeks McEnroe would treat Britain to both the Dr Jekyll of his immense talent and tennis of aesthetic beauty and the Mr Hyde of the anger and frustration of a tethered crocodile thrashing for freedom and lashing out at all around him. The inimitable middle-England demographic which populates this idiosyncratic British sporting garden party responded to this changing of the guard and its louche instigator with the righteous indignation so beloved of MCC members. This was a group to which McEnroe was the diametric opposite in every fibre of his being and one which he could never understand in the slightest, even had he ever wanted to. But in 1981 he took over their precious fortnight and in doing so, to his own regret and that of the Wimbledon devotees, drove Borg out of the sport forever. As Adam Ant had announced his upwardly-mobile arrival on the British pop scene at the same time, an ambitious, shrewd young go-getter from a humble background who had realised his ultimate ambition and changed the landscape, nauseating the older generation but enrapturing the young, here was his sporting equivalent. Here was the future and the 80s embodied.

If McEnroe mirrored a change in popular culture, the year's previous new kid on the block was more a reflection of the ideal attributes propounded by Margaret Thatcher. Steve Davis was the Thatcher model in sportsman form. As the remarkable rise in the British public's interest in snooker took its next step, the unapologetically ambitious young man from the soon to be Thatcher heartland of Essex took his first world title, establishing a decade-long dominance of the sport. At the same time, under the guidance of a like-minded manager, he became the first in the sport to apply the approach of the business entrepreneur to his sporting career, developing his commercial interests in the same cool, efficient and thought-out manner with which he beat all before him on the table, becoming the first to truly transcend his sport. Steve Davis, Essex Man, with an insatiable desire for success and reward driven by a willingness to work hard to improve his own lot, was Margaret's type of young achiever, the Pete Waterman of the sporting world, perhaps. Just weeks before Davis was conquering The Crucible, a new venture called the London Marathon made its first appearance – a huge success, an example of a happy, shared experience and a forerunner of a new philanthropy, from the public and organisations in tandem, which would punctuate a decade often characterised too readily as purely one of individual greed. If McEnroe was an example of the worst unsporting behaviour and Davis the epitome of personal ambition, here was an event that demonstrated that sport could have a generous, communal impact too.

The story of England's football team made its own contribution to the theme, fluctuating from the sort of humiliating disasters which enhanced the shame at home and the disparagement of and contempt for the state of the country overseas, to the slivers of hope for the future later in the year. The spring and summer would bring little other than humbling, unprecedented defeats against nominally 'minnow' nations and a hooligan fringe masquerading as supporters terrorising the cities of Europe. That autumn, however, delivered the victory which would mean the nation's first appearance at a World Cup finals tournament since 1970, and another boost to the spirits looking into 1982. It was just one more of the juxtapositions which characterised the year.

1981 would, however, be dominated by that other proto-Thatcherite who became England's greatest hope of a revival and its definitive sportsman of the 80s. The tale of Ian Botham is told here, not as another *Botham's Ashes* analysis of the wicket-by-wicket detail of the cricket in that infamous series, but in the context of how it helped change the disposition of the public – his fortunes waning and waxing, over many years but never more so than in this 12 months, in tandem with those of the country itself.

* * *

Whilst Botham's feats gave us an instantaneous uplift, the turnaround in the political situation was less visible and only revealed itself 12 months later. Botham's journey from beleaguered, careworn and much-maligned leader to national hero and patriotic figurehead took no more than a matter of weeks, Margaret Thatcher's parallel route from the same dark place to days in the sun would need considerably longer. This is the nature of change in society as against change in sport: in the former, history only rarely happens in a specific moment – generally it is made over time almost without us noticing; in sport, history is made before our eyes which is what makes it so compelling. 1981 was at the centre of a story which, for both characters, played out over almost 20 years and exploring this wider timespan is crucial to an appreciation of how the changes of that particular year came about, why they mattered, and the legacy they bequeathed. That analysis revealed an unexpected additional narrative: an uncanny concordance of timing and content in the careers, the challenges and successes, and the fundamental beliefs of the two most recognisable personalities of a time of change.

Two Gunslingers

'The world goes to those with a sense of individual competition.'

Ian MacGregor,
Chairman of British Steel, 1980

THE US bureau chief for *The Guardian,* Martin Walker, published a review of Margaret Thatcher's memoirs in the mid-90s. In it he encapsulated the perceptions, traits and beliefs which so entwined her and Botham, strange as that double act may seem at first.

> 'To be neutral about Margaret Thatcher requires superhuman detachment. She would not permit it … She rattled us and our complacent ways down to our very bones. Even her stoutest enemies had to confess to a sneaking admiration for a woman who was more than just another politician. She was a force of nature. And she acted upon the instincts of British pride and nationalism that most of us had absorbed in our history lessons.'

Botham too rattled the cricketing and then the wider British worlds to their bones and played to its pride and nationalism. Both were determined to shake their country out of what they saw as its acceptance of mediocrity by the end of the 70s. That country was ready to be shaken too. Not for either the middle ground of bland statements with which no one could disagree. In one of any number of parallel depictions of the two, former team-mate Vic Marks would say of Botham, 'He had the guts to either succeed or fail spectacularly. There was no middle line.' Similarly in *England: The Biography* cricket writer Simon Wilde maintained that no cricketer apart from Tony Greig had a greater talent for crossing swords with the cricketing establishment than Botham. For the rest of his career Botham and MCC would be oil and water, as would Thatcher, Ted Heath and the infamous 'Wets' in her cabinet. Neither stood on ceremony or were impressed by toffs and old-school ties. There were no niceties and few nuances to either character. You may not like what they said, but you knew they believed it. It could take them into difficulties of their own making on occasions, especially with those who were genuinely conservative and preferred the devil they knew, but they were not going to change for anyone. Laurie Mumford of the *London Evening News* described Botham as 'a fugitive from the slavery of convention' and that would fit Thatcher too. Another characteristic Mumford identified which was common to both was an indomitable spirit which often shone through at its brightest when the clouds looked blackest. Both would need that quality more than any other at the moments of greatest peril to come. They could be stubborn to their own detriment but show an unfailing consistency and belief which would sustain through their tribulations and bring them out the other side. In fact, in spite of this and of perceptions, Thatcher considered herself 'instinctive', which is certainly a word which characterises Botham's cricket and his approach to life.

What you saw was what you got. Or was it? Neither was as easily definable as we might think. Many of the things people believe they know about Thatcher and Botham alike are simply not true. She did not take Britain to war in the Falklands to secure her re-election any more than Botham flogged himself through huge charitable endeavours simply to improve his public image. Both were in fact paradoxes. Laurie Mumford's take on Botham, yet again appropriate for both, was that whatever the odds, he refused to surrender to anybody, but beneath the swagger there was a humility and, beneath the unbending determination, a willingness to take advice. Pat Murphy painted a picture of a man of contrasts:

> 'The right-wing Tory and ardent monarchist, yet a social iconoclast; the apostle of self-help, of Thatcherite endeavour, yet with a deep commitment to charitable causes ... anarchic on the cricket field yet regarded on the field by umpires as a sportsman of Corinthian mould; the supreme individualist yet touchingly supportive of team-mates; incandescent with self-belief yet insecure and increasingly reclusive.'

Leaving aside her untested abilities on a cricket pitch, this was Thatcher too. As was the impression Botham's former England colleague Geoff Cook had of him. 'He's a man full of paradoxes. I was struck by his forcefulness, his occasional lack of patience and quick temper, yet he often showed the caring side of his nature.' So, for all people believed they were easily characterised, the opposite was true.

The apparent resignation of many to the country's torpor was not something they shared. Applying the employment-related meaning of that word resignation, one of them would eventually be forced into it, the other steadfastly refused for a decade to bow to the pressure to do likewise. But resignation was not something in the vocabulary of Margaret Hilda Thatcher and Ian Terence Botham. If there were two people more determined to resist decline and turn their nation around, they don't come readily to mind. Another musical artist and unlikely contributor here, Dolly Parton, once said, 'You can't control the wind, but you can sure control your sails.' There were to be winds of gale force proportion heading towards both at the start of the 80s but, close as they may have come to the rocks, they never gave up on their way of riding them out. The choice Thatcher and Botham were to take in the face of the challenges of the time were predicated on an attitude of front-foot attack and no turning back. Neither was a fan of détente. In this they set an example and a tone which their people were to pick up on increasingly, especially through the year of 1981. They were doers who didn't want to look back – moving forward was all that mattered. In an interview with Peter Jay on ITV whilst still leader of the opposition, when discussing pay deals and other matters of Labour's economic policy, Thatcher's strident question to her interviewer (not the last time she would turn the tables on those who thought *they* were doing the interrogating) was, 'Is Britain to be thought of wholly in terms of restraint? Can't we advance?' Restraint was another word which meant little to either of them and was a mannerism in others which meant both would lose patience with a Geoffrey. Thatcher owed much to her first chancellor, Geoffrey Howe, but she liked dash and he was the antithesis of dashing. Thatcher's biographer, Charles Moore, suggests it was Howe's very patience that made her cross. Botham also owed much on occasion to his own Geoffrey – Boycott – but, when batting, Boycott's level of patience made Howe look positively skittish and his degree of dash made the chancellor a ringer for Usain Bolt. This irritated Botham in precisely the same way and was a matter he once addressed (the veracity of the story dependent on whose side of it you believe) by running him out in a Test match before he cost his side any chance of victory and bored Botham to death in the process. Howe would perform his own 'run out' a decade on, when the cricketing analogy in his resignation speech all but ended his leader's career, but the impatience with their respective Geoffreys in the years prior was a clear demonstration of their drive to get things done without procrastination. Charles Moore also saw in his subject 'a horror of wasting time. Such people act and even as they are acting they do not pause to observe how they are acting'. Botham lived this philosophy, wanting to push life to its limits every single day. His wife Kathy experienced this urgency for many years, saying, 'He sees a goal and that's it.' In this way, as in many others, they would live the lives of similar people acting simultaneously in different fields.

Botham was actually to prove himself the ultimate Thatcherite – an incarnation and example of the independent self-achiever his prime minister admired and sought to encourage. Here was someone with no silver spoon in his background who made good through his own efforts and the maximising of his gifts and also through determination, self-belief and a drive for self-improvement, who then enjoyed the fruits of the success that followed with little restraint and no guilt. Like Thatcher, he believed strongly in a society which offered incentives because the growth and strength of a nation came from the efforts of its people. One of Thatcher's more trusted advisors, John Hoskyns, said that 'She had this "let's go for the mountain tops" attitude'. Botham had it in spades as Graham Dilley would find out on greeting him at the wicket at Headingley.

There are many interviews and speeches in which one can find Thatcher's beliefs given expression but a revealing one also exists, now an internet jewel, of Botham confronted by a challenging, youthful BBC audience and one which, not unusually for the nation's public broadcaster, did not come across as representative of all political allegiances. He gave an uncanny impression of his prime minister, revealing both his convictions and his defensiveness at any challenge to them which had the air of an accusation in equal measure. On *Open To Question* in 1986, he would reference his father's defence of freedom during the Second World War to answer a question on whether he considered changing nappies women's work. Challenged on whether it was selfish to so immerse himself in his sport, Botham seemed barely able to comprehend the motivation of the inquisitor and insisted 'It's my job, but I'm also an entertainer and it's flattering that people will pay to come and see that. And if you can entertain them, surely you're making a contribution to society?' Finally, when the questioning moved into the area of his politics he confirmed he was in agreement with a lot of the Thatcher policies, articulating a strong belief in free enterprise. 'I do believe that if a guy wants to get off his backside and go and make something of his life he should have that opportunity. And I fear that under the Labour Party it would be too easy for people to sit around and do nothing and get paid for it.' Thatcher's speechwriters may not have framed it in quite the same words but it would have been no surprise had they scripted the precise sentiments. Andy McSmith references Thatcher's own belief in self-reliance and that she feared this was being diluted by a bloated welfare state which supported those (alongside other more deserving cases) who couldn't be bothered to help themselves.

Had Botham had speechwriters himself they might have scripted this for Thatcher, too. Revisiting this interaction now not only gives a sense of our country's tendency to tall-poppy syndrome in the general antipathy towards a sportsman who had given such pleasure in the preceding years but also, in the plethora of questions which asked Botham to address many of the country's ills himself, rather endorsed the feeling that this particular sportsman had, unintentionally by his deeds in '81 in particular, become relevant in the nation's mind as a spokesperson for society as much as sport. The belief in freedom of the individual and the importance of creating an environment which would encourage rather than deride ambition was not 'greed is good' but 'making and taking opportunities is good' – advocacy of taking personal responsibility for making the most of one's life, rather than relying on the state or others to offer you an easier alternative. Botham wanted to squeeze the last drop out of every experience, in whatever aspect of his life it might be. He wanted to push the boundaries to see what he was capable of. He was talking Thatcher's language. He would say that it was the leaving of the shires for London as a young man that convinced him, as he took it all in, that he wanted to be one of life's successes and to make it happen on his return to Somerset from the capital. 'I wasn't proud. I'd do anything to earn a few quid and wasn't out of work all winter.' His embodiment of the philosophy that it was incumbent on the individual to make change rather than hoping somebody else might do it was never better demonstrated than in his turning of the Ashes series that now bears his name.

Not everyone would share their belief that inequality is not necessarily a bad thing. Whilst both understood the desirability of creating equality of opportunity, to strive for equality of *outcome* was to fool oneself – no such thing truly exists either in life or in sport. If all games ended equal, sport would be pointless. Sport should always encourage equality of opportunity but its whole purpose lies in inequality of outcome. Some perform better than others, some win, some lose – sometimes through lesser talent, occasionally (but not consistently) through bad luck and sometimes through lack of application and effort. Margaret Thatcher and Ian Botham both recognised this within their own worlds. Lack of effort was the devil's work to them. So Botham and Thatcher were indeed a natural fit. The England cricket biographer Simon Wilde was convinced – 'he was completely into her agenda. He fitted it perfectly and would've been proud to be identified with it'.

But Botham also gave the lie to the caricature that 'Thatcher's children' were all one-dimensional, grasping, self-centred and unsympathetic. He would, through his walks to raise money for medical research into leukaemia and the time he devoted to hospital ward visits to the joy of many young sufferers of the condition, prove that a belief in some of Thatcher's principles did not have to be a barrier to philanthropy and empathy. He could also be extremely empathic towards any players in his teams who were struggling and in the same way, for all the portrayals of an ice maiden, Thatcher too had a sensitive side. Dominic Sandbrook highlighted numerous examples of her kindness to her staff and quotes a Downing Street messenger, a lifelong Labour supporter, as claiming he had never known Number Ten as happy a place as it was under her. Nonetheless, both were sensitive to criticism, found it hard to forgive those who they felt had let them down and were capable of bearing the most enduring grudges. Sandbrook noted her tendency, shared by Botham, rarely to forgive a slight and her knack of provoking fierce passions. There was a sense of 'us against the world' in both of them – once you had won their trust and were accepted into the inner sanctum as someone deemed to be 'of the right stuff' their loyalty and generosity of spirit was rock solid but if you were on the outside looking in, you could expect a much less convivial relationship tinged with suspicion.

Aldous Huxley once suggested that 'those who believe they are exclusively in the right are generally those who achieve something'. This was something that both Thatcher and Botham would demonstrate throughout their careers – as the broadcaster Danny Baker once termed it, 'sometimes right, sometimes wrong, but always certain'. That didn't appeal to everyone. Pete Waterman said of Thatcher, 'the thing about her is that whether her policies were right or wrong she followed her policies. She stood for what she stood for – and that angered some people' and had he said that of Botham it would have been just as accurate. On occasion it could make them look foolish and obstinate in the face of reality, but without it they surely wouldn't have withstood the toughest times and come back to make such a mark on the world. They could each be abrasive, aggressive and in Botham's case sometimes physically so. He was sometimes labelled as 'boorish' in behaviour and attitude, but the bottom line was that a nation which had become used to vapid leadership and acceptance of mediocrity was happy to accept a bit of abrasiveness now. In the world of sport in particular, after a decade of sporting sterility the people and media alike were delighted to see someone with a bit of spirit. The electorate would evidence its own desire for the same come 1979.

David Gower saw his team-mate as 'hugely charismatic … literally unstoppable' and never saw him show any sign of weakness, even when he was sure the doubts must have been creeping in in the first half of 1981 when nothing went his way. 'If there were doubts, I would say he hid them well. It was a great trick to master.' Doubts there most certainly were at times, but both knew the value inherent in people's perception that they held nothing but belief. Those of us with fainter hearts are drawn to following those who offer strength. As far as Botham was concerned such fortitude was simply a given – try facing Andy Roberts or Jeff Thomson without it. It was part of a personality which grated with some, perhaps in particular those who were unable to replicate it. In both Thatcher and Botham it was often seen as arrogance – not something welcomed by the British as a rule. Dylan Jones in his book *The Eighties* reproduces some words from the rock musician Gordon Sumner, aka Sting, who was another example of an unapologetic self-improver in the Botham mould and the sort beloved of Thatcher, and another whose success came from unremarkable beginnings in the mid-70s to global stardom by the early 80s. In a response to accusations of aloofness which reflect all three, he said, 'I've been perceived as an arrogant person but I don't see that … I stand on my own two feet. I've always been confident and even when I wasn't I could pretend that I was – which is what I suppose was perceived as arrogance.' As a characteristic relevant to success in the Thatcherite era its potency was demonstrated by the likes of Sting and Botham time and again.

At first glance Thatcher and Botham might appear an odd couple to consider soul buddies. They were certainly disparate personalities – one a workaholic and almost a puritan in her social life if such a life actually existed, the other a force of nature *bon viveur*. Both would burn the midnight oil throughout their careers but in mightily different pursuits. Peter Roebuck would say of his former Somerset team-mate that 'he took heroic liberties, not all of them calculated with minute care', which was both an understatement and an example of a contrast. Thatcher would prepare for every battle with the forensic assiduousness of the trained scientist to ensure she was fully briefed, no matter how much she would like to insist she was an instinctive politician. Forensic was not a word many would apply to Botham's preparation which bore little resemblance other than in its nocturnal nature. For both could survive on little sleep and still perform even if the word 'performance' meant different things to each. Thatcher would use the sleepless nights to study ministerial red boxes and civil service briefings … Beefy was more likely to be found studying a bottle (or three) of claret. The former was predominantly serious and straight, although still able to enjoy a party, if not of the Botham variety. The latter was gregarious and at times irresponsible. Thatcher's skill resided in the mind, Botham's more in the physical, though the mind was also strong in a competitive and sporting sense. Hers was the meticulousness of the trained lawyer; his was the seat-of-the-pants ride of the gambler.

Thatcher's father once urged her 'Margaret, never do things just because other people do them' and both were happy to break convention and challenge the status quo, having no truck with those who wanted to thwart their ambition. Told bluntly by Heath that if she stood against him as leader she'd lose, she revealed 'that remark gave a zest to my competitive spirit.' This iconoclasm in an innately conservative society meant they became 'Marmite' figures – loved or loathed depending on the eye of the beholder. The Pakistani writer Imran Yusuf reflected on Botham when considering this and the mixed relationship many of his countrymen have with him: 'He was – he is – a tremendous character, a massive personality and life force for the game of cricket, and for this reason Beefy should only, can only, be loved. Even if you hate to do so.' They were characters who would forever split opinion. At times of struggle people will look for a target – a figure to blame. This was a fate that befell them both for a time – indeed at around the same times. Although unemployment had been on a steady rise under the Labour government, and accepting that Thatcher's solution to the wider problem was not going to improve but exacerbate that reality for a time, it was easy to make her a scapegoat for the whole issue to identify a target for the understandable anger it brought with it. It would be much the same with Botham and his captaincy in battles against the West Indies – he would become the fall guy for the defeats but to hold him personally responsible for them was unjust.

They were often distrusted by the establishment and their fondness for taking down a peg or two those who are not one of their own but are visibly successful and confident with it. Born and raised in northern shires, a grammar school girl and a comprehensive-educated boy, their upbringings may have influenced their own shared distrust of the existing elite and of consensus, and yet both would eventually find themselves in the House of Lords. They were inculcated with traditional views and standards from early on, Thatcher by her strictly Methodist father and Botham through his parents and his own life experience. Both had had to be patient in gaining recognition, for different reasons, throughout their early years and to fight to be taken seriously. They would be in time. Both would ultimately be loved by the grassroots more than those establishments and one of the reasons they were able to outlast the brickbats and the bad times was that their views often bore closer relation to those of the vast majority of the population than did the views of their critics. Through this both managed to broaden their audiences and supporters through the early 80s in particular. Whilst Botham brought cricket to the consciousness of the public and to people who had never followed England cricket before, Thatcher's election victories of '79 and '83 were driven by a huge political loyalty from those who had never voted Conservative before. Botham always felt that that the world of cricket was harder for him to conquer coming from 'the sticks in the north'. Thatcher discovered soon enough on assuming the party's leadership that the old Etonian grandees who liberally populated her inherited Shadow Cabinet saw her accession as a remarkable aberration on behalf of the party and fully expected that they would be rid of her in short order and before she could affect the sort of change that was anathema to them. The conspiratorial whispering behind her lasted from her appointment until she rid herself of them in the ruthless reshuffle of her cabinet in September '81 and it betrayed an issue of class. A member of all the cabinets of her first term, with the more acceptable background to the upper echelons of his party of Eton, Cambridge and captain in the 9th Lancers, Christopher Soames once bemoaned cattily, 'We've got a corporal at the top, not a cavalry officer.' But those theoretically on her own side who considered Thatcher a 'nine-day wonder' were to be disabused. It's not hard to envisage many members at Lord's of similar upbringings, including those who ultimately appointed him, having precisely the same view of Botham when he became the leader of his national team. Many in the olde-worlde bastions of MCC and beyond saw it as the same kind of ill-judged mistake, which would ideally be rectified sooner rather than later. In both cases there was a distasteful sense that they would never be fully accepted because they simply weren't 'one of us'. Ultimately one would ride these out and survive to change her party and country, and the other would be forced to succumb, but would still move on to ultimate success. The close proximity of their respective accessions to the top jobs in their fields was just one example of a remarkable symmetry in the highs and lows of their careers and their timings – 1980 into 1981 being perhaps the starkest case in point when both came under huge pressure but managed to come through in their different but similar ways.

Competition was more than important, it was critical, and both thrived on that challenge and winning the key battles when others were telling them it was impossible, proving the doubters wrong. The former England Test player, now commentator, Mike Selvey recalled, 'in the lexicon of Ian Botham's existence there is no word for "impossible". He does not do, and has never done, '"can't" … There was no situation so dire that it could not be rescued by his personal intervention, so secure in his mind was the infallibility of what he was trying to do.' Perhaps this is not something the British always perceive in themselves and maybe it's why both were respected even when they were not liked and why they would become such distinctive cultural forces. Such innate strength did however, in both cases, at times mask a certain sensitivity and insecurity. Botham's tour manager on his cataclysmic West Indies tour in 1981, A.C. Smith, saw his reaction to negative media coverage at the time. 'He's fundamentally insecure and very sensitive to criticism.' Both could become defensive and morose in the face of criticism and they weren't without the need of support. It may have been because they could so often sense the whispers and the back-stabbing that those they could truly trust became their absolute rocks – another concordance being in both of them losing those rocks in tragic circumstances just before, and just after, attaining the top job when they needed them the most. Both were capable of what Mike Brearley referred to in Botham as an instinctive but brief mulishness. But despite their strength of conviction both were possessed of another ability. 'Though Botham sometimes initially seems reluctant to listen, he does take a point', wrote Brearley. This was true of both provided the advice came from someone they trusted and saw as one of their own. Charles Moore noted of one of Thatcher's speechwriters, Ronnie Millar, that he was ' a trusted friend who wanted her to succeed and was therefore prepared to tell her things she didn't want to hear'. Such 'rocks' were just as important for the strong character that was Botham. Over the years Brian Close, Ken Barrington and Mike Brearley would all play that role to his benefit.

They were both conservative and yet radical, driven by a deep love of their country. Charles Moore said of Thatcher that the emotional force was not really a doctrine about economic liberty – strong though that was – but a romantic belief in the greatness and a sad lament at the decline of her country. They were both strongly motivated by a desire to achieve things that would put a pride back into the nation and what they felt it stood for rather than suffering the prevailing defeatism. Thatcher herself outlined this in her memoirs: 'The truth, that Britain was now a middle-ranking power greatly weakened by economic decline, seemed too complex for sophisticated people to grasp. They were determined to think themselves weaker and more contemptible than was in fact the case, and refused all comfort to the contrary.' When her Defence Secretary John Nott briefed Thatcher in the spring of 1982 that, if taken, The Falklands 'could not be regained', she was distinctly unimpressed. Had anyone told Botham that, once taken, the Ashes could not be regained he too would have dismissed it as fatalistic nonsense. Thatcher began her 1986 party conference speech with 'Mr. President, before I begin I would like to make clear, the rose I am wearing today is the rose of England.' For Botham, carrying the lions of England on his chest carried a similar honour and importance and in the words of biographer Murphy he had 'a near-primeval loyalty to the Queen'. He was an ebullient national-anthem singer and St George's Day celebrator and would defend his country to the hilt in argument and in battle on the cricket field, and would without doubt have done so in battle off it as well had the need arisen.

In writing a book about three outstanding football managers who worked miracles with three unfashionable clubs and had a significant consequential positive impact on the spirit of their provincial communities in the same period of the mid-70s to mid-80s, I discovered remarkable similarity of method, belief and success amidst some marked differences in personality and concluded that they went on to achieve 'similarly but differently brilliant things'. The synergies between them did not mean they were identical but the will to survive, to prove people wrong, and to reach the top were shared. It so happens that they each reached a high point across 1980 and 1981, Lawrie McMenemy's Southampton turning the football world upside down by signing the European Footballer of the Year and 'small' clubs Nottingham Forest and Ipswich Town wrecking the natural order of dominance in European football. In that remarkable year of 1981 Ipswich, even more remarkably, were named the European Team of the Year. More change. The football analysis also noted that in any period of sustained achievement there are likely to be moments of fate, fortune, call them what you will – those sliding-doors moments that we all experience in the journeys of our lives.

Political historian Andrew Marr puts forward the view that were it not for a Labour Party disembowelling itself and a corrupt, desperate dictatorship in South America, Thatcher's government would probably have been destroyed after a single term. Had the majority of her early cabinet ministers who disagreed with her been brave enough to say boo to a goose she might not even have made it as far as that. Many argue that it was Thatcher's huge good fortune that the wait for the expected salvation which would come from North Sea oil should finally be over on her watch – that without it she could not have laid claim to the country's economic recovery. Richard Vinen notes that 'both [political] parties prayed that they would be in office when the oil started to flow. In 1980 Mrs. Thatcher won this particular game'. Marr described Thatcher as 'bold, verging on the reckless. But she was also extremely lucky'. Many a cricket commentator would say the same of Botham throughout his career, usually as an observation rather than a slight, but if fortune favours the brave, perhaps it does also for the 'bold, verging on reckless'. Fate needs a helping hand – something or somebody to drive it, and these two made that difference *themselves*. Were they both lucky in their successes? At times yes, of course. But, as Peter Roebuck would say generously of Botham 'if he was lucky, he deserved to be and of course luck was not his only quality. He was outstandingly courageous too. Fortune is selective; it favours the bold adventurer'. And so it proved in the stories of the courageous bold adventurers that were Margaret Thatcher and Ian Botham, their beating of the odds and changing of the nation.

I included a quotation from the American Melissa Meyer in my analysis of the football managers which bears repetition here: 'In the end, maybe there isn't such a thing as fate – maybe it's just the opportunities we're given and what we do with them.' Botham and Thatcher continue that narrative here. Roebuck said of Botham that he never doubted his own destiny. Thatcher saw a destiny too. It was how they might get there which was the unknown.

If the harmony between our two leading characters can be encapsulated in one sentence it may well be that of an economic advisor's description of the paradox of Thatcher. 'I was struck by her sense of insecurity, sense of destiny and reckless courage.' A perfect summation.

Alwyn Turner described Botham as 'an unpredictable individualist whose career seemed entirely appropriate for Thatcher's Britain'. Perhaps there was both a serendipity and an inevitability that they and their deeds should come along at exactly the same time. Here is the subtext within this exploration of change – so conspicuous and arresting were the parallels which emerged between them that they became a constant thread. Over the years Margaret Thatcher and Ian Botham – similar and distinct in equal measure, loved and loathed depending on individual tastes – would change the mood and the reality of the country undeniably and forevermore. They were ultimately two figures who came to epitomise both change and the survivor's instinct required to see it through and leave a lasting legacy. Marr said of Thatcher, but could also have said of Botham in 1981, 'the early reverses … are turned into massive, nation-changing victories' and Thatcher herself said, shortly after taking office, 'Nations depend for their health upon the achievements of a comparatively small number of talented and determined people'

Here is that tale. Cometh the hour, cometh the man. And the woman …

PART TWO:

'The Before'

THE STATE OF THE NATION

1974–1979

Down The Plughole

'We were in a desperate way in 1979. We were going down the plughole.'

Lord Carrington, Foreign Secretary 1979–82

'The country had felt for years as if it were stumbling into chaos … and the British tendency to mock was looking as though it might be part of the problem, not the solution.'

Alwyn W. Turner,
Rejoice! Rejoice!: Britain in the 1980s

'Britain's self-image was as a country trapped in an inexorable cycle of post-industrial decline.'

Dominic Sandbrook
Who Dares Wins

IT IS impossible to consider the impact of the events of 1981 and their future significance without a recollection of the state of the nation in the years before and the opportunity that offered a couple of individuals to come to prominence. The current media presentation of the 1970s as a decade is bedecked with the sugar-candy nostalgia of the television programmes which take us back to cherished days of *Multi-Coloured Swap Shop* and *Tiswas*; of proper FA Cup final Saturdays; of three television channels regularly turning themselves off when they could find nothing more with which to entertain us other than the Open University or *For Schools and Colleges;* of Chopper bikes and TicTacs; of cheese fondue and Freddie Laker. Alternatively, we are reminded of dark days of decline, the Winter of Discontent and a slightly quaint but, in hindsight, rather shoddy way of life.

Both are valid portrayals to a point. The 70s probably weren't as depressing for many of those who lived through them as some of the political and economic struggles and the ever-present threat of terrorism on our own streets might suggest. Richard Vinen makes the point that opinion polls in the relatively happy days of the Queen's Silver Jubilee in 1977 suggested that quite large numbers of the British people, for a time at least, felt that the hot summers of 1976 and '77 were the happiest times of their lives and painted a picture of a part of the nation which was conservative with a small 'c' and content and at ease with itself. There was still some optimism when James Callaghan became prime minister in 1976 that prosperity might lie ahead, especially if he could deliver some industrial harmony. It would be a different poll come the winter of 1978–79 when it had become apparent that he couldn't, and that optimism was gone, but upon Callaghan's arrival it is plausible to argue that Britain's decline was seen more clearly by those overseas than those at home. This negative perception abroad would, in due course as it became apparent, be a major contributor to a loss of pride and confidence but for many that realisation took a while to register, certainly if you were, as I was, a young child whose life experience at that stage was sheltered from the reality of the wider world. In my own somewhat protected middle-class Hampshire adolescence I recall long, happy summers, cosy Christmases and just enough financial resource for a wealth of first experiences. They may have been more modest and practical holidays back then – in tents rather than villas – and presents may have been football annuals or *Wisdens* rather than iPhones, but these were what we knew and cherished. Even the England cricket team had its moments, with three victorious Ashes series – against varying quality of opposition – and victory in India thrown in alongside the odd sobering capitulation against terrifying fast bowling.

But there was a problem. The economic and political health of the nation got into a state in the 70s the seriousness of which can be underestimated today. The influence of the trades unions was becoming powerful enough to suggest they were effectively governing the country themselves. The defeat of the National Coal Board by the National Union of Mineworkers in 1974 and the consequent demise of Edward Heath's Conservative government did nothing to dispel that impression. Moreover, it emboldened not just the miners but the TUC in general that in the future no government would be able to move the country in any direction without their acquiescence. It was a different time, when union bosses were some of the best-known names in the country. For a TUC bigwig to be referenced by name in the country's leading sitcom on the understanding that everyone would recognise it would not even get past the script meeting today, but Hugh Scanlon popped up in a 1976 episode of *The Good Life* as a matter of course.

This union power was growing at a time when the country's educational institutions, particularly its universities, were increasingly being infiltrated by the politics of the hard left and it is easy to disregard today just how close the country was becoming to a truly left-wing state. This sense was hardly discouraged by the increasing profile of the likes of Tony Benn and Michael Foot in the Labour governments that would follow Heath. Andy McSmith contends that since 1945 Britain had edged towards becoming more socialist and that within the Labour Party during the mid-70s there was a vigorous movement to give the country another sharp push in the same direction. (I can confirm this given my great auntie was a committed part of it.) To this could be added 'The Troubles' in Northern Ireland and the spreading of that issue onto Britain's streets. To maintain any general feeling of comfort against a backdrop of industrial unrest, plummeting productivity in an atrophying manufacturing base and the carefree public spending of the Labour government, the country was paying itself more than it could afford year after year and storing up a whole heap of trouble. Additionally, at this time there was no disguising how Britain was viewed abroad, by friends and well as foes. On 29 April 1975, not long after England's battered cricketers had returned from an Ashes thrashing down under, the *Wall Street Journal* published an article titled, uncompromisingly, 'Goodbye Great Britain'. It portrayed an image of Britain on the verge of political and economic meltdown – in its opinion because of the Labour government's mishandling of the economy. It saw a toxic mix of weakness in the matters of exchange rates, risk of hyperinflation, collapsing business confidence and punitive levels of taxation particularly on wealth-creating entrepreneurs. In short, the public finances were in a dire state. It warned its readers of the dangers of what it termed 'the welfare state-manic Keynesian syndrome' and to beware the possibility of it happening there in America. After all, if a country once as pre-eminent as their traditional ally, Great Britain, could get itself into this state and accept what it termed the management of decline, they could not consider themselves safe either if such a drift was allowed. It was a sorry picture but more fact than over-dramatised fiction. In 1975 the US Secretary of State Henry Kissinger told President Ford, 'Britain is a tragedy – it has sunk to begging, borrowing and stealing ... that Britain has become such a scrounger is a disgrace.' Meanwhile, at home even the head of the civil service, Sir William Armstrong, told his colleagues that the British government's task was now 'to oversee the orderly management of decline'. To use one of Margaret Thatcher's more famed responses to something she disagreed with at the end of the decade, the reaction to such thinking from both her and Ian Botham would have been a vehement, 'No! No! No!' In 1975 she would start to do something about it.

This picture of a nation fluctuating between happy days and pessimism was reproduced in the fortunes of the England cricket team as another figure of future significance made his first steps. The image of a country in decline was mirrored by England's performances in the period bookended by the struggles of the Heath government – his three-day week, the oil shock and the miners' strike amongst them – and the humiliation of the Labour government which replaced them with devaluation and the plea to the International Monetary Fund in 1976.

An upturn in morale through the hot summer of 1977 and the street parties of the Silver Jubilee was accompanied by a first Ashes victory for six and a half years, notable for the arrival of Ian Botham in the Test side with considerable success. The series was also played against a backdrop of the Packer schism in the game which produced a similar concern for the sport's future to that which found its source in the turbulence of the country's political landscape. It was weak opposition which would then create the opportunity for both Ian Botham and Margaret Thatcher (who was fortunate in the enemies she had both in the Conservative Party and on the opposition benches) to take the reins as the decade reached its conclusion.

England's results since the war had begun to form the pattern which was to show itself most dramatically in '81 – that mysterious correlation between the state of the nation and that of its team. In the austerity of the years which followed the Second World War, Britain lived an existence of rationing and anti-climax as reality bit. From 1946 to 1952 across 14 Test series (plus one-off matches) and 56 Tests, England's cricketers' managed to lose more matches than they won, this despite their win column being boosted by matches against still emerging sides such as India and New Zealand. They lost almost a third of their series and achieved an aggregate score in Ashes Tests, the true measure in the public's eyes, of 11 to 1 against, as another reality bit – that of Don Bradman. The shared journey took its next turn as the national rejoicing at the Queen's coronation was accompanied by a first Ashes victory for 20 years, completed by the nation's sporting hero, Denis Compton, at a packed and exultant Oval. This would begin an era of unparalleled success when England had a good claim to be pre-eminent in the world which would last, with the odd inevitable down moment, through a time of improved living standards until the end of the Swinging Sixties decade. From 1953 to 1970 England won 59 per cent of the 39 series they played, won more Ashes series than they lost and crowned the run with the regaining of the Ashes on Australian soil for the first time since the Bodyline success 38 years earlier, as the 70s dawned and Heath and the country were still in their honeymoon period.

Now came the challenges: as the economy, low morale and productivity steered the nation towards its portrayal as 'the sick man of Europe' so the cricket picture once more reflected the times. From 1971 until the unexpected victory in India in the winter of 1976–77, the Test team reverted to a losing record, defeated at home for the first time ever by India, eviscerated in Australia in 1974-75, fast bowlers Lillee and Thomson every bit as intimidating as executioners of the England batsmen as the TUC and miners' leaders 'opening attack' of Len Murray and Joe Gormley, and their back-up bowlers, Arthur Scargill and Mick McGahey, had been that year for the Conservative government. The humiliation of Harold Wilson in 1976 was neatly reprised that same summer by that of England's captain Tony Greig at the hands of the West Indies side he had confidently advised us would be conquerable. Then came that sunny summer of 1977 and the arrival of Botham. From the start of that season until Botham's accession to the captaincy his rise came in tandem with that of Thatcher. Aided by that Packer-denuded opposition, particularly in the case of Australian sides, the win/loss score would be 16-5 in favour as the fresh, Botham-inspired side took full advantage of their good fortune.

Taking all this into account, perhaps it isn't surprising that in Britain in 1980 and 1981 cricket and Botham would tell the story every bit as vividly as those other elements which would change the mood.

Now I'm Here
1974–1976

'From my youngest days I had an unshakeable self-confidence and belief in my own abilities … though others might have found less flattering ways to describe it.'

Ian Botham

THERE WERE two elements which would combine to create the opportunities for Thatcher and Botham alike. Their rise and success owed much both to the weakness of their opposition, which would show itself most obviously from 1977 to 1979, but also to the failures of the predecessors on their own sides during the earlier years of the decade.

In 1971 the miners' union saw an opportunity to test a new Conservative administration, and possibly to bring it to its knees, submitting a 45 per cent pay claim. In February 72, on its rejection, they went on strike and prevailed at the infamous Battle of Saltley Gate when they successfully shut down a key coking plant. With the government having few reserves to back up any firm stance, they had capitulated, settling at 20 per cent plus fringe benefits. Like the bully who is placated that was never going to be the end of the problem. Margaret Thatcher was taking note of the reasons for and the consequences of the defeat and resolved not to make the same mistake should she ever be in a position to fight a similar fight. It was to be to the miners' own disadvantage in the long term that Saltley Gate and its aftermath would contribute significantly to her ending up in exactly that position. On the very first day of 1974 Edward Heath announced to the country a national crisis that would necessitate the imposition of a three-day working week and the conservation of energy in every home, and the ensuing winter of candlelight and shortages was one from which he never recovered.

The luckless Heath had been assailed by almost as many missiles as his successor would confront at the turn of the decade but was less equipped to see them off amidst a sea of denial and U-turns. To the unions, the miners and the Industrial Relations Act could be added the Yom Kippur War and oil shock of 1973, the Cod Wars, the challenge of entry into the EEC, the influx of refugees from Uganda, and the issue of Northern Ireland. In fact the global oil crisis was seen by the miners' leaders as the perfect moment to strike again, figuratively and literally, and they made no secret of their primary motivation. Not for the last time, it was clear that the living standards of their members was just an incidental part of the greater war. The true objective could be seen in the reported words of the Scottish miners' leader Mick McGahey when asked by Heath what it was he wanted which might bring peace. 'I want to see the end of your government' left no room for misunderstanding. Again, this did not escape Thatcher and if the union was to get its heart's desire this time, ten years on it would be very different.

Heath had been the great hope of the centre-leaning MPs within his party – a man of consensus and of compromise and the sort of statesman unlikely to arouse any great ire in anybody, or indeed to arouse anything at all. This was the sort of conservatism that the Tory grandees believed had successfully navigated the past and held the key to the future. It wasn't a vision shared by every member of his team however, and ultimately it would not even hold the key to the door of No.10 Downing Street. Heath was not a man given to laying the blame for the desperate state of affairs in the country he led at his own door – he was still refusing to do so in resentful retirement a dozen years later. (Heath's relationship with his successor – his gracelessness towards her and his steadfast refusal to praise her – was the opposite to that between Botham and his own successor (and predecessor) Brearley in the years to come.) Had he possessed a semblance of either contrition or self-awareness he would not have asked the electorate to decide 'who governs?' in the erroneous belief that they would decide that it would be best if he continued to do so. Even following the subsequent defeat, a willingness to step aside would almost certainly have stillborn any chance Mrs Thatcher might have had of succeeding him. On such things do our worlds turn. So, in an irony invisible at the time, the miners and their leaders had effectively prepared the ground for their future nemesis to accede first of all to leadership and then to power. In the words of the historian Richard Vinen, 'Heath's failure was a pre-condition of Mrs Thatcher's success.'

It was the forced departure of another captain of the ship which would open the same path to national recognition for Ian Botham, in this case not through his failure but his defection. Tony Greig was about as un-Heath-like a character as could have been found on the planet, but had taken over the leadership of the England Test team from a man, in Mike Denness, who bore a far closer resemblance. Denness was also a man whom the establishment responsible for appointing him saw as a safe pair of hands and anything but a rocker of boats. Unfortunately, nice chap though he undoubtedly was, he was no more possessed than Heath of the strength to overcome the brutality of the challenges he faced. His days were numbered after the obliteration he was unable to counter in Australia that coming winter, and the loss of the first Test back in England in the Ashes of 1975 confirmed the need for a change and that the English public was again ready for a leader with a bit more fight. It was not, however, Denness's loss of the job that would give Botham his opportunity but that of his successor.

Looking back, it is serendipitous that Tony Greig became England's leader just four months after Margaret Thatcher took the helm of the Conservative Party, and from a character whose haplessness he couldn't help but contrast.

Moreover, there was a parallel in the decidedly mixed reaction to both appointments; if many of the traditionalists in the upper echelons of her party found the wholly unexpected arrival of a woman, and one who planned to challenge the cosiness of their existence at that, hard to stomach, there were similarly dissenting voices both in the establishment in English cricket's corridors of power and some of the game's followers, which suggested that a brash South African leading the England cricket team was beyond the pale and, in the wider country's view, just another blow to pride and a badge of decline. What they all really wanted was a similar saviour, but of good English stock. Neither new arrival concerned themselves with the naysayers and for many others Greig was seen as exactly the type required – a forerunner of Botham in his insistence on leading a charge on the ramparts regardless of the odds against. Greig oversaw a recovery of sorts and a display of previously absent backbone in the remainder of that summer's Ashes series without preventing a 1-0 defeat. His gung-ho optimism went rather less well in his infamously indelicate choice of words intended to sound another battle cry ahead of the following summer's Tests against the West Indies and in the hammering that followed, but an impressive victory in India in the winter had Greig's England just about in the positives column overall and set him up for the chance to become one of England's few Ashes-regaining captains in the summer of '77. Just as importantly, unlike Denness before him and Mike Brearley to follow, there was no question that Greig was worth his place in the side. Had Geoff Boycott not taken himself into self-imposed exile for the previous three years he would have had supporters for the role as the only alternative to Greig with the same guarantee of a place on merit. However, even when he returned that summer he was not seriously considered for the future despite a couple of Tests deputising as captain the following winter.

If not his namesake Howe, Geoffrey might be seen as the cricketing equivalent of one of Thatcher's favourite ministers, Keith Joseph – undoubtedly talented but given to introspection and far from the greatest empathiser or communicator, with a tendency to produce the tactless utterance at just the wrong moment. Like Joseph, although he had some committed advocates, there were too many risks attached to an appointment to the top job. If Boycott was Joseph, Greig was Thatcher's Michael Heseltine, all blond looks, dash, rampant self-belief and obvious ambition, but encouraging an air of suspicion that that ambition might just be his undoing. Nevertheless it was dash and self-belief that the people and selectors sorely wanted, not introspection. A world-class all-rounder and inveterate competitor, Greig's contributions were the cornerstone of his teams efforts. There wasn't room, or so it was widely perceived, for two such all-rounders in the side and Greig didn't appear to be going anywhere anytime soon. Therefore, had he not become the prime mover in the Packer project which would split the game for the next three years with the inevitable loss, initially of the captaincy, and ultimately his place, the Botham journey might have been very different. In the same way as Heath's hubris had changed matters for Thatcher, so Greig's commercial ambition did the same for his replacement as England's white charger. The sliding doors had opened and both were ready to walk right on through them.

As the events of 1974 gave Thatcher her first window of opportunity, so they also gave us a first glimpse of Botham. Charles Moore suggests that it was during the course of 1974 that people began to notice Thatcher's abilities. This was now to be paralleled by Botham. The young Somerset all-rounder's name was on a few lips but not many until a match which has moved into legend changed the narrative. That summer the West Indian fast bowler Andy Roberts was a startling new arrival in the county game – his brooding, taciturn manner and truly life-threatening bouncers sending barely concealed apprehension bordering on terror around opposition dressing rooms. Roberts had announced himself via a succession of splintered stumps and broken bones and nobody had found the combination of nerve and technique required to counter him. Roberts's Hampshire had arrived at Taunton for a Benson and Hedges Cup tie in June and long before the end they had it all but wrapped up with Botham's Somerset still 70 short of victory with just two wickets left and Roberts with overs in hand. One of those overs included the ball that hit Botham on the jaw and had him spitting blood and teeth all over the pitch. The undaunted, attacking 45 not out which followed, that took Somerset to a remarkable one-wicket win, was the first notice that here was somebody a little different to your average English sportsperson. From that day on, the name of Botham was sought out in the scorecards and touted as a future hope of England – at that moment being in reference to its cricket team but, in time, translated to that of the country itself.

Aside from those Taunton heroics the summer of '74 had been a low-key one for England cricket fans. A one-sided whitewash of an under-performing Indian side was followed by three rain-affected draws against Pakistan – cricket and weather hardly conducive to lifting spirits. However, as autumn and winter approached, both for those who followed these things and the rest of the public such humdrum events would seem nirvana in respect of what now lay ahead.

The blast could be heard for miles around. It was 5 October 1974 and an IRA bomb had just detonated in a crowded pub in Guildford. It was a chilling confirmation that that organisation was bringing its campaign to the British mainland. When, six and a half weeks later, similar devices exploded in two Birmingham pubs it had become clear that anyone who liked to enjoy a British social life could no longer consider themselves safe in their own towns and cities. If a general murk had descended upon the public mood through the privations of the first half of the year, here was a dark cloud that only intensified the sense of unease and futility. Five days on from Guildford, the second general election of the year, required to address the unworkable hung parliament created by the first, delivered a Labour victory but with a three-seat majority that would leave the government hamstrung for the next two years and the country's politics spitting in the wind.

If futility was now the overriding ambience at home, it was no easier for England to avoid 10,000 miles away. Those who were hoping England's defence of the Ashes in Australia might offer some escapism and relief were to be sadly disappointed. Instead, that domestic futility was reproduced in the England batsmen's attempts to cope with Dennis Lillee and the nasty shock that was Jeff Thomson. In another strange political parallel it was in the same month that England arrived in Australia that the disgraced and disappeared MP John Stonehouse turned up in the same country having sought to avoid prosecution for fraudulent crimes at home by faking his own death and setting off for the other side of the world. Neither of the tourists had any realistic chance of success and both would be found out and returned home in humiliation. Whether or not it was an attempt to justify his own fall from grace and give him comfort that he was well shot of it, one of Stonehouse's last speeches before his incarceration was articulate enough in its picture of the British life from which he was to be temporarily removed, claiming there was 'a tension, a disquiet and a dismay in the nation that can be seen on the faces of ordinary people'. There were soon to be similar countenances on the English cricketers. From the first day of the series on 29 November, waking on each morning of a British winter to daily news of capitulation on the cricket field had a depressing air of inevitability. *Wisden* suggested that the pitch at Brisbane, prepared by the city's mayor no less, 'provided the perfect launching pad for the most lethal post-war fast bowling partnership'. Lethal was the word of the moment: England was battling terror and seemingly insurmountable odds everywhere you looked. The country was getting buffeted and battered home and abroad.

Despite a typically defiant century in the first Test and three further fifties in the series, even the combative Greig was unable to hold back the tide on his own. It did however provide further ammunition for those who believed that it was time for a change at the top which might banish the prevailing culture of 'managed decline' and that this was the character to provide it. Some within the Conservative Party saw the need for just such a change too, to address the election defeats and install a similarly belligerent leader in opposition. The days of Denness and Heath, acquiescence and consensus, needed to go. And two unexpected events once again ran in tandem as the two bedraggled forces limped into February.

On 11 February 1975 there was a rest day in the sixth Test of a series in which by now England were 4-0 down. Two days later they would secure a most unlikely victory at Melbourne by an innings, although aided by a weakened opposition, shorn of Thomson from the start and Lillee to injury after six overs. If supporters hoped this marked a line in the sand and the start of a recovery, the same week would also see a far more significant victory with consequences which would last considerably longer. That 11 February was also the date on which, to the surprise of many and consternation of the grandees, Margaret Thatcher handed her rivals an innings defeat of their own and was elected leader of her party. Some would never let their irritation go. There is a Chinese proverb which says, 'when the wagon of fortune goes well, spite and envy hang on to the wheels'. So it was to prove for Thatcher. Her election occurred in a manner which had many Conservatives wondering how it had happened at all, MP Julian Critchley calling it a backbenchers' 'peasant's revolt'. After all, they had just chosen someone who as Education Secretary had removed free milk provision in schools and was consequently tagged 'the most unpopular woman in Britain'.

Another party member of long-standing, Reginald Maudling, told his young colleague Kenneth Baker, 'They've all gone absolutely mad. It's the darkest day in the history of the party.' In truth, it may well have been the opposite and the view was shot through with both male chauvinism and snobbery. These misgivings of her own team would be mirrored in Botham's own accession to leadership five years later and there were echoes after that appointment in Charles Moore's take on Thatcher's victory – that it was not obvious the party had meant to elect her or were very comfortable with its decision. Such ambivalence bordering on regret meant that neither was likely to be afforded much establishment support when times got tough.

In the same manner as Botham's, Thatcher's appointment benefited from the absence of compelling competition (as would her ascent to Number Ten), particularly in the first round. Had he stood then, the father figure of the party, Willie Whitelaw, would probably have won the vote and had Edward du Cann thrown his hat into the ring at the same time it is believed Thatcher would probably have stepped back and Britain might look somewhat different today. As with Botham, many assumed this would be a fleeting relationship with power before normal service was resumed. Richard Vinen could also have been articulating a view which would be held by many of the equivalent MCC grandees and members regarding Botham as leader five years later when he wrote that, 'Few Conservative MPs would've shed any tears if she'd been quietly ousted after a year or two to make way for a more establishment party figure.' After a year of Botham many at Lord's would be pushing for just such a figure to take his job – one of the county captains with none of the same world-class ability but with the right educational establishments on their CVs. In 1975 the two were at different stages of their careers and profiles, but there were no signs that either would become pivotal figures in the years ahead. Perhaps people should have paid more attention to the relatively low profile single by the emerging rock band Queen, which reached its high point in the UK chart the very same week Thatcher took the reins. Brian May's opening lyrics were serendipitous: *'Now I'm Here, think I'll stay around.'*

There had been one other event which would have a significant impact on our two subjects and their direction of travel, when a third 'gunslinger' had ridden into town to play the king.

Rupert Murdoch's own journey from successful newspaper proprietor to global media mogul, who would effectively come to own and dictate the country's news agenda, was another in which milestones tallied with the key moments for Thatcher and Botham, and both would develop relationships within his world which played no small part in their stories. In 1969, a year before Thatcher's first ministerial post in government, Murdoch satisfied his ambition to own a British national newspaper when he purchased *The Sun*, then a relatively small player in the UK's tabloid market, trailing *The Mirror* by a distance and indistinct from it in its left-leaning editorial stance. Over the next decade Murdoch increasingly saw something he liked in Thatcher and in advance of the 1979 general election decided to back the Conservatives, urging his growing readership to elect her. It was the morning after John Major's election win in 1992 that the famous headline 'It's The Sun Wot Won It' adorned its front page, but it was no less influential in its making of Margaret and championing her programme for change. In 1981 Thatcher made a proactive effort to court Murdoch whilst he added the *Sunday Times* to his collection and to ensure the weight of his support for her at the moment of her greatest peril. By this time Botham was also a *Sun* columnist – a relationship which was to be somewhat more fractious if commercially rewarding and one which did a similar job in keeping the player firmly at the head of the nation's news and sports agenda. Murdoch's newspaper and these two cohorts would become intertwined, all of a like mind. As Roger Domenghetti wrote, 'if *The Sun* embraced the spirit of Thatcherism, Botham embodied it'.

The idea of a new dawn for the cricketers and the country was to be short-lived as 1975 progressed. In the mid-1970s the leadership on both sides of the House of Commons feared the economy was on the verge of collapse and recognised that the old remedies were not working. Two days after Thatcher's arrival as opposition leader, the Labour government settled a 35 per cent pay rise for the miners. Once more, the evidence that Britain's economy and politicians were still being railroaded by union power was not lost on Thatcher. Nor was the realisation that she was by no means a unanimous choice within her own party. Now was the time for digging in. Soon it would be time to change direction.

The relentlessness of the challenges being laid before the country was reflected in its cricket by the fact that Ian Chappell's ruthless Australian side was refusing to go away. Unusually, a home Ashes series of four Tests would begin only five months after the away version had concluded and an element of shellshock remained in many of the batsmen England considered their strongest options. The pessimism in the dressing room and the stands alike was scarcely lessened by the World Cup semi-final between the two countries in June, ahead of the Ashes. The new tournament itself had been an unbridled success played in a fortnight of warm sunshine and bringing together eight different international sides in one country, England, for the first time. The cricket was as sunny as the skies – the moment when the potential of international one-day cricket culminating in such a global event began to gain real traction, even among the traditionalists. It also offered more evidence of the relevance of cricket to the lives of the British with a Gallup poll estimating that 57 per cent of men in Britain had followed it.

Whilst the West Indies were taking all before them and became the real story as Britain's Caribbean immigrant population took over ground after ground, none more so than the hallowed turf of Lord's on the day of the final, the nation had entertained hopes that England might be the first to get their names on the new trophy. (Had they known at the time that such an engraving would have to wait for another 44 years the traditionally sardonic English cricket lovers may have turned away there and then.) Reality took over in the semi-final as Australia ripped out their batting for 93. Though England made a fight of it before their defeat, before us again was the spectre of English batting quivering in the face of any Australian bowler – this time the skilled but less than fearsome unknown swing bowler Gary Gilmour. Two years later Gilmour's American mass-murdering namesake would demand the death penalty be his punishment for his crimes. It was the sort of judgement the English batting had been under for months. The former England captain turned journalist Tony Lewis captured the foreboding. 'The mere sight of Ian Chappell's side recalled the nightmares of the England batsmen during the winter – those 'horror films' viewed in Britain.'

It was, as anticipated, merely the *hors d'oeuvres*. An innings defeat in July's first Test in which Lillee, Thomson and Max Walker were again the destroyers duly followed. England were trapped in a groundhog day with apparently no answer to the question of when it might end. Lewis noted in his diary of the summer, 'England is at war with Australia.

Is there anyone who doubts it? After the innings defeat at Edgbaston we are struggling to rescue national pride.' This is what it meant and this was when the calls for defiance reached their crescendo – the desperation for a new hero to fightback against defeatism. In terms of the captaincy, Greig was that man. Lewis considered 'this is the sort of man England needs in the crisis, someone who projects his will to win and his enthusiasm in the doing'. In the event, Greig's mission was to be unsuccessful, unlike that of the next 'man for a crisis' who would soon step into his shoes. However, it would be a middle-aged journeyman who would become the totem of the summer, gaining the nation's affection as an embodiment of the fighting spirit of the British everyman which had seemingly disappeared. David Steele, white-haired and bespectacled, stood firm against the enemy for the rest of the summer as England failed to get as far as a victory but, with the aid of the weather and a vandalised pitch, managed to stop the rot and were not beaten again. The vision of a conquering hero was in truth one born of desperation. That a man who scored four half-centuries in a losing Ashes series should be voted as the BBC's Sports Personality of the Year was perhaps an indication of that desperation and of how far standards had dropped in terms of where the country now set the bar in defining success.

The famous epithet handed to Steele by Clive Taylor of *The Sun* of 'the bank clerk who went to war' was the perfect example of the nation's harking back to past glories. But this was an image of yesteryear and in the end Steele was to last no longer than the following summer whilst Greig would, in the eyes of some, sell-out England to a chorus of 'told-you-sos' and would himself be gone a year later. The search for the true and lasting hero went on.

If 1975 was the year of the everyman, 1976 was to be the year of grovel, with no indication that the country's diminished standing in the world, cricketing or otherwise, was to be turned around. The word used by the South African Greig in suggesting that when the arriving West Indian tourists were down, they 'grovel', was insensitive and hugely injudicious. Clive Lloyd's emerging side was littered with the talent and athleticism which was to gain them world domination for the next decade and beyond. If they had arrived with the ambition of victory then to that objective they now added the determination to ram the word down Greig's throat without mercy. Providing no let-up in England's suffering of fearsomely fast short-pitched bowling, at times Roberts, Michael Holding and Wayne Daniel were even quicker than those whom they had faced before. A 3-0 home defeat took on the appearance of a three-month Caribbean party, the joyous celebrations of the West Indian fans undoubtedly containing an element of enjoyment in the putting down of the former colonial masters.

The institutionalised racism of the time was represented, and somehow almost inured us all to its presence, by any number of supposedly humorous television programmes. But it's ugliest and most violent strain could be seen in the National Front marches, Notting Hill riots and battles with the Anti-Fascist League which became commonplace. If anything could compensate for the beatings by the dominant Caribbean cricketers in 1976 it was the joy to be seen in the black communities from Leeds to South London and beyond as they partied their way through a summer they made their own and the pride and identity given them by their cricketing representatives. Whilst many cricket fans actually shared the enjoyment in a memorable summer, it did nothing to alter the ongoing self-perception of their own country in decline.

The summer was memorable for more than just the cricket, with the weather once again demonstrating its capacity to influence mood. A sizzling summer of heat is remembered today as one of frolicking in fountains and endless warm summer nights, but for an embattled government it was simply another crisis to manage, with drought restrictions officially declared on 6 August and a public which had been lectured on the need to conserve energy two years previously was now instructed to do the same with water. It took a bank holiday weekend to break the weather with the first rain for three months arriving on 26 August. For the first time but not the last, the British weather displayed its penchant for shadowing the landmarks in Ian Botham's career. That same summer Thursday, to less fanfare than the rain's appearance, Botham played his first game for England in the one-day international at Scarborough. A score of one from seven balls and one wicket at nearly nine-an-over was not a performance to hog the headlines. In the story of the cricket season this appeared of no significance at all. But the journey had begun. In the winter of 1976–77 that journey took the young cricketer out to Australia and the experience helped form him in a way which would come back to bite his hosts in the future. There was no doubt that a winter playing in Australia toughened him up, but it also firmed up some of his views and his character. He saw not only a nation whose approach to life and sport mirrored his own – a determination and will to succeed and a philosophy that you play to win – but, as he admitted, 'After the cynicism of Britain I saw the strength of the Aussie loyalty to their flag.' The patriotism made its mark on him, and he was determined to play his part in bringing that back at home.

The Test series wasn't the only demonstration of grovelling that summer. As England's cricketers bent the knee in a sporting reflection of the state to which the nation had sunk, it's chancellor confirmed it as he was forced to do the same. Whilst the dying throes of Britain's manufacturing industry and the blame for not arresting them have traditionally landed at Margaret Thatcher's door, the fact is that in the second half of the decade Harold Wilson's Labour Party did little to arrest that decline or the country's wider economic woes. The travails of the Labour government, the country's 'sick man' characterisation, with productivity and economic performance lagging behind that of its European neighbours and the utter fecklessness in failing to arrest rampant inflation finally came home to roost. Or rather they went overseas to roost as the new prime minister James Callaghan and his chancellor Denis Healey were forced to go, the month after the West Indies took away the Wisden Trophy, cap in hand to the International Monetary Fund for a bailout loan as a result of the sterling crisis which had seen the resignation of Wilson in March. With inflation still rampant and the pound at a record low against the dollar, it was another moment deemed a national shaming.

Humiliation piled upon humiliation, perhaps the most concerning aspect being that nobody was greatly surprised by any of them. Wilson's resignation and the succession of Callaghan didn't appear initially to be to Thatcher's advantage. Something of a political version of Tony Greig – certainly not in demeanour or character but as a newly arrived skipper aiming to address a country at a low ebb and a generally popular public figure, Callaghan was a man in whom the country placed a degree of hope. In the days when politicians could be considered as such, Callaghan was followed most often by the adjective 'avuncular' and the moniker of 'Sunny Jim', such a disposition being a valid one to apply to England's new cricket captain too. His personal popularity rating remained ahead of Thatcher's right up to the 1979 election and it was felt he would be a far harder man to defeat than the discredited and disinterested Wilson. In fact, the change at the top would ultimately play out in Thatcher's favour and usher her into power. For Callaghan had a problem – one that people had assumed would be a strength but was to become a fatal weakness. He was and always had been a union man and was considered by all, himself included, to be the unions' friend. This was surely what the country and the Labour Party needed – a man who could calm troubled waters and work in partnership to bring to an end to the industrial strife and strikes crippling British manufacturing productivity. After all, had not the hardliners within the trades union leadership admitted that they saw it as part of their duty to remove any Conservative administration by any means possible? And that goal had been achieved. However, in doing so they had become accustomed to getting what they wanted, and the idea prevailed that direct action would deliver this for them whenever required, and the arrival of a Labour government rather than putting an end to this would make it even easier to maintain. In Callaghan they saw their perfect ally. But they were in for a rude awakening. As Andy McSmith recalls in *No Such Thing As Society*, the unions had become used to being treated almost as partners in government and too many strikes had worn away public tolerance. Callaghan understood this. Whatever his political instincts might have been, he was a wise and realistic enough political animal to understand this situation could not stand. A month on from Botham's debut at Scarborough, he made just as notable an appearance at another British seaside town. His keynote speech to his Party Conference in Blackpool played its own role in transforming Britain in that it kickstarted the procession of events which would end with Margaret Thatcher entering Downing Street.

Deciding to build on his evolving image as the safe custodian of the national economy, placed between left and right, and following a Bank of England warning of another looming currency crisis, Callaghan lectured his audience on the need for restraint and cuts in public spending – the rhetoric in the eyes of the unions of the Tories themselves. If the country largely approved, the left of his party did not, the impression growing on the former that the latter cared not a jot about what was best for the country in the face of their own interests – a perception that was to inform many choices come election day. As the conference voted to endorse the TUC's decision to flout his five per cent pay norm and both his policy and his party's harmony collapsed, with unexpected candour Callaghan suggested 'for too long, maybe ever since the war, we postponed facing up to fundamental choices and fundamental changes in our society and our economy' and insisted it was time to address 'the fundamental problems of British industry'.

It was the start of a messy divorce between the prime minister and his supposed heartland of support and it would lay the ground for a winter of great discontent two years hence which spelt the end of his office. By the end of 1976 the country and its cricket team were united in a spiral of decline and depression. Something needed to change and someone required the opportunity to make it happen. Now at the end of the year, though few recognised it as such, Callaghan had presented Margaret Thatcher with her second opportunity after that granted her by Heath. In the coming year another would be offered to Ian Botham. And things would never be quite the same again.

Opportunity Knocks
1977–1978

'It took extraordinary luck to bring Thatcher to power … she was a political opportunist in the best sense.'

Peter Clarke,
Hope and Glory

THOSE WHO make change are often given the opportunity to do so as a result of times of struggle and previous failure. Both Thatcher and Botham were stepping into something of a vacuum. If few people realised at the time what Callaghan's speech would mean for Margaret Thatcher, then the same and more could be said of the impact on the career of Ian Botham of another announcement in the spring of 1977 and the clandestine activity that had preceded it. Reaction to the Packer crisis, as many viewed it, was one of concern for the future of the Test game rather than whether this might open the door to one young England player. Even as late as 1980 it was still filling the more traditional cricket lovers with foreboding, evidence of a lasting impact and the desperate need for the game, and the Ashes in particular, to provide something special which would secure the true game in the public's affection once more and put the 'circus', as Packer's enterprise would come to be titled by the establishment, into its proper perspective. Once again the whole affair would have a mirror nearly 50 years on. The challenge to the current game of franchises, ever-shorter formats and rich global moguls – media and otherwise – fills those who see the Test game as sacrosanct with a similar dread. Again, it was to the Ashes that they looked for protection and salvation and this time Ben Stokes's making no secret that his 'Bazball' approach was in part important to him in keeping the traditional game relevant and exciting was the ray of hope. The series he delivered in 2019 as a player and 2023 as a captain went a considerable way to doing exactly that.

Something similar was needed now and might require a similarly captivating individual to make it happen. For even in 1980 the pessimism was widespread. The former Australian Test player Jack Fingleton, who after retirement from the game became one of its most eloquent commentators, had little time for Tony Greig's role in this – referring to the dangers of 'a lanky man in his yellow coat' and what he might help do to the game. That year in *The Cricketer* he wrote: 'Things are not what they used to be but, sadly, are what they seem and won't change. Whether we like it or not, and I don't, we had better get used to it. Where will it all end? Don't ask me, I think it's just the beginning. The whole world seems to revolve for the good of commercial advertising and I think watchers will eventually revolt.'

Fingleton was not alone in his reservations. Reflecting on his experience in Australia on the 1979–80 England tour, the first without the Ashes as its prize since the previous century, John Woodcock told his readers in *The Times* that, for his liking, Packer's Channel Nine and their marketing associates resembled too much an army of occupation. All in all it was not a positive picture for the game as it entered its next decade.

The story of English cricket has often played out through its divisions – traditionalists versus modernisers, the gentlemen amateurs and professional players, Kerry Packer against the establishment, South Africa's exile and its rebel tours, and so on. The story of English politics is, of course, one of divisions too which may go some way to explaining that symbiotic relationship and the frequent crossovers between the two. Two moments in the year of 1977 – one cricketing, one cultural – carried similar appearances of happy diversions whilst things were about to crumble. In March, Australia played England in Melbourne in the Centenary Test to mark 100 years of such matches between the two. Rather than a forced commercial exercise the event was a resounding success, attended by the vast majority of living Ashes cricketers who had played across that timespan. With Dennis Lillee and Derek Randall producing outstanding performances it became a joyous mix of a celebration of the ongoing quality of cricket and rivalry between the two, and a nostalgic recognition of history. Few knew that the occasion was also being used as an opaque recruitment meeting for an initiative which would threaten to undermine both of those things. The location and nature of the event also reinforced for many watching from afar the contrast between Australia and England in the late 70s, away from the cricket pitch. Here was a place considered a land of opportunity, particularly in the view of those English emigrants leaving in their numbers to seek a fresh start away from the gloom and pessimism of their own country. Sun and sea, a high standard of living – everything seemed the reverse of 1970s Britain and made home seem even greyer. Up to this point the success and ambition of the Australian cricket team were another constant reminder of that difference.

The year of the Queen's Silver Jubilee would bring something similar to the British summer against a backdrop of the youthful, cultural mania of punk – rather overstated in retrospect in terms of the true scale of its social influence but nevertheless seen by some in the establishment and in the shires of middle-England as another subversive challenge to their way of life and a further sign of the country's decaying social fabric and mores. Here was a chance to rejoice in the undoubted current popularity and efficacy of Britain's monarch, of the commonwealth and of the country's history, little more than a year before a winter of industrial and social strife would paint a very different picture of the land. Rod Stewart can be forever grateful for his number one record in the week of the celebrations to the generally held belief that record sales had been artificially manufactured to keep the Sex Pistols' 'God Save The Queen' – less of an endorsement of her majesty than its title initially suggested – off the top to protect the sensibilities of the establishment. The Pistols' John Lydon's referencing of 'England's dreaming' in the song was meant to articulate his contempt for the English tendency to nostalgia for the days of greatness now passed, to mask the reality of the lack of any optimistic future for its youth, and particularly its working-class youth. It was a valid point and was illustrated firstly in the public's rush to embrace the celebration of its royal family and history and then by the fact that such hope was as transient and illusionary as Lydon had suggested. Although John Lydon is unlikely to have been welcomed to membership of MCC, even if his hair was sometimes close to the right colours, and was about as far removed from the cricket establishment figure of Jim Swanton as it was possible to be, at precisely the same time that summer there was an element of 'England's dreaming' to Swanton's reaction to Packer and his paean for what the cricket writer and his ilk believed the game was and should still be.

There is a wealth of detail in the Packer affair, but it is its longer-term implications which have a relevance to this story. Having assumed control of the Australian television channel, Channel Nine, on the death of his father in the mid-70s, media tycoon Kerry Packer was determined to sequester the broadcast rights for Australian Tests from the national broadcaster ABC and made his pitch to the Australian Cricket Board to do so. As with many entrepreneurs, Packer was not used to being denied his objectives and the refusal of the ACB to entertain him simply led him in another direction.

Convinced that his proposition was far stronger than that of the incumbent ACB broadcaster, unconcerned with their reasoning of loyalty to a long established and valued partner and angered by his perception that he was being shunned simply because he wasn't part of the establishment within the game, Packer took another route and he had one thing strongly in his favour. Cricketers around the world had been poorly remunerated for many years when one considered their role in providing the international product for spectator and television consumption. They knew it too and were fed up with being chattels to their governing boards. There were also a few within their midst who were the sort of characters who would not stand idly by in the face of such a situation and were only too ready for a fight. Packer was therefore dealing with an amenable audience when early in 1977 he set about contracting as many of the game's biggest global names as possible to an alternative international game which he alone would televise. In doing so he would dramatically increase the financial returns for his players.

In this initially secret endeavour he successfully enlisted two of those personalities who didn't shy away from confrontation or controversy, who just happened to be the current captains of England and Australia, as his lieutenants and chief recruiting officers. How many of the players anticipated that signing their contracts would see them excommunicated from traditional Test cricket is hard to quantify but it is safe to say that if some were shocked when the bans were duly handed out by the authorities, Greig in particular went in with his eyes open and must have known his England captaincy would be his sacrifice to what the game's establishment – administrators and much of the cricket-loving public alike – saw as Mammon. In the public's perception the defecting players were in some ways comparable to the union members bringing conflict at home in the way their actions might offer them short-term benefits but were souring the majority of public opinion against them and thereby limiting any sympathy for their arguments. Should they not harbour a nagging sense of guilt that they were letting down a public who had always tried to support them in the past? Even if people appreciated the accusation that they would also be perfectly happy to accept more money for doing the same job, that option was not open to them at a time of belt-tightening and the feeling remained that there was a right and a wrong way to go about attaining it.

The cricket journalist Christopher Martin-Jenkins was a true lover of the game and its history. The opening chapter of his book on England and English cricket in 1977, *The Jubilee Tests,* was a reflection on Packer and its implications. He titled it 'Courageous coup or shabby sabotage?' which was evidence of his professional desire to approach the manner even-handedly but also encapsulated the debate the situation had raised. Most lovers of the Test game saw it as the latter. In England it had an additional resonance too. The 70s as a whole had been terrible years for England's traditional team sports and Grieg's was not the only 'shabby sabotage' on show. If the British people, particularly those wealth-creators who didn't fancy being rewarded for their efforts by giving 80 per cent of their earnings to a feckless, profligate government, were fleeing to other countries in increasing numbers, their sporting leaders were following suit, with rather less sympathy. In the same summer as Greig joined forces with Packer, the England football manager, a post which at the time was still deemed in sporting circles to be an honour laced with a sense of duty akin to that of the monarch, also jumped ship. Don Revie's reign had been a conspicuous failure and rather than double down on trying to address it he accepted an offer to work in the United Arab Emirates in as clandestine a manner as Greig. Allied to the Packer affair it simply added to a sense that the equity in the country's two national sports was at an all-time low. What was clear from a cricket-follower's perspective however was that, at a time when high quality sport was an antidote to the depression pervading real life, the cricket they relied upon as one of their few remaining simple pleasures and a treasured part of their summers was in danger of being taken away or, at best, having its quality diminished. *The Times* brought Kerry Packer into its editorial comment, claiming he had become 'our new national obsession', whilst Martin-Jenkins pointed out that his name was on more people's lips than was Callaghan's – another reminder that cricketing fortunes remained a significant bellwether in English life.

If some of the more naïve or optimistic – take your pick – England players hoped they might have their cake and eat it, much in the manner of the LIV golf defectors today, believing there could be an amicable solution found and no bans, amongst those who *did* see the wider implications for their careers, especially the players in the later stages of their international days, a good number opted for practicality. Alan Knott, the world's best wicketkeeper-batsman and an integral part of the England side for a decade, had played more Tests in the previous ten years than any other Englishman, and the fact he would return in 1981 confirmed his career was a long way from the twilight stage. But Knott was phlegmatic and unapologetic about signing for Packer. He was a family man and the offer to both secure their long-term financial security and be able to spend winters with them in Australia rather than in the subcontinent without them was not difficult to accept. Greig himself, with a more overtly commercial vision in mind, would argue that in business (and he saw himself as a businessman in all but name) when the lot of the directors improves, so in time will the salaries of their employees. This he saw as justification enough to claim he was actually providing a valuable service to all cricketers. This was an argument not far from that which the capitalist model, political conservativism and Thatcher herself would propound as part of the monetarist approach, insisting that you don't make the weak strong by making the strong weaker. There was of course a counter-argument to both disciples of this – in Greig's case, that if you destroyed traditional Test cricket you also destroyed the domestic income of the home boards and therefore it would be the players at the next level down the cricketing food chain who would suffer; the counter to Thatcher was even more simple and played out brutally in the years ahead – unemployment. Is it stretching the analogies between politics and sport at the time to see Packer as a form of cricketing Arthur Scargill? Certainly it could be said both were at this time attempting to hold those in power to ransom to get what they wanted, and often using the employees as the pawns in that game. Martin-Jenkins would ask of Packer's motivations, 'Did Packer have their [the players] interests or his own at heart?' The same question could be asked of Scargill and those he purported to be fighting for when many saw a different, individual, agenda in the years to come. In another comparison, some players would eventually lose faith in Packer as their own leader as the suspicion grew that he was indeed all about his own interests, and some would seek to extricate themselves from their contracts and his command. Such a loss of faith would also afflict Scargill from within his miners' union by the time of 1985 as some recognised the motivation of personal aggrandisement rather than the delivery of a greater good.

The authorities' response to Packer was also one that Thatcher would have recognised had she had the slightest knowledge of or interest in the affair. The breakdown in talks between Packer and the game's government was similar to that also playing out between Callaghan's government and the unions. As Martin-Jenkins said of the authorities rationale around the talks, 'If they agreed to give him his way with a loaded pistol at their heads, others in the future might find equally effective bargaining points.' As a summary of

Margaret Thatcher's approach to union negotiation in the future which would forever change the nature of Britain's industrial relations, this could not be bettered.

Bans were indeed handed out by various boards, although inevitably court battles were then waged with Packer supporting his new employees in their claims of restraint of trade. Unsurprisingly for an experienced and well-prepared businessman with the resources required to hire the best lawyers, Packer won the legal argument and threw the traditional administrators into further turmoil and the game's immediate future into confusion. As a result, the action to rule players in or out of both international or domestic cricket were not uniform and led to a patchwork of international teams, some more depleted than others and some for longer than others. Hardest hit in terms of its Test team was Australia. Of their best players, 19 signed to Packer at the start. Although the news of Packer's plan was only brought to a wider audience by *The Guardian* and *Daily Mail* in May, when the Australian tourists were arriving on English soil and therefore the removal of 'Packer players' was impractical and the touring side remained a reasonably strong one, of the 17 who made the tour only four were not signed in secrecy, with the non-Packer tourists left in the dark. Such a division must have affected morale and offered England their opportunity that summer. As Martin-Jenkins noted, 'They were forced to play as if in a vacuum.' By the time of the England Ashes tour down under in 1978–79 – another significant winter in the nation's story – the Australian side was decimated, making for one of the most one-sided and least satisfying contests ever between the two countries.

All of this was to have a significant impact on Ian Botham in three ways. Firstly, it would mean that when he did attain international success the financial rewards and commercial opportunities for him would be far greater; secondly, it created space in England's team for him with the departure of Greig as captain immediately and as player shortly afterwards (even Greig himself, rather disingenuously, implied that he was defecting with the best interests of the future of England cricket at heart, saying 'Ian Botham is going to be a great player and there won't be room in the team for both of us'); thirdly, it meant that when Botham took up that place in the team, the opposition against which he would be aiming to make his mark would be considerably weakened. The defections within the England ranks were sufficient to open up a place in the side for him but not so many as to weaken the team's strength to the same extent as that of their opposition. It was the perfect scenario for the next stage of Botham's career.

So another Australian media mogul had played his part in this story – if Murdoch was the man to open the door for Thatcher, Botham's indirect benefactor was undoubtedly Kerry Packer. In his end of season review of the 1981 cricketing summer, the *Daily Telegraph's* Michael Melford reflected 'after the catastrophic upheaval suffered by cricket at the hands of the Packer organisation four years ago what the game needed, more than anything, was a memorable series between the two ancient rivals, England and Australia. "Memorable", of course, is too mild a word to describe the happenings of the few crowded weeks wherein what had seemed an absolutely assured retention of the Ashes by Australia was dissolved, chiefly by the feats of Botham whose performances will become an unforgettable legend in the history of cricket'. It was not just the performances but that need for them which Melford had identified which enhanced the legend. In a sense, Packer made Botham.

It is one thing to be offered an opportunity, but another to seize it and 1977 would be Botham's time. He first encountered the Australians that summer when they came to Taunton in May. His run-a-minute 59 was supplemented by 39 not out in the match-winning stand and five wickets in the match, including that of Greg Chappell. The two would meet again before the summer was out. Martin-Jenkins's conclusion was that here was 'a no-nonsense cricketer and a no-nonsense character'. From here the sporting summer did as was hoped and added some further uplifting colour to the narrative of the Jubilee. After Virginia Wade had delighted one British demographic by giving them a queen of Wimbledon, her victory arriving as if part of the long-scheduled series of celebratory events, cricket's story was of Geoffrey Boycott's return to arms, his gift to his Yorkshire audience, normally less gushing than those following the tennis, being his 100th first-class century in a home Test at Headingley and the return of the Ashes. Gush they did. Boycott's seminal moment came as a redemption one match after his Test return at Trent Bridge when he ran out Nottingham's local hero Derek Randall by half the length of the pitch. His 187 runs in England's victory there were the minimum penance required. But these Ashes matches had another significance. The bad taste and concern engendered by Packer had been alleviated briefly after England had gone ahead in the series. Martin-Jenkins noted, 'The England victory at Old Trafford lifted the shadow which the Packer affair continued to cast over the summer', which suggested that despite a respite of sorts the matter still lingered in the background, the short-term good news only papering over the longer-term reality. As CMJ would conclude at the end of '77, 'The year which had begun with a magnificent match to celebrate a centenary was ending with a bitterly ironic threat to the future of Test cricket.' The need for that good news was, however, evident in the public interest in that series. Sun and sell-outs were the order of the day, the queues beginning at 5.30 in the morning on Headingley's first day being confirmation that cricket was still very much an important strand of British life. Randall's joyous cartwheel on completing the catch which meant a first Ashes victory for six and a half years had a certain symbolism for a country desperate to find some joy itself. This was the public stage onto which Botham now arrived. His selection for his first Test at Trent Bridge was not as a direct replacement for Greig but the result of an injury to a bowler, Chris Old. It was an indication that at this point Botham was considered a bowler who could club a few useful runs rather than a serious alternative to his former captain as a top class all-rounder. His performance seemed to confirm it – an unremarkable 25 in his only innings but a five-wicket return in his first innings of Test match bowling. The first of those wickets gave notice of Botham's career-long habit of success via outrageous fortune when the one batsman of true world class in the Australian line-up, their captain Greg Chappell, dragged the most innocuous of long-hops onto his stumps. For all his supreme ability, such happy accidents tended to punctuate Botham's more dominant performances. No-nonsense and determined, possessed of innate abilities and not without the occasional moment of help from the gods, this was a combination both he and his soon to be prime minister would retain as their own formula.

But the sight of Botham was more than welcome in the situation in which cricket and England found themselves. It was to his advantage, if not his creation, that he was always likely to be held in greater affection than the Packer players on show if he could produce some signs of international class. That he now did. The venerated cricket correspondent of *The Times*, John Woodcock, at the time reported Botham's debut Test under the headline 'Botham chooses happy time to make impact in a Test': 'The bowling honours belonged to Botham. It was a happy time to make the impact he did having, as he does, no Packer strings attached to him. Thomson [the Australian fast bowler], having just *left* Packer, was cheered all the way to the wicket … as spontaneous an indication of what the public think about the "circus" as there could have been.'

After five more wickets as the Ashes came home at Leeds, Botham's momentum was halted by injury before the final Test, but he had arrived and was named the Cricket

Writers' Club Young Cricketer of the Year. The following year he would add to that the accolade of one of *Wisden's* Five Cricketers of the Year. With Greig having played his last-ever game for England, he was to march through the door which had opened for him over the next two years. CMJ's player assessments at the end of his diary of the summer included a view that Greig's successor, as he now saw him, had already shown his worth but would have to play very well in the years ahead to equal the contribution made by Greig. It is fair to say Botham passed that test and by the time Thatcher was defeating her opposition and moving into Downing Street, he had demolished the weakened sides put in front of him and his star was also ascendent. Nobody was talking about Greig anymore. Soon nobody would be talking about Callaghan anymore either.

Having missed out on the Pakistan leg of the winter, Botham joined his first full England tour in New Zealand in February '78 and kicked off two years of riotous success as the saviour England had been craving. From that point until the last Test before he assumed the captaincy he would score 1,311 runs at an average of 39.72 and six centuries, and take 129 wickets at 18.40 with 14 five-wicket innings. A century, a fifty and two five-wicket returns in the three-match series in New Zealand were the appetiser for a home summer in which no force could stop him. If the numbers were special, it was the mercurial manner in which they were produced which captured the nation. It was about as un-English as it comes. Botham himself recognised the circumstances in which this startling rise had taken place. He would later reflect that the defections of players from other international sides made his and the other young players' early Test careers in this period 'a little less testing than might otherwise have been the case'. This would be at its starkest on the tour of Australia in 1978–79 which had the utmost difficulty in portraying itself as anything like the Ashes. In another cricketing and political parallel, that winter may not have been one of discontent for either Botham or Thatcher, but it certainly was for Ashes cricket and for Britain. It was a time in which both became uncomfortable parodies of themselves, a time of hapless opposition and a time which would ultimately guide Thatcher to power.

The Packer schism was at its most pronounced as England's quest to retain the urn down under approached late in 1978 and unlike 1977 in England there were to be no allowances for the established players who had signed for World Series Cricket to appear regardless. The resulting Australian XIs put forward through the series were scarcely stronger than state sides. Australia being Australia they still found enough new talent to make life more uncomfortable than it should have been for a while and, England being England, they let them. There were some tense battles in the first half of the series in which nobody could seem to stay at the crease long enough to require sunscreen. The home country's irritating proclivity for offering England a nasty surprise in the form of a new fast bowling discovery had not disappeared despite the decimation of their bowling options. For Jeff Thomson four years previously now read Rodney Hogg. Along with his opening partner Alan Hurst, for a while Hogg managed to make England look like they were facing Lillee, Thomson, Roberts, Holding and Croft all at once as they collapsed in a catalogue of heaps.

Fortunately for England however, the Australian batting displayed even less backbone than their own and by the time of the fourth Test in early January it had melted away completely. England completed a record 5-1 away victory without having played outstandingly well themselves, which is not the sort of thing an Englishman should ever decry but there was something wholly unsatisfactory about the entire winter. If this was the Ashes post-Packer then something had to change. There was one footnote to the tour which Botham felt might have stored him up trouble with the establishment for the future. Prior to departure he had suggested that he might not join the tour at all unless his wife Kath could visit for at least a part of it. He sensed he was being marked as a disruptor and that he'd put a few people's backs up on the selection and MCC committees, and his fear they may have long memories was to be borne out.

As England's cricketers were getting on with their work in the sun on one side of the world, there was a lot of work which was not getting done in the dark of the British winter. Callaghan's faltering relationship with a group of unions who had misjudged the situation took the country into a winter with a distinctly dystopian quality. If 70s Britain had already painted a picture of economic and social decline, here it reached the very depths. In months of strikes which impacted on people's everyday lives the most lasting image was of the uncollected rubbish piled up in one of the country's shop windows to the world – London's Leicester Square – with the smell battling sightings of vermin as the source of greatest public revulsion. The pictures would go around the world as apparent confirmation of the total demise of a once proud nation. The horror of the scene before Callaghan was compounded by the knowledge that he had made a fateful decision before the worst began which was to ensure its consequences would be fatal to his hopes of keeping office and would give Thatcher the keys.

His continued lead over Thatcher in the polls of public personal approval ratings through a relatively comfortable first half of 1978 had most commentators predicting victory for Labour should he call an election that autumn rather than waiting for the deadline of the following November. Many in his party urged him to take this course and the fact he blinked in that moment may have helped to change the course of history. As it was, he increasingly looked to be fiddling as Rome burned through the industrial chaos that followed.

The famous photographs of him enjoying the sun on the Caribbean island of Guadeloupe which the newspapers, with glee disguised as indignation, splashed over their pages as the country shivered in a land of cold, dark and strikes were not designed to enhance that positive approval rating. Although the apocryphal attributed words 'Crisis, what crisis?' never passed Callaghan's lips, his apparently unconcerned air on his return was another misjudgement. Calling a press conference at Heathrow and confronted by a question about his reaction to the 'mounting chaos', the prime minister embellished his blithe dismissal of the idea that such a thing existed with a tale of an enjoyable swim he had taken in the sunshine. Unsurprisingly, the next day's *Sun* editorial portrayed a man utterly out of touch. Thatcher seized her moment. In a party political broadcast the following week she began, as is the wont of many a politician, by insisting she was not going to score party political points (rather undermining the title of the programme in the process). In truth, she didn't need to – the own goals were already raining in. Claiming the crisis in the country was much too serious for that, she said she wondered about 'what has happened to our sense of common nationhood and even of common humanity?' More practically, as historian and chronicler of the period Graham Stewart noted, the Winter of Discontent 'fatally undermined claims that a cure had been found for the British disease'. And the electorate knew it. Callaghan had missed his cue in October. At that time the polls showed a clear Labour lead; by March 1979 they were predicting a Conservative landslide. Another Thatcher sliding-doors moment was upon her.

Callaghan still had the option of riding things out until November when the discontent may have become a thing of the past. Or at least he did until 21 March when two 'no' results were returned in referenda on Scottish and Welsh devolution. The Scottish National Party in their pique lost their desire to prop up a lame Labour government and called a vote of no confidence. After frantic horse-trading over the next week the result of the vote came through – the Ayes 311; the Noes 310. By one vote the first election to be forced by a Commons vote in 55 years was called. It was the first British government to be brought down by a vote of no confidence since 1841. If there was some sort of divine fate in bringing Margaret Thatcher to the nation, this was the moment it showed itself most obviously. One vote; one changed country. As unemployment continued to rise, when the election was finally called in the spring the Saatchi & Saatchi ad campaign poster slogan 'Labour Isn't Working', above a staged image of a winding dole queue, struck a nerve. Now the public was increasingly willing to consider a different future as its patience ran out. Was Thatcher, after all, the woman who could bring hope? On 3 May they decided to find out and gave her the mandate to prove it. The country had its first female prime minister. Ian Botham had put his cross against the Conservative box that day and was to remain a staunch supporter evermore.

On 30 August 1979, as Thatcher settled in to her new position of power, Botham's third run in the fourth Test against India, following a blistering century in the preceding one, took him to the all-round double of 1,000 runs and 100 wickets in fewer matches than any cricketer in Test history. One month later one of the country's cultural phenomena of the early 80s aired for the first time. The title of the most successful sitcom at the turn of the decade, *To The Manor Born* could have been appropriated by Botham at this moment. The fact that the TV series ran until the back end of 1981 was a neat synergy. On the 1979/80 winter tour to Australia, against an abrasive Ian Chappell-led side hungry for revenge for the humiliation of 12 months prior and with their giants of the past restored following the Packer resolution, England were glad to have refused to put up the Ashes for a three-match series as they were comprehensively whitewashed. But even amidst England's capitulation Botham's star maintained its ascendance, with 19 wickets and an undefeated century. Ever since his debut, cricket – like life – had been enormous fun. If further proof were needed of a man at his peak it was laid out at the Jubilee Test against India in Bombay in February 1980 on the way home from Australia. In a tour de force unprecedented even in his own titanic two years, he hit a century and took 13 wickets in England's victory. Here was confirmation that if things were to be different against the Aussies in 18 months' time, he was the man on whom hats were going to be hung. He was the *man* who could bring hope.

May We Bring Hope
1979

'You only have to move about Western Europe nowadays to realise how poor and unproud the British have become in relation to their neighbours.'

Sir Nicholas Henderson
on stepping down as Britain's ambassador to France, 1979

'Britain in 1979 was a nation that had had the stuffing knocked out of it … we were widely dismissed as "the sick man of Europe".'

Margaret Thatcher
The Downing Street Years

THE WRITER Martin Amis aligned with the view of Sir Nicholas above about the late 70s in his novel of 1985, *Success,* saying, 'You hardly dare open a paper these days: the news is all of cataclysm and collapse … the world is going bad on us.' Historian Mark Garrett referred to Amis's belief that although 1975, '76 and '77 were years when people began losing faith in Britain and its economic future, the fact that they also featured three long, sunny and warm summers means that today for most of the country's population life is remembered as fun and the memories are predominantly happy ones, regardless of the trouble that may have been brewing. But 1978 to the first half of 1981 were different times. In these years there was no counterbalance to the political ills as the summers turned drab and wet. Garrett himself considers the whole period one of challenge and that the five years from 1974–79 were a dangerous and disorienting time when what counted most was to survive. He paints a picture of a country reeling from the oil shock of 1973, and as its implications sank in its inhabitants sensed that their country had become a more unpleasant place without anyone really noticing.

But there is little doubt that the last months before Thatcher's victory were the darkest in terms of a slide in living standards and public faith in the future, accompanied by weather that reflected them. They were also the times of greatest hiatus for cricket. In both, the desperation was for somebody who, regardless of whether you were attracted or aggravated by their manner, could bring some hope. The economist John Hoskyns, in whom Thatcher was to place considerable faith in the years ahead, had for several years been railing against politicians who talked of widening prosperity but were neither brave nor talented enough to effect the changes required. He believed the British economy had become dysfunctional and in the gloomy context of the mid–1970s reform could no longer be postponed. Garrett also quotes the US journalist Eric Sevareid on *CBS News* averring back in 1975 that Britain was 'drifting towards a condition of ungovernability' and that it was sleepwalking into a social revolution which its majority clearly didn't want but didn't know how to stop. Writing this in 2025 has some strange echoes 50 years on. But there were at least two people in two different fields who agreed change couldn't be postponed, who believed they knew how to stop the sleepwalk and who were determined to do so.

The accessions of both Thatcher and Botham to the leadership of their country, within a year of each other, were firsts of a sort, Thatcher becoming Britain's first-ever female prime minister and Botham England's youngest captain of the century – in fact for 98 years. Firsts can come as a surprise, generate a degree of suspicion and their outcomes be hard to predict. Neither Thatcher nor Botham could be considered a huge surprise. The former's most unexpected moment was in becoming the Conservative leader to what political commentator Andrew Marr called 'general stupefaction', but once she had done so a victory for her party at the next election would guarantee her the top post. The tribulations of the Labour Party for the previous five years had made this more likely than not, so the moment itself, whilst historic, was not a bolt from the blue – more a *fait accompli* through lack of an alternative when she met with the Queen on 4 May. So it was with Botham too. Even he himself was aware that the popular view when he was first appointed was that he had been handed the role more by default than because he showed any signs of being leadership material. But although there were concerns about the timing, some also saw him as the obvious or only choice, unless the selectors wanted to dip into the group of county captains with a claim, but with modest or non-existent Test records. After Mike Brearley the England side wasn't keen to allocate a place to another player not truly worth a place in the side. Botham therefore became that default option.

But if neither was a complete surprise, a degree of suspicion there most certainly was. There were some, even from within the groups that had appointed them, who doubted the longevity of their respective tenures and indeed, some who were not unhappy at the idea that before long they might find just enough rope to hang themselves. And yet many people were drawn to both as potential saviours of the country's prosperity on and off the cricket field. What gave them that pull in spite of the capacity of their personalities to generate antipathy? The answer may be found in the words of the MP Nigel Lawson at the start of Thatcher's government, referring

Two gunslingers. Botham and Thatcher changed the nation driven by a fierce patriotism whether in the Union flag or the three lions

State of the nation. Edward Heath's tenure began Britain's decline in the 1970s. Thatcher seems to be eyeing up the chair.

Another leader in trouble. Tony Greig is comprehensively bowled at Trent Bridge in 1976. The England team's woes in the mid-70s were symbolic of the country's decline.

Opportunity knocks. Kerry Packer's removal of Tony Greig from the England team and his weakening of other international sides gave Botham his chance.

Thatcher was also fortunate in the weakness of her early opposition. Heath, an unelectable Labour party and, in time, Arthur Scargill would be easy targets.

Down the plughole. The 1978/79 Winter of Discontent summed up the perception of Britain by the end of the decade at home and abroad and ushered Thatcher into power.

May we bring hope. Botham celebrates reaching the Test 'double' in record time in 1979, just four months after his new prime minister's own message of hope. Alec Bedser (left) was not to be constant in his support.

Why it would be a ... to make Botham captain

The other side of Ian Botham. Signing on a non-contract basis for … Fourth Division football club, towards the end of …

am sure that the same could well be written about Ian one day. He has a natural feel for the game and, like Gary, would lead from the front by personal example. How well, and how successfully, time alone will tell.

These comments stress the point that I consider Ian, for whom I have enormous respect as a cricketer, could, and will, make a fine captain of England. My concern is the timing which seems wrong.

To be a successful captain or a football manager, the first need is either a very good side or indifferent opposition. Without one or the other, the results on which he will be judged, often quite unfairly, are likely to be indifferent. Clive Lloyd has clearly benefitted from that first requirement and Mike Brearley, until this winter, enjoyed a relatively easy ride.

Too Much Too Young. Trevor Bailey's article questions the wisdom of making a young Botham England captain. Neither Botham nor Thatcher's accessions to leadership were greeted with unanimous support, even from within.

Stand down please. Botham's arrest on charges of affray on 23 December 1980 further strained his relationship with the establishments. By this point both he and Thatcher were under intense pressure to go.

Missions impossible. Early in 1981 Botham's four horsemen of the apocalypse were Roberts, Holding, Croft and Garner. Thatcher's were the economy, the unions, rioting and Northern Ireland.

The traumatic West Indies tour and the death of his mentor Ken Barrington devastated Botham here reading the lesson at his memorial. Thatcher had lost her own 'rock', Airey Neave, in similarly tragic circumstances.

Thatcher's Budget of March 1981 might have finished her, but became her 'Headingley' moment. Geoffrey Howe was an ally now, but would ultimately finish her after all.

Grey days and storms. The weather can have a huge effect on mood and shadowed the lows and highs of 1981 surreally. Rain at Lords in May was indicative of a miserable early summer.

Cultural changes also reflected the nation's mood. As the gloom of the weather, cricket and economics began to lift, the fatalistic music of The Specials was replaced by a very different genre …

… Duran Duran arrived in the top five of the charts the week The Specials disbanded. 'Ghost Town' to 'Girls on Film', a new hedonism arrived to define Thatcher's 80s.

The transformations of July. 2 July - Botham presents his team to the Queen at the start of the Lord's Test. It was a hugely proud moment. The ardent monarchist was clear: 'I'm very British — very, very British.'

to the magnetism of Winston Churchill but as a depiction of what Thatcher offered. 'It is the note of confidence and the message of hope. For all the words about blood, sweat and tears, he offered them [the public] the promise of victory – and that's why they followed him' '. Confidence, hope and the promise of victory. Botham's own draw was as the Churchill of English cricket. The BBC's political correspondent at the time, John Sergeant, recalled that the polarising effect of Margaret Thatcher becoming prime minister was extremely sharp but there was a demographic which did see what might be coming in a positive light. Marr felt that to the inflation-ravaged and despairing middle classes who doubted whether Britain had a future and believed the unions could never be tamed, she brought both faith and hope. Botham did the same for the more optimistic England followers, who had similarly feared for the future as Packer threatened their game and purloined their previous white knight captain, Greig. As Thatcher's chancellor, Geoffrey Howe, introduced his first budget a month after the election victory he had painted a bleak picture and his determination to address it. 'In the past few years … the threat of absolute decline has become very real. That is not a prospect I am prepared to accept.' Acceptance of decline was not in Botham's make-up either.

Whether people were for or against, there were very few who were short of an opinion, such were the characters and profiles of those involved. The new leaders weren't short of an opinion either. In her diaries Thatcher herself referred to the theme of change. 'I was less intimidated [than previous Conservative prime ministers] by the risks of change.' With shades of Botham's England captaincy to come she saw herself as the rebel at the head of an establishment government. One of the most significant consequences of that rebellion and lack of fear would be her clarity on how the scourge of inflation was to be managed going forward. No longer would it be addressed via pay restraint policies and therefore at the gift or otherwise of the unions. Now it would be monetarism and the markets which would be the methods of control. Change does have risks and requires courage and conviction. It requires people possessed of those qualities not simply to instigate it, but to see it through and as a defining characteristic this is almost certainly the one which underpinned their success and its longevity. Belief was fundamental. One of Thatcher's most important policy advisors Alfred Sherman considered her 'a woman of beliefs, not ideas'. Sherman's view was that she was more often seduced by and ready to adopt the ideas of others she admired (hence the large coterie of strategists she wrapped around her). There was something similar in Botham – his willingness to embrace as gospel some of his friends' own beliefs was obvious in his Rastafarian-coloured wristband and blazer phase in the slipstream of his most trusted mate Vivian Richards. He too had a total faith that he could and would win but possibly no great strategic vision of how he would do it, which is where the skills of a Brearley in directing his greatest feats were so crucial. Another analogy … Brearley as Sherman, the man of significant intellect and ideas guiding the force of nature down the right path. But whilst they were happy sometimes to shine in borrowed light, it was their own drive which made the difference.

Thatcher's own role in the change wrought by 1981 may have been based on detail from others but was long-planned and based on a vision; Botham's just happened, though he had long held a desire to knock the Australians in particular off their perch. Botham's role may have been more mercurial, but to put it down to luck would be to misread it completely. The man himself made it real in a way no other English cricketer could have done. Both also saw belief not just in terms of their own, but that of the country – their mission was to turn that around. 'My concern in 1979 was that … the national morale was so depressed it would be necessary to restore our own self-confidence', said Thatcher. 'We intended to achieve a fundamental change in direction. We stood for a new beginning, not more of the same.'

The world's cricketing authorities also wanted a change in direction in the spring of 1979 – after the apology of an Ashes series they had just endured in Australia nobody was in any mood for more of the same. As Thatcher came to power so, in a sense, did Kerry Packer with the Australian Cricket Board coming to an unexpectedly swift – and to many eyes, feeble – accommodation with their nemesis of the last two years. Giving Packer's Channel Nine the rights to all Australian home Tests was the price for getting the game back on track in the same way as some saw giving the keys to No.10 to Thatcher as the price for getting the *country* back on track. This concordance of timing may not have meant anything to Thatcher and her leadership but it was to impact Botham's in a way not visible at the time. The 'rebel' players would be back playing for their countries just in time to populate the West Indies side which would shortly be his opponents in his first ten Tests as captain with many of the most formidable talents on the planet. If he had anticipated the timing, Brearley's intelligence may well have been matched by his shrewd perspicacity.

Thatcher's recollection of William Pitt's words on entering No.10 that 'I know I can save this country and that no one else can' could equally well have been spoken by Botham when he arrived at Headingley two Julys later, or indeed on accepting the offer of the captaincy in the spring of 1980. For if there were doubters about that appointment, and there were plenty, true to form Botham was not amongst them. True to form was sadly not something he was to remain, which would ultimately lead to his departure while his political counterpart survived, but in May 1980 he was convinced he was precisely the man to deliver the same results as his contemporary. The prevailing feeling that we were in a moment of fleeting interest rather than one of true significance wasn't helpful when times became tough. The apparent failures of the next 18 months seemed like affirmations of this widely held view and encouraged few to afford them time to turn things around. Andy McSmith confirms of Thatcher's arrival, 'There was no reason to think her government would last beyond 1984 or make much impact on society.' But she turned out to be a far more determined woman that most people in 1979 realised and possessed of a quality which would see her survive to implement her vision in a way Heath could not. The MP who had for a time preceded Thatcher as the big hope of the right, Enoch Powell, noted 'a remarkable characteristic, which stamps her as a superb politician, is her ability to put up with things and go along with them until the time comes when they can be dealt with'. It would be evident in her prevailing against the miners' leadership and the 'wets' and dissenters in her own cabinet. Botham's character was a little less pragmatic and by the time of Lord's in 1981 he couldn't employ the same patience. Thatcher was undaunted in her determination to drive change and, in a country which had become used to harking back, she was looking ahead. She was very clear that it was the mood and faith of the country she was intending to alter, not just the state of the finances, recognising that it was the air of fatalism which was at the root of the problem. This was the lesson Botham had learnt during that formative winter in Australia. She would later say, 'The economic crisis was a crisis of the spirit of the nation … the economy had gone wrong because something else had gone wrong spiritually' and in her vision for change 'economics are the method. The object is to change the soul'.

As Britain said goodbye to a decade which had been rougher than anyone expected, *The Observer's* Peter Conrad saw 'no apter farewell to the unlamented 70s than the spittle of Britain's punks' and not many bid them farewell – the decade or its most famous cultural expression – with any compliments. There were a few that saw it as that moment of hope – one being a former Labour MP, now Thatcher acolyte. George Brown happily admitted that, 'The great joy for me this week is that we can say goodbye to one of the worst decades Britain has known – a decade of despair and disintegration' and in Thatcher he saw 'a sense of purpose and determination that No.10 has not seen in many a year'. On New Year's Eve 1979 Thatcher made a speech which articulated her personal mission and was a direct exhortation to the hearts of the public. 'As you raise a glass to the 80s … drink with me to the reawakening of Britain. These will be difficult and dangerous years. But we are drinking to a country with a future. The remedy lies not only in economics – the mission of this government is a recovery of our self-confidence and self-respect.'

As the new decade dawned there were to be few concrete signs of that better future and the next two years were to be difficult and dangerous indeed. Historian Dominic Sandbrook suggested that Thatcher was now steering grimly towards the storm. He didn't know it but Botham was heading off on the same course. By the end of the new year both would be facing calls to go.

PART THREE:

STAND DOWN PLEASE
1980

'It seemed as if it could never end. Yet quite suddenly it did. In 1980 Ian experienced sustained failure for the first time in his life and it did not rain, it poured. Suddenly he was under attack from all quarters.'

Peter Roebuck on Botham
The Cricketer, November 1981

FOR ROEBUCK'S summary of Botham's year above, read also that of Thatcher. For those who had entertained hope at these arrivals, 1980 was to be a year of disillusionment. It's start would begin 18 months of despair for those in whom the belief had been invested. By its end that hope and faith had evaporated even for many of those who had been believers. Thatcher, as Botham was to in a few months' time, had gone into her first years in office determined but with her eyes firmly open. 'The forces of doubt and despair were so firmly entrenched in British society, as the Winter of Discontent had powerfully illustrated, that overcoming them would not be possible without some element of discord.' And in 1980, for her and for Botham, discord there was. As they both headed into their first full years of leadership they were each met by an ever more challenging environment. Andy McSmith remembers 'the most significant transformation was in the political and social landscape. Anyone growing up in 1980 was entering a dangerously divided world, the future of which looked uncertain'.

If the recent narrative had been one of opportunity, from here on it was to be of nothing but challenge and people would prove to have short memories and unforgiving natures. As Roebuck said of Botham and 1980, 'Whereas before his indiscretions had been tolerated as part of his Viking spirit, now his failures were held up and scorned. Ian did not thrive in this vexed limelight.' And those businesses which had so welcomed Thatcher as a saviour began to despair at what they saw as capitulation in industrial relations. What were the Tories here for if the union paymasters were to be allowed to continue to run the country's industry as they saw fit? By November the new prime minister whose rhetoric had been so pinned to initiating an economic recovery was forced to raise interest rates by three per cent to an eye-watering 17 per cent. And it wasn't solely the economics which punctured any potential optimism. The Irish Republican Army and its tactics in pursuit of a goal Thatcher was never going to concede on her watch were to feature regularly in the years of her leadership.

On 30 March 1979, a month before that leadership began, the INLA took the life of the man who had done as much as anyone to secure it, her confidant Airey Neave. At the end of August the Queen's cousin Lord Mountbatten met the same fate at the hands of the IRA. It was a reminder that in late-70s Britain you could change the singer, but the song remained the same.

Too Much Too Young

2 FEBRUARY 1980 was a day of some prescience. The first harbinger of what might lie ahead was the confrontation between disaffected local youths and the police in the St Pauls area of Bristol. It would not be the last of its type. The same day, the first of two number one songs by The Specials with a relevance to the narrative reached the top of the charts. 'Too Much Too Young' was still at the top as Botham took to the field in what was then Bombay to begin the match which would take his standing to its very height. His one-man tour de force – that bristling century and 13 wickets – was the highest of the many summits he had attained over the previous three years. It also seemed to confirm this man could do no wrong. The title of that first number one single from The Specials might be seen, with hindsight, as just as eerily well timed and cautionary as their second one would be 18 months on. Whilst English cricket had been in dire need of such an inspirational new presence, and Botham would of course not have had it happen any differently, he had set his bar at a height from which any fall would be more visible and dramatic. When perhaps the most naturally gifted English football player of the 80s, John Barnes, scored a goal for England in the Maracana Stadium in 1984, against the might of Brazil, of such dazzling brilliance that some wondered aloud if he had the right shirt on, he burdened himself with a benchmark by which the public, if not he himself, unfairly spent the rest of his career judging him. He claimed this did not concern him

and he certainly never wished he hadn't scored the goal but from then on anything but genius was greeted with criticism. Had Botham created the same scenario for himself?

'Too young' was certainly a refrain from those, including close personal friends and mentors, who could see what might be coming as Brearley announced he would no longer be willing to tour and the correct assumption was that this might end his captaincy before the 1980 summer of cricket began. The casting of a replacement was not straightforward with no obvious choice standing out and it may have hampered Botham from his first day in the job that it was hard to dismiss that argument that he was in post for want of a stronger alternative. The Gloucestershire bowler Brian Brain wrote in an article in *The Cricketer* that 'the only candidate I can see is Botham." It appeared this view was shared by Alec Bedser and on 31 May England's Chairman of Selectors offered Botham the role and he duly became the youngest England captain since Ivo Bligh in 1882.

In his foreword to Peter Smith's tour diary of the tour to the West Indies the following winter Bedser revealed the rationale behind the appointment as he seemed to be giving his struggling captain a vote of confidence at the end of a troubled tour. 'We decided to give Ian his chance in the knowledge that he lacked leadership experience but confident in the knowledge he would learn as he went along and provide England with a long-term solution.' But the feeling persisted that it was something done on a wing and a prayer and at precisely the wrong time. Only three months later Bedser would take a different view regarding that long-term solution. In reviewing both this about-turn and the decision to appoint him in the first place when it all ended in tears, Tony Lewis was clear that both were not simply mistakes but unfair, arguing 'the timing of the captaincy was treacherous to Botham'. When Botham was gone, Mike Brearley agreed: 'it was callous of them to throw him at the West Indies in his first two series'.

Some people foresaw all along the problems the timing would bring. Another all-rounder, though not of Botham's flamboyance, Trevor Bailey, who many had touted as an England captain in the 50s but never got their wish, gave his thoughts at the time, empathetically but unambiguously, under his editor's heading of:

Why it would be a mistake to make Botham captain

Trevor Bailey enters the controversy on who should lead the country this summer.

'It would be a mistake, which could even prove to be a disaster for English cricket, to give him the post at the present moment. I feel this exciting extrovert would react well to the extra load and would lead from the front by personal example as did Garry Sobers with the West Indies … however, my concern is the timing, which seems wrong.' With the foresight of the clairvoyant, Bailey suggested that to be a successful England captain (or indeed football manager) you need either a very good side or indifferent opposition and Botham would have neither with the recent deficiencies of the England side, despite their results, camouflaged by the weakness of the opposition. 'Even if faultless as leader, it would be no surprise if he loses the next two series.' The second reason Bailey gave also articulated that widely held concern. 'He is too young. It is a demanding post which takes years off careers and England cannot afford to lose Botham early.' Bailey closed by suggesting the wily captain of Essex (Bailey's own county) as a 'safe pair of hands'. In that regard he was expressing a wish which chimed with that of much of the male echelons of the Conservative Party before the equally concerning (to them) arrival in post of Margaret Thatcher. They were expecting a more experienced and less reactionary candidate – in other words, one of *them*. On reflection Keith Fletcher would have been to England what Willie Whitelaw might have been to the Tory party. The fact that neither took the reins as alternative options to Botham and Thatcher was another significant twist in the tale.

The former England captain Brian Close, whose careful handling, as Somerset captain, of Botham's emergence had been a mixture of no-nonsense dressing downs and familial kindness (as the uncle of Botham's wife Kath), was one of the concerned. As blunt a Yorkshireman as there was anywhere, if Close had expressed displeasure on hearing of his niece's choice of fiancé, he was no more enamoured of the selectors choice of Botham as captain now. He urged his protege to turn it down, convinced that it was too early and it would come again. Close was no fool and a cricketing survivor and he anticipated precisely what came to pass. His argument was that the next three Test assignments were against the West Indies, twice, and Australia, both of whom had now welcomed back their Packer players. The prescience of his prediction that Botham would be on a hiding to nothing was topped only by his warning that 'it'll be the worst bloody year of your life'. Although Botham, as a man with a Union Jack stapled to his heart, was never realistically going to heed his wise owl and turn the job down, sadly in 12 months' time he could only admit Close was right. Others would concede it at that point too. If a week is a long time in politics, then a year can be almost a career in sport. A year on, even the inherently sympathetic Christopher Martin-Jenkins began his piece on the Ashes summer ahead with, 'Alas Botham, a raw and brilliant all-rounder, has lost luck and form on the field and proved incapable at times of handling the enormous burden of office off it … this is a tragedy because the qualities which made him famous, not least courage, have not disappeared.' For all the ordeals that were to come, nor did they. For Thatcher the chorus was less 'too young', although Wilson in 1964 was the only younger prime minister to take office since the start of the century, but, politically at least, 'too callow' (she had no experience of any of the significant offices of state) and for many Conservatives (with both a small and large 'c') 'too female'.

If the year had not begun auspiciously with the start of a steel strike on its second day indicating that industrial strife was not yet going away, April gave a brief boost to public morale as the country sat gripped in front of their televisions watching a real-life cliffhanger rather than an episode of *The Professionals*. The matter of the steel dispute was another example of Thatcher's pragmatism when needed and when she judged it was necessary for survival, biding her time until the issue could be resolved in her favour, and her success now was in not getting the government involved. Even then she managed to portray something which went against her principles as something of a victory. Whilst conceding a 16% pay rise to the steelworkers was not helpful in her crusade against inflation, it was well below the union's initial demands and the fact that she had resolved the issue below their level of expectation but without further, extended industrial action was a small but significant step in the right direction. The April settlement was therefore actually seen by many as one of her first victories. Had it been otherwise and the steel strike had won the day, it is, believes Richard Vinen 'quite possible that Margaret Thatcher would not be a household name today'.

A month later brought another little victory. When the SAS's daring relief of the Iranian embassy hostage siege had reached its successful conclusion on their screens, few Britons other than those peeved that the Special Forces had interrupted the coverage of the world snooker final felt anything other than a certain pride that their nation could still perform when it mattered most. It mattered more because not only did it show what even an isolated success could do for the mood of a troubled country but because it was, with the possible exception of the steel issue just resolved, the only obvious success Thatcher's government could claim since it came to power.

With inflation heading to 22 per cent and unemployment towards a million Thatcher needed something to hang her hat on and it wasn't going to be the economy anytime soon. Richard Vinen noted that, 'one leading industrialist was quoted as saying [at this time] that "the removal of Mrs Thatcher would be the best thing that could happen to the economy"'. If it feels slightly strange now that a relatively short-lived if dramatic stand-off such as this could have so captivated the country, Dominic Sandbrook offered a reason as to why it did: 'At last, the lion had roused himself from his slumbers and the fact that the world was watching made the success all the sweeter' and the following day's newspaper headlines included the likes of 'So Proud To Be British' and 'Our Country At Its Best'. For a while at least, Thatcher would benefit from a little reflected glory. It wasn't the last time the country's armed services would provide her with some much needed good news and was, in the opinion of Sandbrook, the first indication of a promising future role as 'the warrior queen, the British St Joan, Britannia incarnate'. The Boadicea persona was something she was very happy to cultivate in the years ahead, playing opposite Botham's St George, but this was the last respite she was to enjoy for the rest of the year as the economic news insisted on remaining unremittingly bad.

In the month that the England selectors handed the captaincy to Botham in what was to prove a triumph of hope over experience, the positivity of the siege's resolution was another false dawn. Nor was the disruption of the snooker the last time the British sporting public would be threatened with the disappearance of one of their few opportunities to escape the gloom by turning to their cherished sporting events. The Soviet Union's recent invasion of Afghanistan had raised the stakes in the Cold War dramatically and further increased public fear of potential Armageddon – just one more brick in the wall blocking any sight of happy days ahead. Unsurprisingly, a debate began about the efficacy of sending a team of British Olympians to a Games to be hosted in Moscow that summer. Politicians and sports fans tend to take rather different positions in such situations, both defined more by self-interest than the pure principle everyone was purporting to hold most dear. The former tend to a penchant for using sport as an expendable sacrifice on their altar of outrage whilst sports fans, especially in the days when their access to live major events was far more rationed, generally favour the pragmatic over the idealistic. 'My life's miserable enough already thanks, don't you dare take my sport away', was an understandable response to the threat of a boycott in the grey days of 1980. Margaret Thatcher was therefore hardly going to improve her already emaciated popularity with the stance she took in insisting British athletes should not compete.

After one of the most underwhelming performances by a British Olympic team in Montreal four years before, public reaction to this position was hardened by the fact that this time there were a number of new talents who had the potential to bring home medals, even in the recently barren blue riband arena of track and field. As with many things throughout 1980, Thatcher was to lose twice over – she didn't get the result she wanted in terms of non-participation and in not doing so she had made herself the bad cop again. Watching Alan Wells, Steve Ovett, Sebastian Coe, Tessa Sanderson and Daley Thompson all subsequently bringing home athletics gold to a grateful public, via the grainy pictures that came with any news from the far side of the Iron Curtain simply reinforced the otherworldliness of that apparently suspicious part of the world, the futility of suggesting that sport and politics could and should be kept apart and, above all, that sport's impact is often far greater than as simply a line in the record books. The *Daily Express* used *that* word again in assessing the impact of these athletes, and specifically Coe and Ovett as they exchanged world records through 1981, seeing them as 'representatives of *change* – individualistic heroes in a society where collective loyalties had frayed'. It suggested that, much like Harold Abrahams and Eric Liddell in Paris in 1924, as portrayed in that year's British cinematic success *Chariots of Fire*, their triumphs were built on character. Again, Thatcher and Botham would have seen something they recognised and admired in the manner of such achievements. They were another expression of their belief in equality of opportunity – the white-collar Coe and fiercely blue-collar Ovett taking different routes to the same pinnacle – but inequality of outcome where striving for victory through self-motivation and unapologetic and necessary self-centredness was a badge to be worn with honour.

In 1981 first Coe and Ovett, then Botham, would drive the transformation of British sportspeople from the gallant, sometimes amateur, losers in the finest tradition cherished by a proportion of the English public to self-made professional winners. In 1975 the former had been represented by that everyman David Steele and his rearguard in the Ashes when those half-centuries in a losing series were greeted as herculean triumphs. The following year, Brendan Foster's Olympic bronze medal gained him hero status. Both were voted BBC Sports Personality of the Year in the mid-70s. Now we had a new breed of athletes who believed second was nowhere and a new breed of sports fans who loved their un-British irreverence and vocalised confidence. At the top of that athlete list would be Daley Thompson and Ian Botham, the most potent symbols of that change. But supreme as Thompson was as an all-round athlete, during his long unbroken record of success Sandbrook agrees that 'even Daley couldn't match the popularity of the best-known sportsman of the 80s'. That he didn't feel the need to name that man in his sentence is testimony to Botham's pre-eminence. The fact that both these characters saw themselves as ordinary, working class and misunderstood in a world run by a patrician establishment only endeared them more to a wider section of the public than any sportspeople of the age. A footnote to the divisive nature of the Games and the British athletes' participation came on the last day of the year when not a single one of the gold medallists appeared in the New Year's Honours list. Sandbrook called it a calculated snub on Thatcher's part, noting her rationale that 'they chose to accept their democratic right to go to a country with no democratic rights. I did not agree with it. I advised them strongly not to go'. Such statements showed the potential dangers of cant which Botham would need to avoid when the subject of South African rebel tours came up two years later.

And mention of South Africa points to the expediency and hypocrisy of which Thatcher could occasionally be accused and was not unknown at times in the choices and utterances of Botham. To upbraid the athletes for their supposed tacit endorsement of a regime which curtailed human rights looked rather shameful when the same prime minister was actively encouraging professionals in other businesses to pursue interests in the South Africa of the time. It was not her finest moment.

Whilst Britain's athletes brought some joy to the summer, a sporting event two months earlier had offered a better illustration of the country's perception at home and abroad. On the plus side, England's football team were making an appearance at the final stages of a major tournament for the first time in a decade but that lost its sheen as soon as their fans were admitted to the stadium hosting their first game and they played out every worst fear in setting about the Belgian fans who were more focused on enjoying the occasion. The sight of tear gas engulfing the terraces and players leaving the pitch with their eyes streaming and throats choking was a tableau encapsulating the now familiar sporting version of the British Disease. If the rest of Europe struggled to understand what had happened to their once proud and respected neighbour, Margaret Thatcher was equally baffled as to the motivations behind such violence on foreign shores. For someone intent on rebuilding Britain's reputation this was anathema of the most perplexing and frustrating kind. Some social historians suggest that the violence was another manifestation of the social stress of the time. It was not a mitigation Thatcher was likely to accept. It was merely the start of another battle she would have to fight throughout the decade – one in which she would find the opposition's motivations just as unjustifiable and destructive as those of the trades unions and one in which she was similarly determined to prevail.

As England's footballers, and to widespread relief their 'fans', failed to get past their group stage and departed Italy in the blink of an eye, their cricketing counterparts were unable to counter the misery. If that assertion that those growing up in 1980 were facing a dangerous and uncertain future, Botham and his new team would soon understand that anyone playing for England in 1980 would be entering an uncertain future in their own version of a dangerous environment. The Packer dispute was now settled, at least to a point where banned players were back and international teams returned to full strength. In the case of the West Indies that was a considerable strength and if England's relatively small number of defectors had previously given them the benefit of being less impacted by the bans, so now they reaped less of an uplift from returning stars. And if Botham had timed his arrival as a player well in starting against both the less historically strong nations and the weakened sides, his step into the captaincy was the diametric opposite.

A captain as fêted as Brearley himself would have found the prospect of what was coming in the next 12-18 months more than daunting; for England's youngest captain of the century, ten Tests against the world's strongest team – onc of the strongest in history – and an Ashes series against a reinforced Australia, were to prove altogether too much. For the Centenary Test at the end of the summer and the following year's Ashes series the Australians brought with them a returning Dennis Lillee. England had not won a series against a Lillee-inhabited team since his very first (and only partial) appearance ten years previously. To those who branded him lucky, Botham could counter by pointing to such slings and arrows. What he could not point to, unfortunately, were positive results. There were certain undeniable upsides to his new level of profile however. In an early indication of how Botham was to become one of the new celebrity sportspeople who would transcend their field and open the way for a new land of riches for the top athletes in the commercial decade to come, there he stood in July in a full page advertisement with a Saab 900 alongside the car manufacturer's strapline, *Botham and Saab 900 – Born to Lead.* Botham's association with the brand would bring him significant financial rewards over the years, but rather too soon the tagline would need to change.

It is a commonality of leadership in both politics and sport that an individual's own fate can be determined by matters outside their direct control. At the start of his captaincy and ahead of the summer Tests with the West Indies, Botham's claim that England could be truly competitive ('I've a gut feeling we can defy the odds') may have looked flimsy but it would have been both unacceptable and out of character to say anything else and in the first Test at Nottingham England had their opponents in a degree of trouble chasing a moderate final innings total only for another set of sliding doors to get stuck in the act of opening. At seven wickets down and still 29 short of victory England had opened up one end to the bowlers in their opponents' vaunted batting order. Andy Roberts was an occasionally effective hitter and had decided attack was the best option. A horrible skier went up and over David Gower's shoulder. The perennially brilliant fielder Gower groped for the ball in the gloom and grassed it and with it went the chance of a momentum-charging win. Given the weather for the rest of the summer it could be argued, harshly on Gower but accurately as it transpired, to have been a series-deciding drop. The second Test at Lord's, traditionally a much anticipated highlight of the summer season of sport, was abandoned at lunch on the final day as a stagnant draw in which England were always behind. 'England behind' had become the general narrative. It was a typical scenario in that cricketing summer and the series never got going thereafter.

As the Two Tone movement reached its apogee in 1980 (Sandbrook identified the middle of the year as a time of 'a palpable shift in cultural temperature'), The Beat would provide another musical commentary to capture the times. Four days before the end of the West Indies series and two weeks after the announcement that Thatcher's economy was officially in recession, they released 'Stand Down Margaret', the title of which requires no further explanation. Lead singer Dave Wakelin's opening words – 'I see no joy, I see only sorrow; I see no sign of your bright new tomorrow' – articulated succinctly the growing public perception that 'may we bring hope' was now consigned to history as an originally quixotic and now forlorn ambition.

By the summer's end there was little sign of Botham's bright new tomorrow either and although this was hardly his fault given the forces stacked against him, the number of doubters prepared to vocalise 'stand down please' in the cricketing leader columns and idle chatter was climbing up at him with the unavoidable trajectory of a Colin Croft bouncer. Seeing only sorrow was also a feature of another cultural and political story of the year – the growing threat to world peace from the Cold War and the advance of a nuclear menace. The public perception of this as a very real global destruction in waiting was not soothed at all by the bleak portrayals, bordering on scaremongering, across the media. A BBC *Panorama* programme on 10 March had created a horror in many viewers and, at a time when pessimism hardly needed a helping hand, just added to the gloom. It was something which would cast an ever-greater shadow across 1981 after the accession of Ronald Reagan to the US presidency and his alignment with Thatcher as a committed 'hawk', believing totally in the deterrent argument which would fuel a decade-long arms race. It would also add another domestic burden for Thatcher in 1981's accumulation of them when on 12 June she accepted some of Reagan's missiles at British airbases at Greenham Common and Molesworth, occasioning more vehement public protest in a year flooded with it and which would last for the rest of her premiership.

On 12 August the curtain duly came down on Botham's first series as captain and a 1-0 defeat. As quixotic hopes and forlorn ambitions go, the idea of victory against the cricketing juggernaut confronting them was a pretty unambiguous example. Botham would argue, at the time and for the rest of time, with some validity proven by the passage of time, that such a scoreline was no disgrace, but the reality was that the main contributor to that final result was the drabbest of summer weather which produced four days of complete washouts alongside numerous starts and stops. After the fleeting glimpse of success at Trent Bridge in early June that snatching of defeat from the jaws of victory was somehow symptomatic. At that moment however, there was a more balanced reaction to Botham's leadership than a groundswell against him. He hadn't yet had enough time to prove himself even if reservations were increasing. John Woodcock reflected that balance in *The Times* at the end of the series: 'The selectors are happy with Botham … though there will be few who have no reservations about Botham's suitability for the job.' Woodcock noted sensibly how the potential runners to replace him, including Keith Fletcher and John Hampshire, had had poor seasons and that 'only three months ago Botham was England's greatest cricketing asset'. This timely reminder of why we had fallen for the bloke in the first place was supplemented when Woodcock reviewed a new book on Botham – such things were another by-product of his increasing fame – by the journalist Dudley Doust, who described Botham's as 'a robust, almost reckless life' but concluded with equal prescience to Bailey before him, that 'future historians may well write of the 70s and 80s as *The Botham Age,* for nothing seems beyond this young man's capabilities'. Admittedly the time lag between manuscript and publication would have been partly responsible for this rather isolated rosy portrayal but it was a useful prompt to the memory that here was a cricketer that should be cherished rather than cast aside. There was also another reason to cherish the man which would get lost in the hubbub of the cricketing debate and Botham's own choice of lifestyle, and it was one which was to resurface throughout his career and beyond, giving the lie to caricatures of someone embroiled in his own ego. An editorial noted, quietly, how on a Sunday that September, at the end of a summer of significant stress and demands, he paid £450 from his own pocket for a helicopter to take him to play in a charity soccer match to honour a commitment that mattered to him. It was not to be the last time Botham's generosity and thought for others was to be turned into positive action.

The downbeat tenor of England's cricketing summer was captured most succinctly by the Centenary Test which brought it to a close. Hoping to replicate the sunshine, the vibrant cricket, the climactic finish and the general bonhomie of its predecessor in Melbourne, this planned celebration of the 100th anniversary of the first Test played in England was to do nothing of the sort. John Woodcock summed things up at the summer's end with 'those who believed that sooner or later one of the Test matches was sure to be played in warmth and sunshine were wrong'. Arlott's retrospective of the season recalled, 'It was, we were assured, the worst summer since before the First World War.' More than ten hours of play were lost to the rain which washed over the bank holiday weekend as it had done on most of the summer weekends before it, and what vibrancy there was on the pitch came solely from the Australians. A Lord's swathed in dark clouds was in ill humour and when the immovable bad light had stopped play once too often for the members' liking a fracas broke out involving some of their number, the umpires and several cushions. If confrontation and anger had now infiltrated the Long Room too, England was in a worse state than it thought. And the cricket team's refusal to act in accordance with the intended spirit of the occasion, deciding against having a tilt at victory and instead allowing Geoffrey Boycott's batting to gradually disperse what remained of the crowd, seemed emblematic of a lack of belief and ambition everywhere. England were going nowhere, and not very fast. On the final afternoon one more connection to a nostalgic past was consigned to history. As John Arlott stood to wave from the commentary box to the crowd acclaiming him on the day of his retirement, he might have been waving goodbye to a mythical era which some felt would not come again. It was an uplifting reception but it still felt like another deprivation in what Andrew Marr coined 'a land of lost content'.

It wasn't just sports-related challenges which studded the summer. Two weeks after England football's shame of Turin came the shame of Westminster as unemployment was announced to have hit a post-war high of 1.47 million. Thatcher's predicted discord was real enough but the overcoming of the forces of doubt and despair was nowhere to be seen. In 12 months' time UB40's 'One In Ten' would lead the protest when this figure had all but doubled, but this week they were in the charts with their bleaker version of Randy Newman's 'I Think It's Going To Rain Today'. Both the title and the words 'pale dead moon in a sky streaked with grey' offered an accurate depiction, meteorological, sporting and political, of the summer of 1980. By its end, what neither Thatcher nor Botham could deny, or convincingly defend though it was their job to try, was the statistical evidence which the media ensured was right in front of everyone's eyes. Thatcher had her unemployment, productivity and inflation figures; Botham had followed his outstanding averages since debut with a summer as captain of 169 runs at 17 and 14 wickets at 37, one solitary fifty and not a single five-wicket haul. He had turned his numbers almost precisely on their heads. They were not to improve either for another 12 months – a period which Thatcher's leadership would somehow survive, but Botham's would not. At the end of the Centenary Test the first significant signs of dissent against, as opposed to concern for, Botham were emerging and Robin Marlar, not one always given to putting sensitivity before trenchant opinion, had written: 'Botham should not be resentful if the rest of the cricketing world points to the inflexibility of his tactical thinking. The end of the game was safe but unheroic.'

In Thatcher, the insistence on no compromise was in time to be seen as a strength; for Botham it was not to be the same saviour. Over the next year or so neither was to be either safe or unheroic and neither was to be shaken from their beliefs or to compromise their characters. Botham titled a full page article in *The Cricketer* that autumn as MY CHANCE TO DEFEND MYSELF. If it was a sign that the leader was beginning to feel the flak, it was also a public statement of his determination not to be derailed by doubters. It was a message Thatcher was about to echo in one of the most iconic political speeches of the era.

Not For Turning

'Our doubts are traitors
And make us lose the good we oft might win
By fearing to attempt.'

William Shakespeare
Measure For Measure

'If you can keep your head when all about you
Are losing theirs and blaming it on you;
If you can trust yourself when all men doubt you …'

Rudyard Kipling
If

THE TRIALS of the summer had denuded even the famed self-belief of Botham and Thatcher. Self-doubt did threaten to creep in – not as to their abilities or the validity of their approach, but whether they would be afforded the time to see them bear fruit – but any that lingered were indeed deemed as traitors. Fearing to attempt was not something either was going to countenance even as the odds against them lengthened and the voices against them grew louder. Defeat was not in their vocabulary and whatever the outcome they would not be lying down and going quietly. It was, in fact, the vocabulary of Thatcher's speechwriter Ronald Millar which would make this clear to those watching, whether in the Commons or the country. Autumn heralded the party conference season and on 10 October Thatcher addressed hers with one of the more famous prime ministerial orations. In a public statement of self-assurance which made it patently clear there would be no change of approach – as she saw it, no loss of nerve – Millar handed her a phrase adapted from the title of a Christopher Fry play. The lady, she insisted, was not for turning. In terms of the fightback that would gather strength through the following year, the speech was probably the beginning of the beginning and its message would forevermore underpin one of the tenets of Thatcherism. The presentation to the nation of a leader who may not yet have had success but who had strength and courage, mattered to many just as much as whether or not they actually agreed with the vision. If the grandees and centrists in her party were aghast, the party members and many conservative voters nationwide found it far more palatable. They had had enough of vacillation. Right or wrong, here at least was certainty. Thatcher's shrewdness had shown itself, turning the condescension of the dismissive group who referred to her as 'that bloody woman' to her own advantage over the next 12 months before she took the knife to it. In the face of it she managed to project a populist appeal to what Peter Clarke called 'the thwarted subaltern class of Conservative loyalists' who recognised her as one of their own, not unlike the great swathe of 'loyalist' cricket fans that outnumbered the small coterie of establishment members and had taken Botham to their hearts as 'one of their own'. A former England team-mate, Mike Hendrick, had his own opinion on what made Botham so popular. 'He's just a bricklayer who's good at something else. He's a man of the people.' In Thatcher's case, the grandees' self-satisfied disdain had now backfired for the long term.

Thatcher's words in Brighton, where she was to produce another speech of strength and courage in the face of adversity four years on almost to the day, may have made a powerful statement, but in themselves they could have little impact on the specific problems she faced. It is often the case, as it was for Heath in the early 1970s, that struggling governments at home have their problems exacerbated by events overseas. In Thatcher's case this now came in the oil crisis forced upon her by the 1980–88 Iran-Iraq war. Despite the increasing benefits soon to come from beneath the North Sea, the quadrupling of the global oil price did little to alleviate her immediate economic challenges as recession became a global rather than merely domestic issue. Dominic Sandbrook argues there was therefore always likely to be a major recession, regardless of Margaret Thatcher and her policies. This was as irresistible a truth as that of the West Indian fast bowlers. As Botham would soon discover in the West Indies, it didn't rain but it poured. Shadows were still being cast as a dark year neared its conclusion. On 17 November came news of the 13th victim of Peter Sutcliffe, aka 'The Yorkshire Ripper'. It was just another reminder that the country was not a happy, or even now safe, place to be living. Jaqueline Hill had been murdered in Headingley, of all places, and the police still appeared as powerless to put an end to the killings which had been horrifying Britain since the middle of the 70s as the government were in addressing the country's gathering ills. This time the regular updates on the news were not so much depressing as terrifying and it all added to a sense of deep malaise. Nothing seemed to be improving. A fortnight after the murder another cloud arrived which was to resound through 1981 in a further challenge to Thatcher's authority and the ultimate test of her 'not for turning' philosophy.

On 27 October the IRA announced that members of their organisation incarcerated in the Maze prison in Belfast would begin a hunger strike. Thatcher was adamant they were convicted terrorists whilst the IRA considered them political prisoners and it was for recognition of that status that the strike was called. Whether either side could envisage what was to come is doubtful but it would become one grisly chapter in 1981's story. For now, Thatcher was to get an outcome which offered some respite, the strike being called off in the week before Christmas. *The Sun* suggested to the nation, in characteristically insensitive fashion, that 'the "surrender" is a big victory for premier Margaret Thatcher's defiant stand'. If it was indeed a victory, and one sorely needed however fleeting, it had only won the first-leg. Botham's run up to the festive period was to contain no such relief.

One benefit of being a high-profile cricketer as opposed to the prime minister was that there were downtimes – fallow periods when limbs and mind could be rested, holidays enjoyed and stock could be taken. Botham had that advantage. At the end of a long summer his autumn could, for a time, turn down the volume. It also helped him that the next assignment would not begin in November as most England winter tours did, but well into the new year in the Caribbean. As Thatcher was making her case in Brighton, so Botham would insist, when asked, that yes, he was the best man for the job; no, he didn't believe the burden of captaincy had affected his form and yes, he was looking forward to spring in the West Indies and a competitive series. There was no appetite from his selectors to make a change as yet and an uneventful winter preparing for the task ahead would have avoided any great debate as to his suitability for it. But if his change in his fortunes had brought trials on the pitch, what happened on 23 December would cap an arduous year and lead to a trial of a very different sort.

A Long December

ON THE evening of 15 December Botham, who had been training and playing for Scunthorpe United to stay fit for the upcoming West Indies tour, joined a night out with his team-mates for some pre-Christmas drinks. If his playing of football prior to an important tour loaded a rifle with ammunition for a media of ex-players and tabloids looking for reasons to doubt him and boost circulation, what happened next stocked up an entire arsenal. In defending his friend, goalkeeper Joe Keenan, against aggression from some locals Botham became embroiled in an altercation. It would not have been in character to take a step backwards, especially when he felt palpably in the right. High-profile celebrities can, however, be obvious targets for those wanting to make a name for themselves. Allegations were made and two days before Christmas the captain of England was arrested on a charge of affray and assault causing actual bodily harm. For those wanting to shift newspapers it was Manna from heaven; for those who believed either that he was unsuitable material to hold such an august post or just that the bloke was too big for his boots, it was perceived validation and further grist to the mill following a driving ban for travelling at 120 miles-an-hour earlier in the month.

The sportswriter Simon Barnes has no time for the idea of the sporting 'role model' or the idea that some of Botham's errant behaviour over the years saw him as having somehow failed everyone. He was to suffer more of his fair share of the country's tendency to what Barnes calls 'mock, pompous indignation'. But for all that, it was not a happy way to end the year. 'Uncle' Brian's prophecy was halfway to reality. At the year's end, *Wisden Cricket Monthly* ran an editorial which so captures the mood and the yearning for something better, written in a cricketing context but with a far wider relevance, that it is worth revisiting.

> 'As the sun went down on the last day of 1980 it took with it not only the first half of the inhospitable English winter but also a year of lamentable frustration which began with an unsatisfactory Australia-England series. Then came a summer in which umbrellas saw more usage than cricket bats. The Centenary Test created little worth remembering. Farewell 1980 and good riddance.'

If the goodbye to the year just gone was one which found not a single redeeming quality, the consideration of the year ahead mixed similar realism with an invitation to redemption:

> 'Not that 1981 has begun all that promisingly. English cricket has been embarrassed by the publicity given to the alleged escapades of its young captain. But let the sun of the Caribbean bring out the best … and beyond the West Indies? An Australian visit. The new sun has risen. What annalistic deeds will it take down with it this time?'

What indeed.

Wisden was not the only one looking forward and attempting to see some sun on the horizon. On the same day as Botham's arrest and the day after Thatcher had told the ITN news that she looked forward to the recession coming to an end during the next year (and it did). *The Sun* carried a report of her speech the day before in which she looked ahead in much the same fashion as Botham was viewing the upcoming West Indies tour – a mixture of the coldly realistic and the optimistic designed to keep onside those who were beginning to doubt. 'Premier Margaret Thatcher revealed her dream yesterday of a happy Christmas ... in ten years' time. That is how long she reckoned it would take to put Britain fully back on its feet. For 1981, her outlook was: the country faces another hard time. But she predicted that if pay deals were reasonable this winter, there was a real hope that a year from now things would look distinctly brighter.' A depiction of Botham's vision ahead of a battle against formidable odds in the Caribbean but then a winnable home Ashes series could have run pretty much word for word. The wish to look forward was not confined to these two gunslingers. Considering what was happening in British popular music at this moment, on 20 December the journalist Paul Morley wrote, 'There is definitely a new mood spreading. Something can happen in 1981.' And so it did. But right now the Christmas greetings were no jollier for Margaret Thatcher than they were for Botham. The day after his arrest, Christmas Eve, *The Times*'s front page showed little festive spirit, announcing that Britain's jobless total had reached a post-war high of 2.13 million, that it was 'an exceedingly bleak end to what has been an exceedingly bleak year' and that 'Mrs Thatcher said there is no instant solution.' Labour may not have been working, but the country was beginning to wonder whether Thatcher was someone who could deliver any solution at all. She could sense the growing doubts. 'By the end of 1980 I began to feel that we risked forfeiting the public's confidence.' She was right to be concerned – across the country the mood could scarcely have been gloomier. Nor was there much respite for those more concerned with the happy traditions of the festive period now upon them. That the Christmas number one they all had to accept was the 'let's buy it for Grandma to save us having to think of anything else' single from the St Winifred's Girls' School Choir rather than a John Lennon song was an indication to some as to just what a pretty pass things had come to. And why a Lennon song? Because the second week of the last month of a depressing year witnessed perhaps the most numbing, dispiriting moment of the lot. In his final ever interview that December, Lennon had been looking forward with more optimism than he had felt in years and professed the hope that 'perhaps in the 80s everybody'll say, "Well ok, let's project the positive side of life again".' Days later, as Mark Chapman turned away from the Dakota building in New York on the night of 8 December, he did so saying 'I just shot John Lennon.'

PART FOUR:

A YEAR LIKE NO OTHER

1981

Four Funerals and a Wedding

AS 1981 dawned, the aftermath of John Lennon's murder took people's faith in the future to a new low. Alwyn W. Turner suggested that his death appeared to symbolise the passing of a kindlier, more familiar Britain and *The Times*'s leader column saw it as the death of the optimism of the 60s when Lennon represented the aspirations of a generation. That generation had now grown up and its optimism at this moment was hard to locate. It also felt, on top of the miserable economics of the 70s, like a cultural full stop. People were going to have to deal with a different reality. A light went out on 8 December 1980. *The Sun* concurred with its soon to be Murdoch stablemate. 'Lennon's death really does mark the end of an era … even though he hated all that schmaltz. In any social history of the 60s John Lennon is a more important figure than any other Englishman … he changed the way in which life and events were regarded.'

Lennon biographer Ray Coleman suggested that few deaths had resulted in so much reflection and the world felt diminished by the loss of an individualistic spirit. There was now a vacancy for other such spirits to fill. It would be glib to suggest either Botham or Thatcher as Lennon replacements but undoubtedly the times and their peoples now needed a little more of that individualism and inspiration. There was also a connection in terms of their view of life and that belief Botham and Thatcher shared that people should be their own motivators and not look everywhere else for leadership.

Lennon never wanted to be a guru or a god and his exhortation to those who wanted to 'follow' him, 'Make your own dreams and do things for yourself. I can't wake you up. *You* wake *you* up', would have found favour with both. But now there was a pall over the new year. It was not a happy start. Lennon's career was another which had every appearance of reflecting and influencing the years it spanned. When the increasing antagonism between Lennon and Paul McCartney led to the break-up of The Beatles at the end of 60s it drew down the curtain on a decade of a positivity and feel-good factor missing since the end of the war and on a British phenomenon which bestrode it. The more acerbic and withdrawn approach he chose from 1970 confirmed that the fun was over and the next ten years would be less idealistic and optimistic ones. But like the country at large, he seemed to see the dawn of the 80s as a moment of potential change and to look to creativity and contentment once again. He was tired of the age of ill humour. It was time to look forward, now living happily in New York and feeling he had managed to divest himself of the goldfish bowl existence of which he was so weary. On the very day that the Yorkshire Ripper had struck for the last time, Lennon released his sixth solo album *Double Fantasy* to much critical acclaim. It marked not only his return to full-time recording after a five-year hiatus but his return to his most productive and creative self. The album was awash with references to his happiness, his love of his family and his rediscovered enjoyment in his own existence. Its first single had a title and a sentiment in which his native country wanted to believe. 'Just Like Starting Over' was released a fortnight after Thatcher had stood up in Brighton to insist the 80s would see a different Britain. If it was tragic that it took his murder to guarantee the song's place at the top of the charts by the middle of September, it was just as galling to many that it should be replaced there before Christmas by the saccharine nonsense of 'There's No One Quite Like Grandma'. That one of the most legendary and definitive songwriters of the century might have his eulogy interrupted by infants from St Winifred's School felt like, and still feels like, a moment of typical British perversity.

The miserable countenance of the first half of 1981 would be coloured by three further deaths within seven weeks of each other. Botham's soul-destroying loss of Ken Barrington in March was felt by the entire cricket-loving community. Then in early May came the more portentous death of IRA hunger striker Bobby Sands and the fury it brought with it. Within a week the world had lost another figure whose legacy would live on long after his passing in Bob Marley. If Sands was a totem for one group of believers with a grievance, Marley was, if less controversially so, another rebel with a cause – one who was an inspiration to a diaspora whose sense of injustice was to become so visible through the year. And yet, in amongst the grief and the burials came a wedding which would change the whole tenor of the year. On 24 February it was announced that the heir to throne had become engaged to a young English aristocrat. The interest generated by the pictures of the unknown and demur girl barely able to engage with the cameras was out of proportion to the news itself but that had its reason. The following morning the *Daily Telegraph* report suggested that 'for a nation more than ever starved of symbols of hope … the royal example becomes more important'.

The moment was here and gone quickly, subsumed by the travails in every other walk of life. When the pomp returned at the end of July however, the impact was more enduring. The disagreement between *The Times* and *The Guardian* over the true impact on the country of the marriage of Prince Charles and Lady Diana Spencer was probably influenced by their respective political leanings. Those who still believed in a leftist, big-state approach didn't want to recognise or acknowledge any signs of happiness whilst Thatcher was in power and it wasn't something their media wanted to convey within their broader agenda. 'Radiance and romance may bring a smile, but they change nothing' Eeyore-ed *The Guardian*. That may have been a view shared by some of their readers, but overall they had misjudged the significance of a revival in spirit, from death to glory. Whether they liked it or not, one late July day – allied to a couple more on the cricket fields of England – would shift the mood from the deathly spectre of a year which seemed to be destined to go down as one of the more depressing in recent history to one which now puts its legacy in a very different light. Four funerals and a wedding acted out the story of 1981.

January: Imagine

ON 4 January 1981 a transformational year began with a low-key meeting. It was one Margaret Thatcher had been seeking for some time. If there was any other political and cultural force who would shape the 80s alongside her and Botham it was Rupert Murdoch. Murdoch had begun his journey to hegemony over the British media in 1968 and 1969 when buying the *News of The World* and *The Sun* respectively, outflanking Robert Maxwell in the process. *The Sun* was then, and would remain by inclination for some time, a left-leaning and relatively unsuccessful newspaper but it would soon become yet another totem of change. Murdoch went to work. In 1978 *The Sun* overtook the previously unassailable *Daily Mirror* in circulation. Just as significantly, Murdoch and his editorial team had become as exasperated with the socialism of the 1970s as had the majority of its vastly increasing readership. In 1974 they had made an equivocal and half-hearted endorsement of Ted Heath at the election, noting that if the Labour Party had anyone who could run it properly, the paper and the voters should still ideally be behind it. 'All our instincts are left rather than right and we would vote for any able politician who would describe himself as a Social Democrat' ran an editorial.

By 1979 there was no such dilemma as *The Sun* went unapologetically Conservative. 'VOTE TORY THIS TIME' screamed the paper's headline on the morning of polling day on 3 May 1979. By the following morning Thatcher stood triumphant in Downing Street. So began a truism of the next 45 years and counting – that Murdoch was now Britain's political kingmaker and his market-leading publication his vehicle. Without his support you wouldn't win elections. That Thatcher had that support as she came to power is regarded as instrumental and can be seen as one of the more significant factors in the decade of change. (The theme of change in 1981 didn't leave *The Sun* untouched either as Kelvin MacKenzie replaced Larry Lamb as editor and instigated changes which were to make it, according to the journalist Bruce Page, 'more outrageous, opinionated and irreverent than anything ever produced in Britain'.) Support can, however, be transient and Murdoch's was motivated not just by belief but by expediency. He was there to sell papers. If he played a role in Thatcher's fortunes in the 80s he did the same with Botham who became a well-remunerated contributor and shifter of copies. Botham was to discover soon enough that he who pays the piper calls the tune and he would always struggle to accept the contradiction in the paper lauding one of its employees and using his successes to their own ends and then hanging him out to dry when the 'anything goes' tabloid circulation war exploded, contributing as much to his dark moments as it did to his highs and practically dictating his profile in the country at any given time.

Thatcher too saw the potential for harm if her benefactor could not be kept onside when times got tough. At the start of 1981, with the difficulties which had beset her the year before and the plans she had for the year ahead, she knew the relationship could make or break her. Charm offensives may not always have been seen as her forte but if ever one was required it was now. Murdoch's desire to close his deals to buy *The Times* and the *Sunday Times*, and to have the political green light to do so, made their lunch more a matter of mutual benefit, but for Thatcher its success would have long-term repercussions and play a role in her premiership surviving not just the year but the rest of the decade.

Thatcher's ascendancy may not have been guaranteed, but fortunately nor was that of the girls' school choir. On the day Thatcher met with Murdoch, they lost their unfathomable perch as the mourning of Lennon placed his best-known solo tune at number one. 'Imagine' again seemed somehow appropriate in terms of the best people could do at that moment. Might it also be the harbinger of better news in a fresh year? The following day suggested, briefly, that it might. On the first of many days of change in 1981, Peter Sutcliffe was arrested. He had been interviewed by police in the past but this time when he was stopped whilst driving with false plates they realised they had their man. Two days later Sutcliffe admitted the murder of 13 women and the terror of the Yorkshire Ripper and the peril of any woman out on her own in the north of England of the last five years was gone.

The first month also ushered in political changes of consequence. On 20 January, the United States inaugurated its 40th president. Ronald Reagan was deemed by some to have won the presidency through his celebrity as a hugely famous and popular screen actor. He was to prove over the next eight years to have more to him than that. It was another happening which may not have been recognised as such at the time but was a notable one in Thatcher's future. Reagan shared her distrust of liberalism and centralism at home, and socialism both at home and abroad. It would be the start of a beautiful friendship and a meeting of minds which would sustain each other through the rest of the decade and make the world a very different place.

If there were changes afoot in American politics, within the week of Reagan being sworn in an even more dramatic revolution was born in the UK. The arrival of Michael Foot as Labour leader the previous November had had two effects.

Firstly, it made Thatcher's position more secure. As Andrew Marr reflected, 'the Tories might be hated, but Labour were now unelectable', and one of Foot's own parliamentary colleagues admitted he epitomised and compounded all the problems of a party coming to be regarded as old, out of touch and irrelevant. The *Daily Express*, not renowned for its love of socialists, was nonetheless probably somewhere near the truth, or understating it, when it claimed that Labour now had a leader whose views scared half the country to death. The time was right neither for a slightly decrepit and elderly politician to convince the public that he was the man to put in charge, fierce intellect and brilliant oratory notwithstanding, nor for the vitriolic, internecine battle for the deputy leadership which would last until September.

One of the combatants in that bitter confrontation was another character who made for a perfect opponent given the inherently conservative nature of the British. Tony Benn's 'extremism and combination of privilege and working-class affectation made him an easy target' remembers Richard Vinen. His future party leader Neil Kinnock, by no means a centrist himself, would call Benn's approach to policy 'a fantasy that insults adult intelligence'. People were after stability and a clear vision and this represented neither. Foot's arrival was not going to move the opposition any closer to the centre where a group of senior, ambitious party notables had become disaffected with the policies, in-fighting and vision of their own leadership. British politics hadn't seen the birth of a new party of significance since Labour's own emergence in the first year of the century but the second consequence of Foot's election was to produce one. The Gang of Four, as Roy Jenkins, David Owen, Shirley Williams and Bill Rodgers were billed, were another bringing change to 1981. In the last week of January the four announced their departure from the Labour Party and issued the Limehouse Declaration which would launch the Social Democratic Party officially in March.

This was not an insignificant moment of evolution. If Labour, or indeed Thatcher, underestimated their potential impact on the year ahead, if not far beyond, they were in for a shock. As the new party made huge inroads into the popular vote in Warrington, then Croydon, then Crosby, everyone had to sit up and take notice. 1981 was at it again and, as Graham Stewart noted, the mould of British politics looked ready to be smashed to smithereens. In modern day Britain, Nigel Farage and his Reform party might yet hope of being cast in the same role in the sequel. They might be less buoyed by the fact that the new party would decline through 1982 as the novelty wore off, which purely in terms of electoral recovery and the securing of a vast majority in 1983 would be as important in Thatcher's recovery as anything.

February: A Coiled Spring

'They came rolling along, one almost overtaking the other, building up like a giant snowball tumbling out of control down a hill.'

IAN BOTHAM'S depiction of the 'snowball' of problems which gathered momentum throughout his disastrous tour of the West Indies which ran from February to April could just as easily have been a description of the incessant issues assailing Thatcher and the country. In January, following the disturbance in Bristol the previous year, came the next precursor of another snowball which was to come rolling along, with one flare-up almost overtaking the other, for much of the year. Thirteen black partygoers died in a fire in Deptford and the perceived casual nature of the police investigation into it led to angry protests in the area through to March. If, as Graham Stewart suggested, the anger felt towards the police by immigrants was not replicated in the country generally, that scarcely mattered as the former was enough to present a clear picture of decay and negativity and the spring of 1981 carried an escalating atmosphere of menace, danger and despair.

It was indeed a 'coiled' spring, and not just one embodied in the actions of the West Indies fast bowlers as they gathered themselves in their run ups to unleash their thunderbolts, but one where increasing and almost unmanageable pressure was building in tandem with the relentless drip of criticism and tension associated with an array of challenges daunting enough to dent the belief of even the most confident souls. Both leaders found even their more traditional support was ebbing away. As Thatcher's backbenchers were suffering a decline in morale in Westminster, so Botham's own backbenchers in the dressing room were beginning to lose faith out in the Caribbean, their morale dwindling in the same way. It served only to increase the sense of isolation in both of them. When Botham's close friend and Somerset team-mate, Trevor Gard, visited him later in the tour he found someone he didn't recognise: 'I'd never seen him like that – withdrawn and negative.'

Cricket's capacity to embroil itself in internal controversies, each of which tended to come with warnings of the end of the game as we know it, displayed itself once more on the first day of February. When Botham talked of things which came rolling along, he was not referring to one which did so quite literally. In a one-day international against New Zealand at the MCG, with the visitors requiring a six off the last ball to win, the Australian captain Greg Chappell instructed his brother, Trevor, to roll the ball down the pitch underarm to make such a feat impossible. Not for the first time in history, nor for the last, the game's authorities and its followers erupted with outrage as they cited the 'spirit of the game', which then as now was specious hypocrisy to some and critically important to others. That this should happen in coloured clothing under the broadcasting auspices of one Kerry Packer simply increased the conviction of many – maybe branded as traditionalists but most, in truth, simply followers who loved the game – that cricket had cast off its soul and was on a one-way journey to destruction. The sport needed something uplifting – an inspiring contest of great cricket instead of controversy and conflict whether on or off the pitch What it got was the precise opposite and caught in the crosshairs was an unfortunate Ian Botham.

Botham was tasked with managing a tour of the Caribbean – in theory one of the more acceptable assignments for English cricketers – which evolved into a stream of barely credible nightmares. The 13th day of the month was not a lucky one for either Botham or Thatcher. At home it was announced that British manufacturing output was now at its lowest since 1968; in Trinidad England began a Test series which started inauspiciously and got worse. Both Thatcher and Botham were faced with Four Horsemen of the Apocalypse. If Thatcher's were the economy, the unions, inner-city rioting and Northern Ireland, Botham's came in the form of Andy Roberts, Michael Holding, Colin Croft and Joel Garner. Perhaps fearing what these messengers of doom might do if given chance to draw first blood, Botham invited the West Indies to bat first and by the end of the day his team hadn't taken a solitary wicket. His bowlers' productivity was no better than that of his nation's workforce. Five days later England had to swallow their pride and an innings defeat. The parallels kept coming. Back home it was the day on which the National Coal Board were forced to bend the knee to the miners, announcing under considerable threat of unrest that they were backing down on their stated plan for 23 pit closures. VICTORY TO THE MINERS! shouted the front page of the *Daily Mirror.* Victory to the West Indies too. Dominic Sandbrook saw the parallels: 'Whether your sphere of interest was politics or sport the story was the same – one of bad news.' Neither defeat suggested that England's two captains were making any progress against their nemeses. In Trinidad the toss decision was perhaps the wrong one but probably inconsequential in the grand scheme of things. This was mission impossible.

For a start, as in the summer England were facing what was, by common consent, an almost unconquerable foe. If the battery of West Indies fast bowlers had been tough to handle on home pitches, those waiting for them on the tour, glistening like glass and fast as lightning, dialled up the challenge from difficult to genuinely frightening. Both that bowling attack and the baying stands of supporters egging them on were coiled springs of their own, seemingly stretched to greater and greater potential force throughout the tour. At its end, the previously unfailingly positive Botham was losing that virtue. It was, he rather uncharacteristically understated, 'a tour that will not spark many great memories when I look back on it in years to come'.

It was a lambs to the slaughter assignment as Botham took out a vastly less experienced team than the one they were about to encounter. He was lampooned for the fact he had said in advance that his team could win, but what was he supposed to say? At this point Botham's famed belief that nothing was impossible was still intact and he *did* believe, in the face of the doubters. There was no Brearley, Knott, Underwood, Hendrick or Edmonds available when what both Botham and Thatcher needed in the spring of 1981 was trusted lieutenants. Botham's on tour were Peter Willey, Bob Willis and Brian Rose – two of whom had to leave the tour before it reached its most critical point. After their departures Botham stood isolated and alone. Thatcher felt this way early in '81 as she looked at her cabinet and took of stock of how much support and backbone there was there. John Hoskyns's own eyes told him that early 1981 was when Thatcher first began to suffer the isolation of high office. Like Botham in the West Indies she needed stout hearts and total backing. Her solution that autumn was to be the new broom reshuffle, bringing in younger faces who were committed to her and her way. Botham may have wanted to do the same but was not in charge of such decisions and anyway, against the world's most dominant side, picking young, inexperienced players was a more difficult way to go. In the manner of Thatcher's early cabinets, Botham found himself 'saddled with players I didn't want, didn't rate and who weren't up to the job'. Thatcher could, in time, bring an end to that problem but the England captain could not and had to put up with a horse-trading selection process in which for every player he insisted upon he seemed to have to accommodate one on the whims of his selectors.

It was a tour beset from the start by difficulties that rained down on the captain as he suffered the same spring of unforeseen and uncontrollable trials that came Thatcher's way. For a start, one thing you might reasonably expect and look forward to on arriving for a tour of these islands in the spring is some sunshine – the odd tropical downpour for an hour in the afternoon perhaps but otherwise blue skies and playing conditions not consistently to be found at home. It was, after all, the dry season in that part of the world. But again 1981 and the weather decided on something different and unprecedented monsoon rain curtailed the warm-up games. Somehow in this most depressing of spring seasons back home, the Caribbean weather was reflecting its grey pallor from many miles away. When practice on decent pitches was sorely needed as minimum preparation for the daunting task ahead, England were met by the most unseasonal weather anyone could remember at the start of such a visit. In the first seven weeks they managed just 17 days of cricket. It was not a propitious beginning. In the circumstances the mauling they took in the first Test was understandable. To some anyway. Not everyone was of a mind to offer Botham sympathy for the size of the task. Henry Blofeld was singularly unimpressed in the *Sunday Express*. 'He captains the side like a great big baby. His attitude is astonishingly naïve and he is letting his country down.'

Given Blofeld is still with us today, and in one piece, it is safe to assume he didn't encounter the great big baby anytime soon after that little critique. When times are toughest you need support – Botham would later say that his early career had taught him a vital lesson which was that when you're on the way up there is no shortage of friendly faces, but it's when the nastiest stuff hits the fan that you find out who your true friends and fellow believers are.

Thatcher was constantly battling her most experienced colleagues. In 1980 she had stated that given six strong men and true she could get through what was ahead. In March 1981, in Westminster and in the Caribbean, both she and Botham found themselves well short of that number. Early in the tour he lost two of his own strong men and true to further deplete that pool. Bob Willis was a hugely experienced Test player on the pitch, a hugely amusing and supportive man off it and one of Botham's closest friends. Brian Rose had far fewer Test caps behind him but had shown strength of character to garner runs against the same attack in the summer and was also a shrewd captain of Botham's county Somerset. As a result he was another man Botham knew well and trusted. That both should be forced home would have been a blow to Botham on any tour but their absences were to become more significant given the troubles ahead. Willis's was to prove more than just significant.

The imbalance in the relative strengths of the combatants alone would have made any success heroic. (His opposition captain was aware of that too. Clive Lloyd would reflect that 'unfortunately he was relying on pop-guns against our heavy artillery – there was nothing he could do'.) What followed over the next month would make it impossible. The shadow of South Africa and apartheid had followed the game ever since the D'Oliveira affair of 1968 and caused it as much angst as Packer. For the Asian and West Indian boards this was, understandably, a particularly sensitive issue. It was not one over which Botham had any control and although the English cricket authorities supported and upheld South Africa's exile from Test cricket, as demonstrated in 1968, they were not prepared to be dictated to when it came to which players they wished to select. In his editor's notes in the 1982 edition of *Wisden* John Woodcock mused on the use of sport by politicians for their own ends when the opportunity arises in a section titled 'Politics Take Over'. This time it was cricket's turn and Botham and his side were to be the pawns. 'Given half a chance the politicians will use it as a means of applying pressure on South Africa to renounce the system of apartheid.' The subtext being an obvious hypocrisy in allowing them to take a public stance on the issue without it impacting economic matters such as trade and therefore saving them from decisions that would be a more significant demonstration of a commitment to force change, but a more painful one for themselves. 'In February this led to the team's evacuation from Guyana ... and for the next few days [whilst discussions went on across all the islands which England were yet to visit] the West Indies board and those in charge of the England team were bystanders, no more.' Sport and politics do mix – believe it. Woodcock went on to paint a future as threatening to the game as had been visualised at the time of Packer.

As talks took place all over the world about various tours – New Zealand to the West Indies; England to India – there was a real prospect the international game could be split in two with the dividing line being one of colour. Those who could foresee this outcome realised therefore that Guyana in February 1981 was more than the cancellation of a Test match, rather the starting gun in a race in which the game might soon run out of track. So widespread was the concern that in the same almanack the former New Zealand captain Walter Hadlee wrote an essay on 'The Escalating Effects of Politics on Cricket'. Before the year was out, we were to see the effect of *cricket* on *politics* to a far more positive end, but for now this was the burden which sat unfairly on Botham and his management team as politics and cricket came together again and caught them in the eye of the storm. The matter of South African apartheid was one of valid importance to many politicians, but different governments, in different cultures approached it in very different ways. Woodcock was right that the suspicion remained that for some it was one on which points could be made and profiles enhanced as a matter of some expediency and that sport was an easy and high-profile target around which to make it a debate. It would be unfair to suggest Thatcher was such an opportunist, as ever having firm and constant views on the subject, but nevertheless over the coming years the whiff of hypocrisy which accompanied her stance on the matter would not make for her finest legacy.

The Caribbean islands were then renowned for a certain rivalry in the quest for global standing and some had a reputation for political volatility and active public protest. In the early 80s Guyana was such a place and it was administered by one Lester Bird, who was not going to let a rare chance to play the global statesman and enhance his profile pass him by.

Once again fate would play a part. Had Bob Willis not broken down, there would have been no need for a replacement. The most deserving substitute was deemed to be Surrey's Robin Jackman, England qualified but a South African by birth, who still returned to play in his native land during most English winters. In this he was not actually alone within the playing party which was already in action on tour so, perhaps naively, this was not thought of great import by the management and no attempt was made to conceal it. Fortunately Jackman was a man of some fortitude, but even his resilience would be tested by the events of the rest of the month. Resilience was something which by the end of the tour in April Botham's England were showing on the pitch as well as off – something often forgotten in the rush to trot out Botham's captaincy record. But in the dark days of February that was a world away.

On 25 February a Jamaican radio commentator suggested to the Guyanese government that they would be in breach of the Gleneagles Agreement should they admit Jackman to the country for the upcoming second Test. It was a piece of mischief-making which Guyana knew they had to take seriously now it had become a public debate. Jackman's visa was subsequently withdrawn and the tour itself was in serious jeopardy. Whilst days of negotiations went on above their heads England's players were left in limbo and under threat, minus one of their number, in a place in which they were clearly no longer welcome, not knowing if any more cricket was going to be required of them at all. After the thrashing in Trinidad it was a scenario to further sap morale. Botham stood helpless and emasculated at the helm as he and his players were confined to their hotel under armed guard. The Caribbean paradise was now more akin to hell. *Wisden* was clear that as the dust settled in later weeks, it became even clearer that the case of Jackman was being used by the Guyana government to make a political point. The Test had been abandoned but, close though it came, the tour was not and on the penultimate day of the month England left Guyana after a show of solidarity which reflected well on both the tour captain and manager. As the plane left the tarmac cheers reverberated around the cabin originating from a sense of release that the bad stuff was out of the way and they could get on with a happier tour. The worst was over, surely? It was a vain hope.

Beware the Ides of March

SHAKESPEARE'S 'IDES of March' exhortation in *Julius Caesar* that the emperor should be wary of what lay ahead is now used liberally to warn others of potential dangers and possibly unforeseen consequences. Had it been uttered during the first two days of March 1981 it would have been far from inappropriate. On the month's opening day the IRA hunger strikes returned, initially in the person of Bobby Sands, an IRA 'soldier' who had been imprisoned in the Maze. The following day New Cross in London was the location of a confrontation between local black youths and the police ending in what some considered to be rioting. At the time, the events of both days were newsworthy but there was very little sense of what they presaged. By mid-summer both had evolved into bitter, violent, destructive, rolling dramas depicting a country at war with itself and exacerbating the immovable mood of melancholy.

At the Maze, this time it wasn't just Margaret Thatcher who wasn't for turning and two desperate months later Sands would, in many Irish eyes, martyr himself, dying amidst a blaze of publicity and angry demonstrations. The Irish nationalist population erupted, whilst on the British mainland reprisals were more an expectation than simply a fear. From April to July the violence of New Cross would be replicated, then ratcheted up, in scenes across inner cities which shocked the nation. It was against this background of domestic misery that Botham and Thatcher would now face the toughest challenges of their careers, the outcome of which might well dictate their futures and the surmounting of which would need a level of support conspicuous by its absence. Whereas the prime minister was aware that her 'team' contained dissenters, Botham believed he started and ended his tour with a happy dressing room. If that is a genuine belief it shows he was not aware that not everyone within his ranks was convinced by his leadership. Comments made by his friend Bob Willis after he returned home came from the right place and were overblown by the media but nonetheless were harmful coming from a man deemed close to him. Another strong character, John Emburey was 'not happy' with the team talks on the tour feeling too much focus was on the West Indies' fast bowlers and not enough on themselves.

Any prospect of greater joy when the England players got back on the pitch was crushed in a 298-run defeat in Barbados in the second (previously third) Test which confirmed, after the loss of the Guyana match, that the Wisden Trophy would be retained by the West Indies at the first available opportunity. The match has gone down in history for its second day which started with the awesome and ended with the tragic. In the morning session the thankless nature of England's task was laid out for all to witness in arguably the fastest and most unplayable over in cricket history. Ever since his return four years previously, Geoff Boycott had been the potential safety net on the not infrequent occasions that England's batting was falling apart. He may not have been the first of their batsmen that people would leave the bar to watch but whilst he was there, there was at least some glue to hold things together. One thing Boycott did have was possibly the finest defensive technique and highest concentration levels in the English game. It was, therefore, both a sadistic and compelling watch as Michael Holding, bowling at the speed of light, had him jumping, swaying and failing to connect with any of the first five balls. The sixth ripped out his off stump and sent it flying towards the sightscreen like something from a long bow.

If it was compelling for those in the crowd, it was positively chilling for the dressing room. If Geoffrey couldn't lay a bat on this, what chance did anyone else have? It is highly likely that in that room there were any number of intimations of mortality, which was something the evening was to bring into sharp relief. For the atmosphere on the party island was about to turn into that of a wake. As *Wisden's* David Frith reported, 'such morale as had survived the previous gruelling month now shrank before the greater nightmare'. To employ a quotation from Claire Foy's Queen Elizabeth II in a recent television drama, unhappiness is only unhappiness until something worse comes along and you realise it was happiness after all. So it was to be for Ian Botham and his team as Barbados was about to wrest from Guyana the mantle of lowest point of the tour through what *Wisden* called 'the greatest tragedy of all'.

Deriving from the Latin word *iduare* meaning 'to divide', Shakespeare's ides therefore refer to the 15th of the month – the date of the death of Caesar. In an appalling coincidence it was another fatality which was to bring Botham to his knees when he woke up on that date in 1981. The night before, after the second day's play, England's much-loved assistant tour manager, one of the finest batsmen in their history, Ken Barrington, suffered a heart attack and passed away. When Botham got the news he lay awake far into the night. His love and respect for Barrington was born of so many aspects of his mentor's character, some of which Botham knew he shared, some of which he probably wished he did. Sadly, he had almost seen it coming – understanding how much English success meant to the man and noticing in the days before Barbados that the stresses of Guyana and the rest of the tour were gnawing away at him. Botham had urged him to try to relax but Ken was one of nature's natural worriers. One thing which always risked Botham having to hold back his right hook was the propensity for the swathe of ex-players who surrounded the game – whether within it as coaches or administrators or in the media – epitomised in his bête noir Fred Trueman, was the 'in my day …' attitude which insisted nothing in the game was remotely as good as it once was.

Barrington was a marked exception to this, and Botham never forgot him for it. Botham admired his bravery and his determination never to throw in the towel. 'I liked the uncompromising attitude and the way he wore his colours on his chest.' Both Barrington and Botham loved their country with a passion and would fight for it with all their hearts. Right now it felt like the loss of a man with an honourable patriotism was just another suggestion that such a thing was either no longer considered an attribute or that it was simply slipping away with the times. Botham would later say that not only was Barrington his boyhood hero and role model but 'he took a lot of the load off my shoulders'. In terms of the job itself and the next few months trying to make it work, this was what he was to miss the most. Now those shoulders had to bear the additional burden of breaking the news to his squad. The tour manager A.C. Smith recalled walking down the hotel corridors with Botham as he visited the various rooms and how 'it must've been the most soul-destroying walk either of us had ever taken'. In different and less tragic circumstances there would be another soul-destroying walk to come four months later.

Reading the lesson at Barrington's funeral was something Botham considered an honour but was also just one more thing on his mind to undermine the concentration needed on the field. In his tribute to Barrington the *Daily Telegraph*'s cricket correspondent Michael Melford wrote of his devotion to his job of passing on his experience to the present young England side, 'not just as an assistant manager and coach but as a lovable, utterly loyal member of the team who was never unkind'. Melford's article quoted some of Botham's stunned reaction: 'To me he was everything. We were very close friends and I used to visit him a lot. There is no way I can describe how I feel.' Botham's chairman Alec Bedser, who had played with Ken many times for England, added his own thoughts. 'You couldn't have a better companion. Absolutely reliable. A wonderful chap to have around.' Something, at least, on which Bedser and his captain could agree. John Woodcock gave his own perspective at the end of the Test.

> 'In the overwhelming sadness which resulted from Ken Barrington's death, the loss of the Third Test seemed an irrelevance as did, suddenly, the many earlier setbacks on an ill-fated tour. Countless people in Barbados felt they had lost a friend. Quite simply, a light went out in many places and the sadness showed on many faces.'

Those faces included two belonging to England's more senior players. Graham Gooch remembered, 'He was a friend, a pal, and a father to us all. It was one we never recovered from on the most ill-fated tour cricket could have known … Ken was one of the finest men I have ever known … there was pain and tragedy emerging from the saddest game of cricket I've ever played.' Team-mate David Gower later recalled 'a tough tour, for many reasons' and the death of Barrington as 'a terrible tragedy and a big blow in particular to Ian, who regarded Ken as something of a father figure'. Gower would remember how when he was first in the England side with Botham he was 'brash and bullish and capable of making decisions for himself' and far more confident than Gower felt himself when confronted with the challenge, when he first lost form, of having to recover it on a public stage. This was Botham's challenge now as that famed confidence began to ebb.

Gower also talked of how Botham occasionally needed restraining and a well-timed word from someone he respected would divert him away from the more harmful excesses of his character and belief. It was Mike Brearley who played this role with the guile and empathy of the trained psychoanalyst. Thatcher's equivalent wise owl was Airey Neave, the man who had driven her leadership campaign and whom she could trust and confide in like no other. He was her Brearley but also her Barrington and the similar loss of her own 'rock' to the INLA assassination shortly before e winning the election which completed the rise in which he had played a huge part, was another remarkable parallel in their struggles when Botham lost his own mentor.

When, 11 years later, Thatcher was to lose another similarly trusted friend and supporter, Ian Gow, also to the IRA, her words then summed up Botham's own sense of deprivation perfectly. 'Ian's combination of loyalty, shrewdness and irrepressible sense of fun was to see us all through many difficult moments … his death was an irreplaceable loss.' Add to the disappearance of Barrington from his life as a leader, the more temporary loss of Willis earlier in the tour and leadership was suddenly as lonely a place for Botham as Thatcher was to inhabit in her own way after Neave. For all their presentation of strength and fierce determination, both were more in need of reassurance than was generally assumed. Peter Willey was an uncompromising north-easterner and a man anybody would want on their side in tough times, but he felt Botham's attempted solution to the problem was a mistake. Willey felt he was trying too much to be 'one of the boys' when true leadership required a more removed persona. It was understandable that such a gregarious character as Botham, one whose greatest joy was to be a team-mate who went round cutting the toes off people's socks, would get drawn back to the group at this moment but it was to be a significant part of his undoing. This new loneliness of command was not a good fit for him. Here was one aspect in which he differed to Thatcher who may have wished for the occasional helping hand from trusted friends but had no interest in club-ability, especially with a club in which she so clearly didn't belong. The resultant distance she put between herself and those under her command may have been one reason she was to survive when Botham wasn't. Another was the differing reactions to the perception of the near-impossible challenges laid before each leader.

In *Thatcher's Britain* Richard Vinen suggests that, unpopular as Thatcher was, there was an underlying appreciation that the economy would have been close to unmanageable for any British government in this period. Although it appeared that at the time of the 1979 election it was in reasonable shape (it was industrial strife that caused Labour the image problem), it masked huge problems which she was to inherit. And though there may have been a similar understanding that nine Tests against the West Indies would have taxed any captain, sport tends to be about the results and the record card and patience is a rare bird. This inconsistency of reaction was hardly fair on Botham but it made a significant difference.

Barrington's loss was an emotional one certainly, but the impact it had on Botham as a captain did not go unnoticed by some seasoned observers. Journalist and career-long admirer and supporter Frank Keating, for one, saw a change which the captain never reversed, finding his leadership without Barrington 'essentially too haphazard and off the cuff'. Some of Botham's team were beginning to see it that way too. It hinted at one element which was a shared challenge in leadership for both him and Thatcher – that of man-management. It was a new experience for both at the highest level and wasn't to prove one of their strengths. Botham was not lacking self-awareness on this. 'It was the hardest part of the role and one at which I believe I got better as time went on.' Reflecting later on that insistence of Close's that the timing of the captaincy was wrong, he admitted that the sensitive management of others was a foreign language to him. Botham attacked life and cricket in an uncomplicated way based on that self-reliance which he and his prime minister felt was missing in too many. He recalled struggling with those players who needed an arm-round-the-shoulder approach – it wasn't the way he had been brought up to approach the game. Soft words of encouragement were not his thing … or hers. An admission that this was an issue for him at least showed some self-awareness on the matter; Thatcher never offered one and instead rather dismissed any suggestion of it as an issue. Others were prepared to articulate it however – the ever-helpful Geoffrey Howe acidly recalling that 'unlike most men, she hadn't appeared to learn that you don't rebuke officers in front of other ranks'. If that said more about the sensitivities of those officers than it did about her, it was still an internal expression of doubt about her ability to manage characters different to her own. But there was something in it. A more trusted confidant, John Hoskyns, didn't hold back on telling her: 'You lack management competence. You break every rule of good man-management … The result? An unhappy ship and this demoralisation is hidden only from you.'

Similarly, the issue Botham was beginning to suffer in his own dressing room was not made apparent to him directly. It was this clandestine and, in their eyes, cowardly element of the dissent which they found most unacceptable – straight-talking as they were themselves. Botham would say of his critics, much as Thatcher would say of the 'wets', 'they can say what they like about me as long as they say it to my face rather than say it behind my back and then run'. Not too many in the squad, Peter Willey a notable exception, were brave enough to do so or be as forthright as Hoskyns. Willey would be the man to challenge him on it and would later reflect that 'Ian wanted everybody to be able to do things as easily as him.' Often great achievers don't make the best managers or delegators – holding a conviction that people at that level should be able to 'get on with it' as *they* did, assuming they should all possess the same sense of character and belief. In fact, as Derek Pringle, one of those who would in the future have to try to replace Botham, said that as a result of his talent and the apparent ease with which he applied it, loved though he was, no player aroused feelings of envy and inadequacy in his team-mates they way Botham did, making for a captain as intimidating for some as he was inspirational to others.

Christopher Martin-Jenkins's end of tour piece was a succinct summation of a miserable few months and clearly identified the moment which had the most impact on the captain. 'Ken's sudden death … was the worst by far of all the hammer blows of ill fortune which afflicted a generally disastrous England tour.' At its conclusion, Botham's insistence that the result had been a decent achievement was not altogether delusional. Even his chairman was prepared to take this line. Bedser, albeit with perhaps one eye on defending his own choice in the first place, gave an element of support to his captain. '2-0 is a better record than many predicted and English cricket should prove better for the experience.' Which was very much Botham's view. 'I led the team out of Jamaica with my head held high.' But whatever his sense of his own performance, insisting captaincy was not an influence on his form, his own figures were no better than Thatcher's economic and unemployment statistics and the facts were piling up against him, managing only 73 runs in seven Test innings (0, 16, 26, 1, 1, 13, 16) and no five-wicket innings. Even if the courageous rearguard action to come in the final two Tests gave some him some justification for believing more positive times were around the corner should he be given time, little in English cricket is long term and much can be fickle – public opinion and nervous selectors alike – and two Tests later Bedser decided his 'long-term solution' who had achieved 'better than predicted' results should be removed from the captaincy.

Unfortunately for Botham his own numbers had given Bedser the bullets he needed.

John Woodcock's prognosis for Botham when his tour finally ended the following month – 'to hang on to the captaincy he will need to overcome strong, not to say bitter, opposition' – would have applied to Thatcher as well at the moment of her own courageous rearguard that month, for at the same time Thatcher was being dealt exactly the same hand, fighting a battle which had the potential to end her leadership in much the same way. Four days before Botham received the devasting news of his friend's fatal heart attack, Thatcher had lived what could have been her own 'Lord's moment' – equivalent to that which was to see off Botham in four months' time, but which in the end became her Headingley innings.

The importance in history of the March 1981 budget cannot be overstated. The opposition to government policies reached its peak at this moment as it would for Botham's captaincy in the second Ashes Test that summer, but Thatcher had decided the time was right for a Botham-style counter-attack. She had said on her accession to the party leadership that 'this country has been on the defensive for too long'. Now she intended to address the matter. If there were just a few shafts of light, if you wanted to look hard enough, (both inflation and the pound were now falling slowly), historian Dominic Sandbrook's picture of the weeks leading to this budget had most commentators 'peering into the gloom, seeing only darkness ahead. The news, as usual, was awful'. The comparison to Headingley come July stretched as far as those commentators, the weather, and the canvas on which there was nothing appearing other than bad news.

In that Test match, had Australia taken any of their numerous opportunities to put England to bed once and for all the series would have been done. In Whitehall, the 'wets' who had been looking for the issue on which they might defenestrate her formed the majority of her cabinet and had they seized their moment and rebelled, Britain's future would have looked very different. But they had all the backbone of Australia's batting at their mutual moments of destiny and Thatcher stared them down in the most Bothamesque manner. Even one of their own number, Jim Prior, would admit 'we were wet in the true sense of the word'. Richard Vinen saw the strength of reaction and the shock in face of one of the most revolutionary pieces of economic strategy of the century. 'Raising taxes in a recession was against all economic thinking and there was real astonishment when the 1981 budget did this.' No budget in modern history had received a worse reception. A famous letter was drafted by 364 economists and sent to *The Times* castigating the approach, predicting economic collapse and urging change. But if they thought this would be enough to oust her, they were wrong. One of the weaknesses of the protest, which rather gave credence to Thatcher's 'not for turning' rhetoric, was it didn't set out any alternative policies to those of the government. It is easy to criticise when not responsible and with that foremost in her thoughts Thatcher became increasingly contemptuous of economists. Botham may have felt the same way – how simple it was for those who didn't have to find a solution to Andy Roberts or Dennis Lillee to sit back and pontificate on it. He grew increasingly contemptuous of those who did so.

For all the significance of the Falklands the following spring, the budget here and now was her greatest confrontation and both she and her acolytes knew it even then. Chancellor Nigel Lawson claimed that she saw this later as her government's finest hour – her equivalent of the Battle of Britain. The economy did not collapse – in fact it began its recovery soon after the budget and in the second fiscal quarter of the year economic growth crept into the black. But Thatcher herself understood its potential implications. Biographer Charles Moore was clear that she knew the dangers and that the courage to stick with it would be pivotal. 'So fraught was the run up with disaster and the promises of further disaster to come, she was forced to confront the possibility that she might actually fail, and fail, at that, dishonourably, by abandoning what she believed.' But with the support of her closest advisors she stood firm, saying to Alan Walters, 'They may get rid of me for this but at least I shall have gone knowing I did the right thing.'

In terms of sentiment it would be reprised a few months later at his own moment of destiny when Botham, understanding it was time to stand or fall and if it were to be the latter he would go down on his own terms, greeted his new partner at the crease at Headingley, Graham Dilley, with 'You don't fancy hanging around here for two days do you? Let's give it some humpty.' This was a more typical Botham phrasing of the same exhortation Thatcher had given over her budget, 'I ask all who have spirit … to stand and join with me.' To be fair to Dilley, then Chris Old and Bob Willis, had they not joined with him at Leeds there would be no story to tell. The outlook in the moment of both events was not good. The 500-1 odds against England as Botham conspired with Dilley are well remembered. Perhaps less so is just how dire matters looked to even one as committed as Thatcher ahead of her career-defining budget. 'I shall never forget the weeks leading up to the 1981 budget. Hardly a day seemed to go by without the financial scene deteriorating in some way.' For Botham hardly an over had been going by without the England scorecard deteriorating in some way at Headingley.

If the upside of Botham's Headingley moment would be immediately obvious, that of the budget was less discernible, but upsides there were in the end as some of the more perceptive commentators noted at the time. At a headline level the budget was very unpopular, but some of the leader columns were more favourable. Although the front page of the *Daily Telegraph* on 11 March was uncompromising and gave a flavour of the immediate reaction, HOWE SAVAGES CONSUMERS, in its Sunday sister paper two days later a more balanced, even positive stance was apparent. In his column, the City Editor Ivan Fallon noted the shockwaves, followed by the protests of the wets and cited it as a critical moment if Thatcher and Howe could come through it. The *Financial Times* was also perceptive enough to see what Thatcher prevailing might lead to, writing 'this could indeed be a favourable leading indicator for economic recovery', and years later the journalist Anthony Howard insisted that 'in the end, history did vindicate them'.

Thatcher's newly appointed Chief Secretary to the Treasury Leon Brittan was quoted in Fallon's column and offered some words which would have fitted Headingley just as neatly: 'Pessimism is at its greatest just when it is becoming clear that things are changing … it is not yet clear, but there are signs – quite a few of them. Another six months could make all the difference. It is a great pity that only Sir Geoffrey and a few others are prepared to see it through that long.' Whether Thatcher would get those six months was by no means assured at this moment but in the end it gave her nine years. Had Botham been given the same six months from March 1981, who knows, his own long-term survival might have been assured after all. Fallon's fellow columnist Jock Bruce-Gardyne was also looking ahead and suggesting a moment of change, the headline to his 'Viewpoint' article being BRICKBATS IN THE SPRING, BOUQUETS BY THE SUMMER. Yet again, if his sports editor had borrowed this at the end of July, it would have served just as well for him.

The March week of Barbados and the budget was when self-certainty and how much of it they had left would be tested the most. At that moment Andrew Marr suggests 'any normal politician would've flinched'. Any normal cricketer would've done likewise and the parallels didn't end there. Thatcher's suggestion at this critical juncture that 'even some of my own supporters would not wholly believe in the strategy until it started to yield results' would have had its own reflection in the England dressing room at Headingley until a gradual realisation came upon the players that something might be in the process of changing for the better. In Thatcher's case, as opposed to Botham's, she was aware that yielding of results might not arrive for some time but, as Marr points out, she saw attack as the best form of defence and 'in the economic storms of 1979 to 1981 she had simply charged on ahead'. What mattered in surviving the budget furore intact was what this did for Thatcher's reputation as a fighter, a survivor and even a winner, and in reigniting her own self-belief. At the end of his tour Botham would also profess that he had emerged with *his* self-belief enhanced – if he could survive this he could survive anything and he truly believed he had proved his mettle as she had. Looking back, it was a perfectly reasonable argument, but not one, unlike Thatcher's, which the media was ultimately willing to endorse. In *Bang! A History of Britain in the 1980s,* Graham Stewart noted how Thatcher's budget did start to affect key economic indicators, particularly in a welcome depreciation in the value of sterling, and that 'along a particularly dark tunnel there was a far off glimmer of light'. Botham certainly believed in that glimmer too. He had come through his 'budget moment' and the worst of times with a degree of credibility. Or so he thought.

April:
The Good, The Bad and The Ugly

HAS THERE ever been a peacetime month in Britain of greater contrasts and conflicts than April 1981? Well, yes, try July 1981, but that was still to come. A remarkable month of weather accompanied the fleeting moments of light and the ultimate victory of the insistent clouds. For a couple of weeks at its start the month tried its best to provide some happy relief. The 29th of March had ushered the month in with the positivity of that first London Marathon and its example of communal action for the greater good in a mood of fun and togetherness. Running, as a happy diversion, was suddenly all the rage – the following day a new British film was released telling the story of two British athletes and their victories at the 1924 Paris Olympics. But *Chariots of Fire* was more than that. It was nostalgia for stirring deeds and a patriotic nation, painting a picture of another generation – the Roaring Twenties, post-war joy, the decadence of Cambridge, punting and champagne, Gilbert and Sullivan and a British approach to sport of 'play up and play the game'. It's huge success confirmed how much people needed such escapism and heroes. When an *Evening Standard* review talked of the film expressing many traits it felt Britain was crying out for once more, it listed amongst others: love of country, loyalty to the team and unselfish excellence in the pursuit of honour. If these were indeed what the country needed it is little wonder that Botham, as 1981's Harold Abrahams, was taken to its hearts in the way he was. Moreover, Dominic Sandbrook recalled that, much to the chagrin of its left-of-centre production team, *Chariots* was seen as another symbol of Thatcherism, given her 'romantic sense of history and intense belief in Britain's unique destiny', and it did no harm, by association, to her advancing image as Britannia incarnate. Like many of the creations of 1981, it resonated more than it may have done at any other time because of its audience's desire for a little less depression and a little more revival.

The relationship between sport and cinema didn't end there. Five days later the equestrian equivalent of *Chariots* was played out live before a vast television audience. So uplifting was the story of Bob Champion and Aldaniti's victory in the Grand National that it would be immortalised three years later in the film *Champions*. The parallels in the tales from different generations were clear: the surmounting of enormous barriers – in the case of Aldaniti those physical ones in front of him on the day as well as those of ill health which had gone before – to achieve remarkable and emotional victories. In the determination not to be beaten and defy the odds the affinity with Thatcher and Botham's 1981 were there too. April's first Saturday was one of the more uplifting days in people's recent memory, especially for a country still wedded to the enjoyment of competition – of the serious or less serious variety – and tales of success. Richard Osman and Louis Theroux were both referring to the unexpected growth in popularity of snooker at this time when they agreed that watching sport is less about the act and the action themselves, but about the stories behind them and the characters involved. (They would be validated later in the month when the only man with a claim to challenge Botham as the most Thatcher-relevant sportsman of the decade, Steve Davis, was changing that sport forever.) Sport is at its best when it is drama and if it can include a truly emotional thread, so much the better. Champion had recovered from cancer and his horse from a serious leg injury which most in racing believed had ended his career. Now they delivered one of the most famous and stirring comebacks in sport to win a race which at the time was still a national event in more than just name. A large part of the country interrupted their daily lives for an hour to join one of the most anticipated annual shared experiences and that day they were rewarded with the sort of inspiration that sport can bring.

There was another iconic shared television experience that April beloved of many, though dreaded by some, another traditional landmark in the rhythm of their year, idiosyncratic though it may have been. The Eurovision Song Contest was, in 1981, still seen as competition worth winning and should you do so it could be considered a badge of national standing. It may be stretching a point to suggest that the UK only winning it once in the 70s was another illustration of national decline but by now any sort of success was going to be welcomed. The frothy foursome that were Buck's Fizz were perfect for a tilt at the prize and 'Making Your Mind Up' duly won the evening. It may be hard to comprehend today that such a thing mattered a jot to the nation's mood but in April 1981 it most certainly did. It may be even harder to imagine, but had either Botham or Thatcher noticed the song, they might have chorused the line 'trust your inner vision, don't let others change your mind'.

An English fightback of sorts was happening 3,000 miles away in the Caribbean too. After the thrashings of the first two Tests in February and March it was widely anticipated that the last two would go much the same way in the aftermath of the Jackman affair and the Barrington devastation. But having dug in for a battling draw in Antigua at the start of the month, England defied all expectations as the tour drew to its end – not with a victory but with a highly creditable rearguard in Jamaica in which both Gooch and Gower demonstrated the skill and courage to counter the West Indies bowling at last with 153 and 154 not out respectively. Whilst not identifiable as a corner fully turned, it was England's cricketing contribution to the hope of better times ahead. After he and his team had shown an ability to survive the turmoil of such an embattled tour, perhaps Botham was back in credit. *Wisden* closed its own tour report with 'England's tour may have been ill-fated and unsuccessful in itself, but the performance at the end of these two young men seemed to symbolise a more prosperous future.'

Back at home, these few weeks of metaphorical sunshine were graced by unseasonal sun and heat. By the end of the month that would have changed to equally unseasonal heavy snowfall. The mood would have changed once again too. Within a week of these little victories, two further clouds appeared to block any rays of hope. On the tenth day of the month the hunger striker Bobby Sands, now in serious ill-health but as determined as Thatcher that he was not going to concede, was elected as a member of parliament in a by-election triggered by the death of the MP for Fermanagh and South Tyrone, Frank Maguire, the previous month. This was more than just an embarrassment for the Thatcher government – it was an invitation to exultant triumphalism for the nationalists in Ireland and a reminder to the British people that this blackspot in the everyone's lives was not going away.

That same evening the tension which had been simmering in the Brixton area of London predominantly between black youths and the police finally turned to violent confrontation. The causes of the next three days of riots which were propounded were various – racial, social, unemployment-related or a reaction to discriminatory and heavy-handed policing – but the scenes brought to the public on the evening news on 10, 11 and 12 April were like nothing they had ever seen on their own streets. Molotov cocktails flying through the air, masked youths setting fire to upturned police cars, the police responding with the vicious wielding of truncheons, and shops trashed and looted. This was more downtown Beirut or the most depressed suburbs of Compton, LA, not England's supposed green and pleasant land. Although the truth was that such unrest in London, and other cities to come, was more the result of long-term decline and poor police/community relationships than it was of Thatcherism, a feeling that their society was on the cusp of complete collapse was spreading through the public with every day that passed and that would inevitably be added to Thatcher's perceived crime sheet. What the hell was going on and when would it end? Once again the striking contrasts of the year were manifest. Many of the diaspora which made up the Brixton community would have been in the stands at the Oval the previous summer rejoicing as the West Indies put down their colonisers and doing the same for the past two months as more of the same dominated the sporting news from the West Indies. Railton Road, at the centre of the riots, was just seven miles from the starting line of the London Marathon. In less than a fortnight those seven miles had seen a journey from the joyous nature of a new communal and philanthropic event to a community experience of a very different nature.

The trials continued, political and sporting. Should they stay or should they go? On 23 April the *Nine O'Clock News* announced that the unemployment figure had just past 2.5 million and it seemed we were back where we started. Perhaps Thatcher *wasn't* the woman after all. And the growing narrative in the sports media at the start of an Ashes summer was that perhaps Botham wasn't the *man* either. Frank Keating wrote that 'by his return in April Botham was facing a different type of prosecution [to the pending one in the Crown Court] in the public prints, one questioning even his abilities as a Test player and certainly as a Test captain'. Botham wasn't completely without support however. On 19 April England's former Test captain turned accomplished cricket journalist Tony Lewis gave a fillip to the man under pressure in a generous article titled WHY BOTHAM MUST

STAY AS LEADER. It was a considered piece and a long one, but so relevant that it is worth revisiting here:

> 'Cricket lovers, normally a generous lot, have one perversity – they love to mutilate their captains. Will the cricket lovers not stop their baying this time before the current captain, Ian Botham, is destroyed altogether? Will none of his critics, all screaming for blood, not stop to realise that a 25-year-old novice captain was sent out to face a non-stop thundering West Indian cannon-fire armed with only bows and arrows … it was not Ian Botham's captaincy which lost the series 2-0. This is not to write that Botham was faultless … the truth is that his long run of success came when England played Tests against countries who lacked their World Series players. It gave him an exaggerated fame. If there is any blame to attach it is to the selectors. Not many agreed with the timing of Botham's elevation. Let us hope they have not ruined him. If they want to finish him off completely they will now dispose of him. Botham has courage … he believes in himself, but if that is taken away …? Ideally therefore Ian Botham should continue this summer with an experienced man at his shoulder and England should move into brighter days.'

It was not to be for Botham, despite Lewis's endorsement, but had Mrs Thatcher been in the habit of perusing the sports pages she might have considered recruiting Lewis to her press office. She was not yet free herself of those 'who love to mutilate their captains' as she sought to 'move England into brighter days'.

The Dispiriting Buds of May

ONE CONCLUSION of Trevor Harley's work on weather and mood is that 'grey is the colour most associated with depression'. 1981 was now to offer one of the greyest, coldest early summers on record and as an accompaniment to the depressed feeling pervading the country, and the early anticlimax of the Ashes series, it couldn't have felt more appropriate. May is traditionally one of the happier months of the year – especially for those whose summers are enriched by our national summer game. When once every four years it heralds the arrival of Australian cricketers for an Ashes tour it feels happier still. The blossom is out, the days are getting longer and from countless lofts around the nation, pads and bats are being retrieved to be whitened and oiled. It is a month of darling buds, a month of anticipation, a month of lifted hearts. This one, however, begged to differ as if determined to play its role in the melancholic tenor of the year. It was one of the dampest Mays in living memory and resisted all attempts at a positive start to the cricket season. By the end of the month Gloucestershire were still waiting to bowl or face a ball in the County Championship. The *Daily Telegraph*'s Michael Melford wrote at the end of the summer that 'the first part of the 1981 season had been no advert for the game. May had been wet, June cold, and the cricket correspondingly unattractive'. In fact, the cricket would continue to reflect the weather and everything else around it for the rest of the year, for bad and for good. For now, like the summer itself, the season just couldn't seem to get started. Things improved in time for the traditional Australian tour curtain-raiser against Lavina, Duchess of Norfolk's XI in the bucolic setting of the grounds of Arundel Castle. If one of cricket's enduring appeals to the English soul is its refusal to leave behind the mythical England of days gone by, a more quaintly English event than this one could scarcely be called up. But before it could be used to celebrate a nostalgically imagined way of life, the month was to be shrouded in deaths.

On the fifth day of May Bobby Sands died of his hunger strike at the Maze prison. There was outrage in catholic Ireland and no little disquiet in Britain. Surely now Thatcher would find a way to compromise, a negotiated way out of this macabre quicksand? It was not to be, even when a week later Sands's fellow striker Francis Hughes passed away too. Never mind the economy, this was by some distance the most powerful gauntlet thrown down before her 'not for turning' entrenchment. It was easy for her to be portrayed now as the unfeeling autocrat who would put creed before compassion and it was not likely to improve her overall popularity. But some demurred at such a view. For them, here was a politician who was prepared to defend a belief and a principle in the face of personal attack. As Thatcher would insist, crime is crime and murder is murder and neither is political – they are crime and murder. To be able to remain firm in the eye of such a storm, to significant personal disadvantage, was a characteristic many admired in their leader after years of perceived weakness and vacillation. In time, the hunger strikes would be seen as an important test passed, if nothing so tragic could ever be described as a victory. In between the deaths of the two IRA men, news broke of the loss of another political revolutionary, though one of different method and very different popular acceptance. The death of Bob Marley on 11 May at the age of just 36 was just one more sadness for people to bear. A man who preached peace, love and emancipation was hardly one the world could afford to lose at the time. Marley's passing as a result of a rare skin cancer (the numerous conspiracy theories of establishment foul play which tend to accompany the deaths of activists and revolutionaries can be seen as just that in this case) was yet another fateful event within a fateful year, occurring exactly a month after the Brixton disturbances. The musician and film director Don Letts, a Londoner born to Jamaican parents and both a vocal presence in the quest for black rights in Britain and a fellow-Rastafarian confidant and friend of Marley, stressed the musician's importance to the black population in England as a voice articulating their struggles and the need to push back against them. Marley had joined the West Indies cricket team in giving them examples of success of the Caribbean people to counter the prejudices, biases and lazy characterisations they endured every day. Letts's understanding of where the violence of the riots germinated can be seen in his recollection of his own London upbringing and mistreatment at the hands of the police. 'A lot of us took that for normal. It was just what we had to deal with. There weren't no culturally enlightened policeman. It was the Wild West and, believe me, we weren't the cowboys.' Letts produced videos for, and managed, several punk bands in the mid-70s and was no stranger to the idea of anarchic protest against the country's injustices. He recalled that his interest in punk was not initially shared by his friend but gradually Marley came to understand and assimilate it. The subsequent sharing of stages and musical ideas between Marley's reggae and those of punk, mixed with the original Ska music of his Jamaican homeland, are things Letts credits for the emergence of Two Tone at the time. But it was in more than the development of a new musical genre that Marley's value to his fellow 'Babylon' dwellers lay. Marley's music came to global attention as a result of its acceptance and success in Britain more than anywhere else and he made England his second home – in fact, for a time, his first home. This not only gave him a clear understanding of the frustrations of his people there but made him immediately accessible to them and brought an intimacy of relationship which exacerbated the pain when he left them. That it should happen at the start of the summer when those frustrations finally boiled over is coincidental but potentially significant. It was one more blow to a group already angry and now deprived of their figurehead and release valve. Letts makes a claim for Marley which may seem a little overblown but which, shared as it was by many of his peers, reinforces the scale of the loss which could be considered relevant to what the rest of the year brought. His view was that Marley experienced for himself, in the era of his upbringing in Jamaica, the worst of British colonialism and when he came to Britain he fought against its domestic equivalent – in short he came to 'save the world'.

The month was still dull, cold and grey as the Australians and the England captain met for the first time as Somerset hosted them at Taunton. Anyone still hoping to read good runes for the summer ahead would have noted Botham having Graeme Wood caught behind in his first over. The question of how he might fare with the bat was then washed away after nine overs of Somerset's first innings by the rain which never abated. The summer's cricket was still in its coma. The football season, on the other hand, was just over, save for a few internationals and in the interwoven worlds of sport and politics there was one final chapter to May that would usher in a coming month of storms. Any chance that Britain's reputation abroad, that had been tarnished by the rampaging of some of its citizens through the cities of Italy the previous summer, might be restored disappeared in what was to acquire, from a media gorging on stories of national humiliation, the obligatory sobriquet of 'The Battle of Basle'.

Humiliation it was for the country in every respect. Firstly the team stumbled to a first defeat against Switzerland in 34 years, losing a World Cup qualifier which made their goal of finally reaching the finals tournament for the first time in a dozen years distinctly precarious. Then, sadly to little surprise, a group of those who had followed them out to the Swiss city proceeded to run amok in their drunken frustration, taking it out on the city and its people in and outside the stadium. The distorted belief many of them harboured that 'victory' in such a confrontation gained their country some sort of warped respect may have had some element of desperation born of a nation sick of its own decline but it was a pathetic, Little Englander attitude shared by few. Thatcher and Botham wanted to restore patriotism to the nation but this was, as Dominic Sandbrook identified, 'a particularly joyless kind of patriotism shot through with surly resentment' and an expression of the disappointments of the age and a national sense of inadequacy which some felt could only be addressed in such a fashion. Football was denigrating the name of English sport by acting as a mirror reflecting a troubled society but in a far more depressing way than the cricket team. If this was English football, the English were going to have to look elsewhere for something to feel good about. The Union Jack on the cut-off t-shirts which were a conspicuous symbol on the trail of destruction, once stood for British courage, pride and success; now it was an emblem of shame around Europe. On the BBC Bobby Charlton's naturally rheumy eyes were close to tears. 'I'm certainly not proud to be English right now.' The England captain Kevin Keegan agreed, admitting he was ashamed to be English. The FIFA official at the game, Jacques Georges, articulated the thoughts of many at home and abroad when he advised 'your so-called fans are a disgrace to their country' and Thatcher's own Sports Minister, Hector Munro, concurred, 'this continuing disgraceful behaviour reflects very badly on this country .'The best solution the FA secretary Ted Croker could come up with was to stop English citizens travelling abroad – it had come to this. The British were rioting from Brixton to Basle. The country had gone to the dogs.

June: Grey Days and Storms

'The sky was as black as you could imagine.'

Geoff Lawson, Australian fast bowler

SO, THE British disease epithet which had now been a go-to headline of the newspapers for years was splashed over their front and back pages once again in the first days of June. The impact of this latest example on people's self-perception and morale was not positive but, worse somehow, it was no longer a shock – it simply washed over a public possessed of a dulled resignation that this was their country in the 1980s. What was less widely reported was the first news of another ailment, from another country this time, which would now add another name to the list of world-changing happenings of 1981. In California, gay men began to turn up at medical centres complaining of various symptoms of illness. The first references to a new disease came in the first week in of June. A Los Angeles journal published an article which introduced its readers to something called Acquired Immunodeficiency Syndrome, a condition caused by a virus it termed HIV. Within two weeks the first death deemed to have been related to the disease was reported in the same city. If this news also failed to cause any great stir in popular consciousness at that moment it was not due to the same sort of weary acceptance, rather a lack of understanding of the genuine shock to come.

1981 was indeed a year like no other and before it was over the first case would be diagnosed in the UK, the word epidemic would be in common parlance and another narrative which would define the 80s had begun.

If May is traditionally that month of anticipation of the summer ahead then June is the one when it is supposed to arrive in all its glory to be celebrated by something of a national garden party. If there was a moment at which the country might rediscover its joy and its pride surely it might through the summer season now upon us which mixes pageantry and sport annually in a quintessentially English manner. The month of The Derby (of course, in this most singular of years it was won, to accompanying gasps of astonishment at one of the race's greatest ever performances, by a horse called Shergar), the Trooping of The Colour at Buckingham Palace; the ostentation of Royal Ascot, steadfastly refusing to pay heed to any talk of national decline; the first Test matches of the summer and all topped off by the definitive English blend of royalty and sport at the citadel of Wimbledon. England expects nothing less than sunshine, strawberries, stirring sporting deeds and days of joyful, communal revelry. What it got in 1981 were grey days and storms.

The West Indies had come and gone and Ian Botham had survived. Now was the time for our knight, former slayer of the old enemy on fields across the world, to lift English hearts once again. The Ashes were here. Unfortunately, any confidence in a vision of a revived Botham bestriding the series was rather undermined at the outset by an obvious lack of faith from his superiors. In a replication of Thatcher's position after her budget, he sensed the rumbles – a growing feeling that the rug was about to be pulled from under him. His mate Viv Richards had felt on the recent tour that 'there were a few people happy to see Ian go down'. Nevertheless it wasn't in his nature to give up without a fight. Whilst he couldn't honestly employ the same words Thatcher would later use when she was being ousted from office, fighting her own fight in the Commons, assailed by the opposition – 'come on, I'm enjoying this!' – the gunslinger within him remained and Brearley's recollection of one of his all-rounder's strengths paints a similar picture. 'He enjoys duels, indeed he provokes them.' It was something both would use to get the very best from themselves knowing that their qualities showed themselves best in confrontation. Pat Murphy said of Botham, 'When it comes to shouting down opposition in a crowded bar, Ian is in a class of his own', as indeed was Thatcher in the sometimes bearpit atmosphere of the weekly Prime Minister's Questions session. They glorified in the fight. But this was one duel the captain was not destined to win. After an unremarkable one-day series had been lost by the odd game in three the selectors handed the opposition clear evidence of apprehension in England's ranks when they appointed Botham as captain for the first Test alone. If there was scant support from above him, some members of the public were still onside and let it be known where they thought the real problems lay. Mr Andrew Sanger-Davies of Romsey sent his letter to *Wisden Cricket Monthly* 'In Defence of Botham' suggesting, 'If he is indeed so relieved [of the captaincy], it is the selectors and not Botham who should hang their heads in shame.'

To add to Botham's troubles he now had a professional trial to endure as well as the personal one due to take place at Grimsby Crown Court in September. His situation was scarcely improved by the media's decision to make a mountain out of a molehill concerning Willis's 'criticism' (more accurately, concern – for his friend as well as the side) of his captain. *The Times*'s back page headline on the morning of the first Test was not much of an endorsement of Botham's positive take on the summer ahead. WILLIS LIKELY TO BE DISCIPLINED AFTER BOTHAM CRITICISM was unlikely to increase dressing room harmony. And even if the matter didn't bother either party involved nearly as much as the press would have liked it to, it must still have hurt the captain to some extent that his mate and key lieutenant should go public at that particular time. It certainly didn't quell the debate at a time when energies might have been better spent on getting off to a winning start. For all the playing down of the comments, the facts couldn't be denied given the local radio interview Willis had given, echoing his thoughts in the West Indies. 'I don't think Ian should be captain simply because I'm convinced his form has suffered dramatically.' Not malicious or inaccurate, nor a direct criticism of his abilities as captain, but unhelpful and ill-timed nonetheless and Botham could have done without it given the non-committal nature of his appointment at the start of the summer. The naysayers were refusing to shut up. The day before the first Test, Thatcher's cabinet held a meeting which she had finally acceded to after yet more pressure from the 'wets'. They wanted a discussion on economic strategy which, in their language, meant one more chance to force a U-turn. That they did not share their leader's belief or optimism was transparent after Jim Prior's opening gambit that, 'I don't know how we're going to get through the coming year.' Another future Thatcher cabinet member, Kenneth Clarke, was a parliamentary secretary for transport at the time and was no more upbeat looking back: 'By 1981 we were so unpopular I was not only concerned we would not win the next election but whether the Conservatives would actually survive as a national party.'

Pessimism was not restricted to Whitehall. Frank Keating noted how even Botham's intrepid self-confidence was dented at once by the Test-by-Test appointment. If that transferred into both his cricket and his captaincy it was understandable. The clouds refused to clear. They refused to bypass Trent Bridge either as his cricketing probation period began. Given the fates of the year so far it was no great surprise to see him lose the first 50-50 battle of the series – the toss. By the end of the first day 14 wickets had fallen under leaden skies – an appropriate start to an Ashes which is remembered as spectacular but was in truth for the most part one where ball dominated bat, and was populated by dogged batting in generally murky light rather than a feast of glorious run-scoring. Here was the perfect appetiser. England had been hustled out for 185 having been put in to bat in the semi-darkness, as Terry Alderman announced himself as an unexpected problem with his first four wickets of a record-breaking series. 'The sky was as black as you could imagine and about 100 feet above Trent Bridge' remembered the Australian fast bowler Geoff Lawson. Botham himself had managed a single before what felt like the inevitable cheap dismissal – the days when he strode to the wicket offering hope and expectation had long since disappeared. When England had taken four Australian wickets by the close they were back in the game – maybe even ahead, suggesting their total had actually been a fair effort in the conditions. But the sort of day followed which seemed to have been following the captain around for a year. What also followed him around now was the ball and they were not a happy series of meetings. Having dropped the opener John Dyson the previous evening he now grounded two more chances, giving lives to Trevor Chappell and Allan Border. On the television Richie Benaud for once stated the obvious: 'Nothing will go right for that man.' Not today, not for a year. The chances were going down faster than the country's manufacturing output and with the same air of inevitability.

Border's would be the wicket England prized the most throughout the summer and passing up the opportunity of dismissing him early that morning would be fatal. Although Botham's misses were the greater focus of conversation given the high-profile examination he was sitting, the most glaring was wicketkeeper Paul Downton's dropping of Border shortly before his captain. The most regulation of chances fell out of Downton's gloves to general consternation. Border's 63 was hardly one to set the pulses of the crowd racing but was in keeping with the whole theme of the Test – and ultimately it would win it. Dennis Lillee and Alderman dismantled England again and although their captain manned the bridge with a game but forlorn-looking 33, that was the best any England batsman could manage. It suddenly looked like being a long summer and much of the public's optimism born of desperation was all but extinguished. The fightback was over before it had begun as, it appeared, was any hope of a love-affair between crowd and team. As the former's irritation grew and became vocal, England bowler Graham Dilley responded with hand gestures not born of respect. The country's discord was spreading from the streets to the cricket. Dialling up the frustration, hope was briefly reawakened as Australia crawled to 122/6 but the difference in the catching, a skill which often travels in tandem with confidence and belief, was indeed the difference. One country was possessed of those qualities; one patently wasn't.

At the end of the Test, John Woodcock's conclusion in his *Times* commentary put him in the opposite camp to Tony Lewis in a representation of the split in the public view, but also the reality that there were now far more on the Woodcock side of the argument. His piece, not unkind but unequivocal was headlined FOR BOTHAM'S SAKE AND FOR ENGLAND'S, IT'S TIME FOR A CHANGE:

> 'It is a good thing Ian Botham is a resilient character, given to arrogance, though not unpleasantly, which comes from possessing an exceptional talent. He is also I think, only mildly sensitive. Were it otherwise he would be finding it barely tolerable to live with the pressures of his present existence. He has a resounding contempt for the press and a burning desire to make fools of those who are gunning for him.'

Whilst Woodcock might be underestimating the level of sensitivity, might the above description remind us of anyone, given to arrogance though not unpleasantly so, and battling the pressures of her then existence? Woodcock continued: 'I feel England might benefit from allowing Botham to concentrate solely on his own cricket. This too is how his players see it.'

If Woodcock was articulating a growing view at the time, it was his last sentence that was surely the largest writing on the wall. There was writing on other walls too – in some ways equally as concerning; in others, showing the first signs of hope. The very next day Woodcock's paper produced a headline for its 'Parliament' section which would have raised some eyebrows. MORE JOBLESS, BUT WORST OF RECESSION IS OVER. It was going to take a while for this to express itself in a way that would convince the public to believe it but the effects of Thatcher's riding out of her high noon in March were being recognised.

Christopher Martin-Jenkins's *hCricketer* editorial after the first Test was another attempt at a message of hope, even if the wish was rather the father of the thought. 'If the optimists are vindicated, the miserable weather of May and early June will be forgotten when the 1981 season is recalled in the future.' At the time it was a good try from the unfailingly sunny CMJ but something of a Hail Mary. Two months later it became a truth. One of the advantages of following sport, especially after yet another disappointment, is that there is usually something else about to happen which offers a chance to move on. It is an addictive trait which keeps many of us coming back with the angel of hope on our shoulder no matter how many times it hurts us. It has the potential, if rarely borne out reality, for an immediate change in fortunes and in mood which is less frequent in everyday life. The day following England's uninspiring failure to get the summer going in Nottingham, the annual fête that is Wimbledon began. We had just passed midsummer and seen nothing of to justify that name. The added pleasure of this event, at a time when there was little hope of British participation by its second week, was enhanced by being able to enjoy it for what it was without the tensions of partisanship. Maybe this was just what was needed as an antidote to Ashes cricket – something in which you didn't have to take sides. Nothing could really spoil the pleasure of Wimbledon. That was the theory anyway. Once again 1981 would have different plans. For a significant proportion of the English public Wimbledon is more than two weeks on the grand slam tennis circuit. It is something totemic – a symbol of all that the country is supposed to do well and the values it likes to think it is known for; an immaculately presented tableau on which the finest in the world are hosted royally and we witness heroic stories of character and comebacks, of victory from the jaws of defeat. All this we expect to be played out in the proper spirit, writ large over the players' entrance with the characteristic but unabashed self-importance of the 'club' – Kipling, triumph and disaster and all that. These things are sacrosanct.

All started well. The blue skies which had just started to peer out at England ironically from behind the clouds in the last hours of defeat at Trent Bridge, graced Wimbledon's first day and that upturn in mood was in evidence in the stands. However, the tennis-following equivalents of Sir Simon Redtrouser were about to have their genteel world turned upside down by that 22-year-old from Queens, New York City. They do things differently there. John McEnroe already had two grand slam titles to his name, won in the cauldron of Flushing Meadows in his own city where he felt truly at home. When it came to tennis they did things differently there too. The appreciative claps of applause and tapping of Tupperwares which were the soundtrack to a Wimbledon match were replaced here by a raucous din on court liberally sprinkled with language which would see your All England club membership cancelled in a trice. The young New

Yorker may have struggled to understand most things about Wimbledon but there was no misunderstanding in him about the tournament's standing, providing the most sought-after title in the global game.

McEnroe had been battling to secure that title since a precocious debut four years previously in which he reached the semi-final as an unseeded unknown. Standing in his way was the undisputed king of the grass, Bjorn Borg, who by 1981 was on a five-year winning streak and was the darling of the crowds. Well as they got on together, he was also the diametric opposite of the American in terms of character on and off the court, offering up a courteous and taciturn alternative to his rival's brashness. Possessed of a sublime talent, McEnroe's frustration at not being able to depose the champion was growing – visibly and audibly – year-on-year and his irritation was as much with himself and his awareness of his contrasting on-court behaviour to that of the Swede, his self-knowledge that it was indefensible much as he might attempt to defend it publicly and his inability to do anything about it, as it was with Borg's capacity to find a way to beat him on grass. In the previous year's final they had played out perhaps the greatest tennis match in history – certainly its most enthralling tie-break – and so astonishing was the tennis and the fact McEnroe illustrated that against Borg he tended to suppress any tantrums, that the approbation from the stands which was all he had ever known was transformed during the match to acceptance bordering on admiration. Certainly there was no shortage of sympathetic applause when he came up agonisingly short.

After all, the English in general and the Wimbledon clientele in particular love nothing better than a gallant loser. Part of the crowd's embracing of McEnroe now was surely relief, in the assumption that he had learned how to do things in their corner of the world and from this point on a new relationship of mutual love and respect would be forthcoming.

It was against this history that McEnroe began his first round match, the day after Botham's first Test had ended in defeat. In the unlikely event that the Kipling quotation above the player's entrance to Centre Court had inspired McEnroe to study the rest of the poem, there was at least one line that went unheeded that day. 'If you can talk with crowds and keep your virtue ...' There followed a match against fellow American Tom Gullikson splattered with McEnroe gamesmanship, conduct violations and volcanic verbal eruptions which has gone down in the annals of sport and, unfortunately, for a long time defined the man. The middle classes in the stands were at first slightly amused, then aghast and finally outraged at the whole performance. If there were some who would be willing to forget when he finally won the title two weeks later, there were plenty more who would not. Though there may have been a little more justification this time, that pompous indignation of the members hit the fan. On the letters page of *The Times* the following day one such tortured soul, a Miss D.K.M. Kirkpatrick from the predictable location of the Hampshire shires, upbraided the newspaper in a way which pigeonholed McEnroe alongside another of the summer's mischief-makers, the IRA – one of the year's more unlikely conflations of the sporting and the political. 'You disgust me. Evil and outrageous activities appear to guarantee the perpetrator his photo on your front page (latest example McEnroe in duplicate, June 23). Are you not aware of the heavy responsibility that you and the rest of the media bear, by this publicity, for the present lamentable decline in social behaviour? Equally, publicity given to IRA activities amounts to culpable complicity.'

McEnroe may indeed have been a rebel and one of Irish heritage but this was a comparison too far. In an exploration focused on cricket and society and on 1981, does the McEnroe story really have relevance? It does, because it was one more illustration of the role sport played in the unruly year and its narrative of change, for here was a changing of the guard at an English citadel, and not a popular one, which did nothing to reduce the general sense that social order was a thing of the past.

The sunshine which had occasionally blessed the tennis was a transient friend. By the end of June reality and solemnity had returned to greet the arrival of the month of July. It was to be the most transformational and contradictory one of recent memory dominated at first by the height, or low point, of the country's woes and then by its sporting Lazarus who was about to make real Kipling's imagined hero through disaster and triumph. In the salad days before his captaincy and before a small matter of the West Indies arrived at his door, Botham had, since his debut, managed eight centuries and 17 five-wicket innings. Now in 11 matches as captain he had 276 runs at an average of 14.52 and 32 wickets at an average of 33. The contrast was blatant and unarguable. This was not the 'lead from the front' skipper in which blind faith had been placed. However, as the mid-point of the year was reached, not everyone was willing to join the pervading fatalism. Some were determined to see hope and believed that the very act of hoping was the prerequisite to a turnaround in fortunes.

On the first day of July the essayist Lincoln Allison published *Condition of England* in which he sought to spell out a few home truths, urge people to stop feeling sorry for themselves and present a different perspective. Allison reminded people that in his opinion, relatively speaking there were many reasons for contentment with the national lot, reminding his fellow-countrymen that they still possessed certain 'collective goods' – a land and a unique way of life – of inestimable value. English culture, he argued, was 'the richest and most resilient in the world', and the English environment one of the most satisfying. In this he may have found some doubters on the day of publication but he refused to be cowed by the prevailing pessimism – the villain of the piece being:

> 'the negativism of fashionable thinking about the current state of England: healthy self-criticism has become debilitating self-denigration. Chief offenders are those in the communications media for painting current affairs in the blackest colours. A steady diet of pessimism has planted a false consciousness of failure'.

The time of Allison's desired change of mood was coming. We were reaching the point Thatcher had always envisaged in her first conference speech as prime minister. 'We are coming, I think, to another turning point in our long history. We can go on as we have been going and continue down. Or we can stop and – with a decisive act of will – we can say "Enough."'

It might have been a message to Botham come this July. One senses that even in his darkest fortnight at the start of the month, Botham would have nodded at much of Allison's call for optimism. He was soon to make it real, but not before first hitting the bottom. It was a month in which he could have continued going down, but became one in which, with a decisive act of will, he said, 'Stop. Enough.'

2 July – 28 July: Ghosts

'The images of those few weeks in July 1981, rioting and mobs juxtaposed with pomp and celebrations, were the most emblematic of how divided society had become.'

Alwyn W. Turner
Rejoice, Rejoice!

'The news from home is unredeemably bad; economic decline, rising unemployment, hunger strike deaths and violence in Ulster, riots in many towns in England. The hopes I entertained exactly two years ago that we might be going to turn over a new leaf under Maggie have been dashed. Our plight is worse than two years ago because we appear to have tried something new and it has failed.'

Sir Nicholas Henderson, Ambassador to Washington
July 1981

'Botham's fall came at a time when his political heroine's popularity was at an all-time low.'

Dominic Sandbrook
Who Dares Wins

AS THE ambassador's words above indicate, even many of Thatcher's friends were now struggling to find anything good to say about her. Botham's 'friends' were about to turn against him too. The sense was England's cricketing hierarchy had also tried something new and it had failed. On 2 July Botham walked into the Lord's dressing room having been advised by his chairman of selectors that his continued appointment as captain had been extended for this second Test only. It was the equivalent of the prime minister being told she might be relieved of her duties after each and every debate in the House. However, whilst her grip on power was by now hardly less precarious than Botham's, she had no similar bench of judges who might sentence her on a whim or at a moment's notice. Hence she lasted out the coming tumultuous month and he didn't. The noise around Botham – his fitness both for office and for performance – was now deafening. That very day the *Evening Standard*'s good luck message to the team and captain came in the form of the headline BOTHAM MUST GO. The fact that the BBC's *Newsnight* programme should lead one episode with a debate on 'The Trial of Ian Botham' showed just how far cricket and its principal character had infiltrated the mainstream.

Pages of copy and hours of airtime were given over to what had become a national debate no less febrile than that over Thatcher's government and the state of the nation. Pontificating editorials were supplemented by commentaries by all and sundry, some of which were more personal than was just. Even the more considered opinions from respected sources were coming down increasingly against him, such as that of Michael Melford who suggested after Trent Bridge that Willis should take over as captain – a bold or foolhardy suggestion given the fast bowler's recent battles with form, injury and no-balls. That in itself probably gave the clue to Botham's continued, short-term appointment in the role – the selectors didn't particularly want to back him but nor could they think of anyone else. Botham himself has said he had already made his mind up that if his selectors wouldn't give him at least the rest of the series in charge he would resign at the end of the match. His state of mind as the Lord's Test began must have been less stable than was ideal. And yet England were to give a better account of themselves and by the second afternoon could consider themselves well on top, At 284/4 they controlled the game. Unfortunately they were to follow this with two windows to the future as they lost their last six wickets for 27 (including that of their skipper for a three-ball duck) and then, having still entertained realistic hopes of a lead, let the last two Australian wickets add 77. Nevertheless by the end of day four England held a lead of 95 with only two second innings wickets down. The chance of forcing a victory on the last day may have been slim but at least there was one, if England could pile on quick runs. Such a thing had not so far been a hallmark of the series and over another dull weekend of weather the batting in the match had been familiarly grey. In today's Test game the idea that neither team would approach three runs-an-over across an entire match would almost be grounds for the docking of match fees, but it was an appropriately turgid reflection of much else going on around it.

Frank Keating described the first Test as 'miserable' and the second as 'pallid', which were two adjectives applicable to more than the cricket. On the day the Test had begun more riots broke out both in Southall and in the Toxteth area of Liverpool. The latter was as violent and shocking a confrontation between locals and police as had been seen in Brixton but this time it was to last significantly longer, not finally subsiding until near the end of the month. By now a bubbling tension could be sensed across many of Britain's inner cities as frustration against a perceived lack of opportunity for an alternative path and inflammatory policing, allied in some eyes by an element of copy-catting, simmered ready to erupt. All the misery of the recent past was welling up to an explosive release valve. Front and back pages brought nothing but further pessimism for the whole week. Monday's *Daily Telegraph* editorial foresaw a long hot summer of unrest. 'The present troubles may prove brief; if they are not tackled firmly and immediately, however, they could well do irreparable harm to the nation.'

The headline to *The Sun's* article on the morning of Tuesday 7 July was an encapsulation of the nationwide sense of futility. It was also to have a true resonance for Ian Botham that very day. NO JOB, NO MONEY, NO FUTURE was the none too optimistic banner. By that evening Botham would have no job … and there was considerable doubt as to whether he would have a future. For 7 July would see Botham's own pressure cooker blow its lid and ultimately offer him his own form of release. It would be his last day as the captain of England and by the following morning he would be sharing the newspaper front pages with news of the riots as the bad news once again linked arms. He would later admit it was the lowest point in his life. *The Sun's* features page that day had Jon Akass claiming WE ARE GOING THROUGH SOMETHING NASTY, DEEP AND ENDURING. It could have been a description of Botham's experience of 14 months of captaincy rather than news from Toxteth, and Botham knew he was no longer willing to see it enduring.

As he strode to the wicket in England's second innings the characteristic windmilling of his blacksmith's arms sought to convey a sense of purpose. His side had lost a couple of quick wickets in the quest for quick runs but with the game relatively safe. As would be the case throughout his career Botham was thinking of the approach most needed by the team's situation rather than the one which might boost his own standing. Never one to be dictated to by what he termed 'step and fetch it' bowlers, he had predetermined that the left-arm spinner Ray Bright was to be attacked. The fact he was on a pair and still on trial to an unjustifiable extent was no matter. At this moment his prime minister's words from four months previously could have been ringing in his ears. 'They might get rid of me for this but at least I shall go knowing I have done the right thing.' This was ever the Botham philosophy and he essayed a sweep shot to Bright first ball only to hear the stumps behind him breaking. It was, in his mind in and reality, a justifiable shot. It was also a remarkably unselfish one but it would not be perceived that way. As Botham returned through the white picket gate and up the pavilion steps through the sparsely populated members' seats, he reached his lowest ebb. If Thatcher's own Battle of Britain moment of her recent budget had been greeted by derision and loud catcalls of the sort McEnroe had induced three days before, Botham's Waterloo was met with a deathly silence – not a hint of applause, not a word of sympathy, barely even a look in his direction. It was a moment he would never, ever forget and he knew then that he was done. His recollection of the emotions he felt in that specific moment mirrored those of Thatcher in her early days as prime minister and conveyed their shared sense of isolation. 'It was the feeling of being deserted which affected me deeply. I never felt as lonely as I did that day.' Such a by-product of leadership, which to some was failing leadership, which both had to experience, was at odds with the gregarious Botham in particular. Perhaps a return to the ranks was not such a miserable prospect after all. To those who had expected and rather wanted him to hang himself in the role and those possessed of the British urge to bring even their own heroes down a peg or two, after four years of success and stardom this was the moment of just fate which Mrs Thatcher's own 'wets' were still wishing upon her. It was a reappearance of the attitude Botham had experienced from the older pros in the bar after that first heroic deed against Andy Roberts in 1974: 'Today you're everybody's hero. Just remember that tomorrow they'll have forgotten you again.' It

7 July – 'the lowest point in my life'. A less proud moment after bagging a pair on the last afternoon. Botham never forgot the response that afternoon from the MCC members and his selectors.

11 July – The Specials' 'Ghost Town' reaches number one as the riots continue to rage – perhaps the most apposite chart-topper in history.

PATHETIC!

England's Test men scrape bottom of the barrel

vies clobber Sussex

19 July – rock bottom. The Sun *reflects the nation's view on England cricket's contribution to an unremittingly depressing year …*

The Daily Telegraph

Australians meet their Agincourt

22 July … three days later the mood is rather different. Patriotism is back as Australia 'meet their Agincourt'.

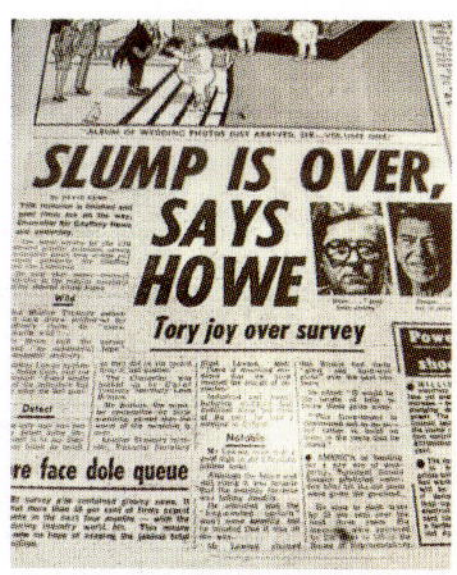

SLUMP IS OVER, SAYS HOWE

Tory joy over survey

re face dole queue

Here comes the sun. 26 July. The economy joins the cricket in ending its slump, as the chancellor claims the recession is over.

28 July. The police holding back rioters in Toxteth on the last night of the disturbances which have stunned the country …

… 29 July. A police cordon of a different kind the following morning as the royal wedding and the much-missed sunshine combine to change the mood.

All Britain goes wedding barmy

PRIDE OF FACE!

PATRIOT

Fans paint the town red, white and blue

UNBEATABLE QUALITY! UNREPEATABLE

29 July. *Pride restored.* The Sun *greets the royal wedding day.*

heroes begin a new Test

BOTHAM

PRINCE CHARLES and Lady Di have set a fine example . . . now England's cricketers must keep the red, white and blue flying today.

And I can't see us losing the initiative we grabbed from the Aussies in the heart-stopping Headingley Test victory.

I have never doubted the spirit of the England side. But that victory at Leeds has really put a right royal spring back into our step.

We are on the march and I expect everyone to be performing at their peak during the Fourth Test at Edgbaston.

But Aussie skipper, Kim Hughes, has a crucial job on his hands in trying to motivate his players after their sensational collapse at Leeds.

IAN BOTHAM

Let's put on a royal show

England's performance—and his refusal to make excuses — must have

30 July. Botham, sensing the moment, urges England to keep the party going in his ghosted column on the morning of the fourth Test.

2 August. A nation changed. A febrile crowd bask in the sun, pomp and circumstance after Botham has secured another miracle at Edgbaston.

Heroes. Botham gives off an air of contentment and confidence some thought they would never see again, in February 1982 ahead of a year which saw him reach his very peak.

The British are coming … home. Joy and flags as troops aboard the Canberra *are welcomed home from the Falklands.*

Last hurrah. Botham celebrates his last Ashes win on 28 December 1986. Hindsight would suggest this would have been a good time to say goodbye …

Botham heads to court and an England ban after a charge of cannabis possession. 1984 to 1986 were years of trials and triumphs for he and Thatcher alike.

Thatcher won her second landslide in June 1987. Like Botham, she had difficulty in accepting the wisdom of leaving on a high.

Treachery with a smile on its face. Thatcher leaves Downing Street after her forced resignation on 22 November 1990 …

… the day after, England began their first Ashes without Botham for 15 years, left out by his captain Gooch (left). He appears to be struggling to see what's coming.

Their impact on their country was huge. They had restored Britain's self-belief at home and abroad.

Something changed. 'What is not in doubt is that they were the architects of change and true icons of the age'. Andrew Marr's summation captures the essence of their stories and of 1981.

was one element of a certain type of British character which Botham could never fathom or embrace, but now it seemed to have won the day. Botham's wish to attack and set a total was vindicated for a time as Australia lost their first three wickets for 17. But the ennui returned as the draw was played out. Fairytales and happy endings didn't happen anymore, or so it appeared. But wherever the celestial cricketing Hans Christian Andersen resided, he was busy composing something barely credible even in the realms of such fiction.

Was the glorious bright weather that suddenly appeared that Tuesday evening a sign of sunshine after the rain for the man himself? Botham would claim that the moment he announced to an eager press at the end of the game that he was resigning the captaincy, a huge weight lifted from his shoulders and looking back there is no reason to doubt it. There was, however, something genuinely sad for those to whom he had brought so much joy over the past few years in his countenance as he made his statement. The swashbuckling have-a-go hero looked utterly spent. It was easy in that instant to doubt whether we would ever see again the force of nature that was the young man who had arrived in the team to make such an impact in the Ashes of four years before. It would transpire, however, that he had indeed 'done the right thing'. Coping with the situation was not helped by the fact that everything in his sporting life to that point had been one continuous story of success, the tough West Indies tour notwithstanding. It was a new experience for which he had no point of reference or understanding. At the end, there was still sympathy and understanding for the experience which had been thrust upon him following Mike Brearley's abdication, like a latter day version of King George VI when handed the crown by his own brother and with similar debilitating results. Martin-Jenkins saw 'a raw young sergeant-major thrust into the role of a commanding officer for battles against a superior enemy … that such a dynamo should have been worn down so soon, even if he can be recharged, is a tragedy for English cricket'.

Thatcher was no less in need of a recharge. If Botham had just experienced the lowest point in his life, those close to Margaret noticed a similar change in demeanour – tired, withdrawn and more morose than was her normal disposition. John Hoskyns saw her as completely bombed out at this point and one member of her political office, David Wolfson, described her as 'almost a zombie', bearing that same haunted look as Botham had worn at his Lord's resignation. As parliament broke for its summer recess the morning after Botham fell on his sword, Thatcher's trusted press secretary Bernard Ingham recorded in his diaries, 'The mood is one of desperate worry and the party left for another summer recess in profound agitation, depression and gloom.'

There was a suspicion that within MCC some held the unnecessarily vindictive view that Botham had got his comeuppance. Being sure of oneself, successful or not, is not universally popular as a character trait in Britain. We can be either suspicious of it or jealous and harbour an unspoken desire to see it dented. The residual antipathy some hold for Botham and Thatcher to this day assuredly has at least some of its roots in this. The best Botham could hope for at this moment was to take that route of dignified resignation and so he did. In the end the general consensus was that Botham had come out of the whole business a degree better than many others and left the post with his dignity intact. Once again Tony Lewis offered his support to Botham in his Sunday column and portrayed his employers in much the same light as the political section of his paper did Thatcher's 'wets', asking what he had done to get caught up with 'a committee which is currently orbiting footloose in Never Never Land without base, policy or credibility'. If they were already doing a fair impression of those Tory dissenters they were to embellish it with the sort of U-turn which had been the latter's holy grail, returning to Brearley as captain for want of any better ideas. In fact this time they did actually have the approval, even the encouragement, of Botham who had put forward Brearley's name generously in the immediate aftermath of his resignation. Their adoption of that recommendation would be one of their wiser decisions. But as for their departing leader, sadly, unbelievably, those above him had not done with him yet. When the time came for the chairman of selectors to speak to the assembled media to react to the magnanimous and helpful gesture his captain had made just moments earlier, in one of the crasser utterances from the English cricket establishment – and that's up against some serious competition – Alec Bedser informed them that they were going to sack him anyway. The following morning's *Daily Telegraph* suggested that this was always the most likely outcome for a mismatched relationship and that its sympathies lay primarily with the captain. 'To the traditionalists Botham was always a rebel who wore the wrong clothes or said the wrong thing.' Even now when, to most minds he had said the *right* thing, his bosses had stumbled forward to say the wrong thing for him anyway. It was a final punch to the solar plexus and totally unnecessary given the man was on his way to the floor anyway. Not too many expected him to get back up off it either – certainly not immediately anyway. They were underestimating the man. Lewis wasn't: 'His agony is over … it will be no surprise if he does not recover his play in time for Headingley … but his talent is natural and will not disappear.'

Where a deposed captain of England did have one advantage over a political party leader however, was that it had always proven nigh on impossible for those leaders to return to the ranks and still be able to effect change, whereas cricketers did have that opportunity, although they were very rarely able to seize it. Had Botham's preference to replace him as captain, Brearley, not made it one of his first acts on getting the job to ask Botham if he would like to play in the very next Test, and been given the authority to make it happen after Botham's affirmative response, that opportunity would not have been open to Botham either. The offer of a role in England's desired fightback was soon to look like one of sports most exaggerated examples of sliding doors. When Thatcher was eventually cast aside by her own team it was the end of the story – in sport, there is often a shot at redemption. For Botham, instead of the possibility of his last chapter, the story was only just beginning. He recalled the very next game he played after his resignation-cum-sacking, for Somerset, back in the bosom of a family that understood and still cherished him. He also admitted that even he was beginning to have a few doubts about himself. A short moment of silence was followed by a growing applause from the crowd. 'After the bleak times I'd endured this morale boost was the most wonderful antidote.' It shook him out of his depressed mood and resolved him to enjoy life and cricket again, treating it as a moment of release. It was Botham's own moment of change and it was to bring sweet rewards. *Wisden Cricket Monthly* tried to find a shaft of light. 'If by the end of the summer the series is won, and if Botham has boomed back to his form which once made him the world's most exciting cricketer, the pain will not have been in vain.'

Whilst Margaret Thatcher was still urging people to believe that the country's current pain would not be in vain either, yet again the political and social hiatuses of the year shadowed the cricketing ones, the nation's woes following the team's, Thatcher's in tandem with Botham's. The day after the latter's resignation, the miners under Arthur Scargill challenged the government's pay limit with a 23.7 per cent pay claim in a clear laying down of the gauntlet to the prime minister and then two of the summer's most depressing stories entered another chapter. Joe McDonnell became the fifth of the IRA Maze inmates to die as a result of the hunger strike which seemed no nearer a resolution than it had been in the spring. He would be followed by a sixth death five days later.

Still neither Thatcher nor the IRA leadership would move. The same news bulletins which brought news of McDonnell's fate also showed images of the start of the next round of rioting, this time in the Moss Side area of Manchester. By now such pictures produced less a sense of shock than one of numb sufferance and bewilderment. If there were answers out there somewhere Margaret Thatcher didn't appear to be the one to find them. Her insistence that terrorists were terrorists and crime was crime was most widely perceived now as cruel intransigence and a refusal to acknowledge the truth of things. As Botham continued, in the face of all the statistical evidence, to insist that there was no effect of captaincy on his form that time wouldn't cure, so Thatcher seemed mired in the same self-delusion. This was the case despite the fact that both contentions had at least some validity.

On the 11th, as the riots spread to six further cities, one of the most referenced of the cultural reflections of the public mood – coincidental but strangely felicitous – was that arrival at number one in the singles chart of The Specials' 'Ghost Town'. This would go down as *the* depiction of the place at which the country had now arrived – dark, brooding, almost apocalyptic in its portrayal of the here and now and its pessimism for the future. It was a brutal and yet brilliant creation and will forever be linked by a certain generation with the year in which we heard it, even if it was rather lost on some. David Jacobs was the sort of Radio Two DJ this world was leaving behind and as the cameras came back to his presentation of the 900th edition of *Top of the Pops* on 8 July at the end of the video, his summation was: 'Oh dear, that wasn't very cheery was it?' It could have been Peter West closing the highlights of the last day at Lord's 48 hours before.

There was one more conjunction to come between the cricket and the world around it as the metamorphosis approached. The week before the third Test match began in Leeds the rioting reached the city's Chapeltown district. As

Roger Domenghetti noted a week before the Test 'the social unrest seemed to be following the cricket around'. The clouds that went with this were also to settle on Headingley – both meteorologically and in the crabby nature of the cricket which was still being served up – when the match began. Leeds was now appropriate in more ways than one. For all the grandeur and profile of Lord's, Yorkshire was the place which best illustrated the bond between cricket and the English. As Tony Lewis looked forward to the Headingley Test back in 1975 he wrote, 'There is no other part of the world where cricket is so much an integral part of life.' In 1981 this was one thing that *hadn't* changed.

Nobody could foresee what was coming next. The *Daily Telegraph's* retrospective of the cricketing summer later in the year was not guilty of any great over-embellishment when it claimed, 'Many of the events that followed had not happened for around 100 years and will not happen again anytime soon.' What appear to be the worst of times can actually have a cleansing effect. What was around the corner for Botham was more appreciated, by him and those around him, as a result of what he had just been through. In the same way as some economists believe the shock of the early 1980s actually saved British industry from even more severe sclerosis, so the shock that Botham was about to inflict upon the Australians was all the more stark given the pale nature of what England had produced for the previous two years. The fact that there were absolutely no indications that one of the greatest stories in English cricket history was about to unfold made the dramatic renaissance more pronounced and the sense of elation and uplift even greater when it came to pass. As *Wisden* recalled, 'The match ended in a way to stretch the bounds of logic and belief', but 'none of this had seemed remotely likely on the opening day when the familiar slate-grey clouds engulfed the chimneys which stretch away from the Kirkstall Lane end.' For the first two days the crowd made up a patchwork of colour within the gloom, but a colour which has never brought much joy to the cricket-follower – that inimitable image of a crowd huddled in their lame, flimsy cagoules and anoraks in those pre-Dupont days, watching their lame, flimsy batting line-up capitulate. Even the Australians in their dominance were scarcely setting pulses racing. For today's generation, gorging on a diet of Ben Stokes, Harry Brook and 'Bazball', the idea that the Aussies first innings which just touched 400 might take two days, would be beyond their comprehension and akin to a prescription of Mogadon.

Wisden described Friday's second day as 'pedestrian in the extreme'. Such was the funereal pace of the cricket that when David Gower put down Trevor Chappell the slow motion replays were barely distinguishable from the real thing. By tea on the first day the Australian total had ground it's way to 97/1 – a score England might expect to make from the first ten overs today. The only saving grace for those who had been at work that Thursday and missed the 'action' was that these were the days when Peter West or Richie Benaud introduced the BBC highlights at about the same time the country's milkmen were climbing into their floats, so only the mad keen or the just plain mad would consider putting themselves through the re-run. It didn't look any better second time around in its abridged form either. Highlights they weren't. Still England steadfastly refused to take the chances that came their way. At 90/1 Botham dropped Chappell; at 112/1 he did the same for John Dyson who went on to a century. The fact that the man who had spent four years taking the most breathtaking slip catches was now shelling the most straightforward ones was cruel evidence that things were going from bad to worse, captaincy or not. For the true optimist there came the first sign of something on the second evening when Botham wrapped up the innings, from 332/4 to 401 all out, with his first five-wicket haul (6-95) since the last Test before he became captain. That one of those wickets, that of the captain, Kim Hughes, should be caught and bowled off a leg-stump half-volley might perhaps have been an indication that 'Golden Arm' Botham was back and a change of fortune was in the air. Another came the following day as Botham made his first half-century since his first Test as captain. From the commentary box Christopher Martin-Jenkins, for one, thought he had seen something. 'It really looks as though the shackles have dropped from his shoulders since the burden of captaincy has been lifted from him.' Whether or not shoulders can actually be shackled is by the by – the vision was to prove correct.

That was the only ray of sunlight that Saturday. 18 July may well have a case for being the nadir in the long-running narrative of decline. PATHETIC! screamed Monday's headline in *The Sun* even after a rest day had given everyone the chance to calm down. The truth was that England had now won only two Test matches since May 1979 – a reflection of the general resignation to managed decline now at large. It sat rather neatly with the latest news that in precisely the same period Britain's manufacturing output had fallen from 29.3 per cent to the depths of 25 per cent. The outputs of the nation's team and workforce were battling for inferiority month by month. As responses to a challenging opposition total go, England's batting was, politely, feckless. Citing the difficulties of the pitch, the commentators were suggesting the damage had been done in letting Australia score well above par with a listless performance in the field which both reflected and influenced the crowd's mood. The frustration in the stands and in front of the country's televisions was enhanced by the fact that the tumble of wickets was no longer the result of the alarming pace and hostility of the previous years. Instead it was induced, as it had been all summer, by the type of controlled, nagging seam bowling at which England were supposed excel. Dennis Lillee was no longer the tearaway speed merchant of six years before but had adapted his persona and method to those of a canny and skilful deployer of seam, swing and change of pace. England may have preferred the previous incarnation. If anything, he was out-cannied by his opening partner Terry Alderman who would end up with a record haul of wickets for an Ashes series, barely breaking sweat in doing so. As a long-suffering England supporter I've been deflated several times by the ability of the Australians to find a bowler we've never heard of to appear from nowhere and prove utterly unplayable. The role would be taken up by the likes of Ryan Harris and Scott Boland in years to come but for now Alderman bamboozled England by the simple means of bowling straight down the pitch. His biggest patsy was the unfortunate Graham Gooch whose confidence he sapped and who could claim the rare and unwanted achievement of being out twice on the same day as England followed on in the evening. The lack of a counter-attack, of something which might give the Australians at least something to think about, had drained any optimism from the crowd. There was little hope for the rest of us if the never-say-die Botham felt on the Saturday evening that even the most incurable optimist would struggle to find any blue sky behind the clouds over Headingley. The day, the match and the Ashes were done and once again the country was subsiding with barely a whimper.

This was something not lost on Botham. It wasn't in his DNA to bow the knee, particularly when Australians were involved. He may have sensed that others had thrown in not just the towel but the shampoo and hairdryers as well and he remembered the atmosphere on the Monday morning as having all the jollity of a funeral, the ground cold, dark and windy and littered with empty seats. This was his own budget moment – sink or swim but either way, go down fighting and, once again, 'doing the right thing'. Mondays have rarely been a day to lift the spirits and by the afternoon England sat famously at 135/7, miles away from even making their opponents put their pads back on and those 500-1 against odds lit up the scoreboard in the darkness that had the umpires glancing skywards. Salvation was not to come from that direction, but another. That grey Monday afternoon it felt like the whole country was a metaphorical 135/7. No way back. Once again CMJ played the role of optimistic cheerleader. 'Now, what a triumph it would be for him if he could still be batting at six o'clock this evening' greeted Botham's arrival at the crease. One sensed it was something to say, with tongue not far from cheek, rather than a serious prediction of what was to come. At tea, with the scoreboard 176/7, even a sage (and an enthusiastic punter) as wise as Richie Benaud was calling the game 'all but over'.

Simon Barnes once wrote of Tim Henman that 'he can find in moments of greatest trial the greatest of his ability … look for your strengths: you will find them in the same place as your weaknesses'. This is where Botham looked now. What happened next is a matter of folklore and in no need of repeat description here other than to recall that Botham's 'ah well, what the hell' charge to 149 not out changed, as CMJ had said, at least the *character* of the match. Botham himself noticed that slowly, imperceptibly, the mood of the two teams changed. During the afternoon the commentator suggested the crowd would be 'relieved to be watching the home team at least putting up a fight here'. It was what the whole country had been wanting to see. By the evening session, a crowd which had believed they were witnessing just one more low in the country's forecast were now streaming back into the ground. The commentator Tom Graveney saw in front of him '… a disillusioned and critical crowd brought to life. From waiting for the final rites of the Ashes they were suddenly behind a rejuvenated team'. There was more rejuvenation the following morning, the last of the Test. Two things were suddenly visible which had long been absent. The first was some sunshine, the second the sight of Union Jacks in the crowd. Both suggested that the times were a-changing. Many years later a film revisiting this series, *From the Ashes*, would open with two lines which recalled a reconnection in this moment between team and public: 'Sometimes it takes a single ray of light to lift the gloom. Things that give us the feeling that we too are winners.' The injured England bowler Mike Hendrick watched 'the way it was being received nationally. Everything stopped'.

Keating called the innings 'almost operatic in its resonant boldness' and Martin-Jenkins 'a joyous abandon as he just smiled his way through one of the most amazing innings of all time'. Whether it was actually Keating's bold counter or simply CMJ's nothing-to-lose piece of gay abandon didn't really matter in the end. And it was another moment of chance which ensured that the heroics would not end up on the cutting room floor as a forlorn rage against the dying of the light and defeat. Bob Willis's issues with injuries and no-balls had reduced his effectiveness in the first two Tests to the point where one of England's potentially most potent weapons was firing blanks. The assumption he might be left out at Leeds was confirmed with the selection of Mike Hendrick in his place. It was only when Hendrick reported himself unfit that Willis had a reprieve. On such happenstances do remarkable events turn. Now Willis, a man-possessed and superbly handled and cajoled by Mike Brearley, blew away the Australian batting as the rabbits caught in his headlights gradually realised what horror was befalling them. Without the fast bowler's brave contribution the summer's history would assuredly not have been written the way it was. As CMJ pointed out at the conclusion, 'A little before this time yesterday English cricket was being buried … Willis bowled Bright to complete the victory which had saved a moribund series.' Indeed, a moribund year to date. *Wisden* wrote: 'At the end, the crowd gathered to wave their Union Jacks and chant patriotically eight days in advance of the Royal Wedding.' What they also did was sing 'Jerusalem', the seed of which may have been sown by those who had viewed the recently released *Chariots of Fire*. The uplifting hymn had as good as fallen into disuse before its inclusion as the climactic accompaniment to great British sporting achievement at the film's conclusion. The idea of a crowd of Englishmen and women chorusing it spontaneously at Headingley or anywhere else in the Britain of just a few weeks previously would have been preposterous. And yet, although many a watcher of English cricket today may curse its adoption now that it is played at the start of every single day of international cricket in England, on that July afternoon the marriage of a piece of patriotic nostalgia from the cinema and another English sporting fairytale on the cricket field seemed perfect. *The Sun* now changed tack as swiftly as the rest of us, and in Andy Beckett's words 'seized on it as a national allegory'. Such lines as 'the bulldog breed bared its teeth again' were very much that newspaper's language but did capture the pride in the fight that many thought had been permanently displaced. The *Telegraph*'s editorial the following day reminded us there was another association here too which had been getting tighter all year. With the prime minister overseas at a leaders' summit in Canada, it pondered, 'This was a perfect Test match which England won against the odds – at one stage 500-1. Perhaps, on reflecting on this apparent impossibility in Ottawa, Mrs T. may sleep a little easier.' In other words, Botham had shown Thatcher the way. The same newspaper's commentary before the royal wedding and the next Test arrived, suggested she was following that lead. 'There are enough straws in the wind to make it possible that Mrs Thatcher can – against all odds – hold the pass for a little longer. For all of us it is a time to hold breaths and hope.'

If further proof were needed that Botham and cricket were now resonating into life and politics, the referencing of Headingley by the Conservative backbencher Charles Morrison to the Home Secretary Willie Whitelaw – a man in a job currently desperate for happy news – surely provided it. Being a politician, of course he was using it for his own ends and to make a barbed but weak point to his leader. 'Don't you think their achievement demonstrates again how often it is possible to snatch victory out of the jaws of defeat subject to a change of tactics?' The flaw in the analogy being that tactics had scarcely come into it at Headingley – rather the belief of one man that the battle could be won and a determination to disprove those of lesser faith. Once again Thatcher's own backbiters had not only missed their target but made her point for her in the process. So the cricket was the talk of the town. In Botham's recollection the team began to realise after the match the impact the epic events had had on the nation amidst tales of a day of untold and unjustified 'sickies'. His partner in the initial turning of the tide on the Monday afternoon, Graham Dilley, remembered 'driving down the motorway you realised what had been achieved. Given the state of the country in 1981 it was something people could latch on to'. Even so, the longer-term significance of Headingley was still opaque – indeed it may have had little significance at all without the supporting cast of events that were now to back it up. It is worth remembering that it was enjoyed sardonically more than triumphantly at the time in the way that seems to have been copyrighted by English sports fans. Although England cricket supporters are a philosophical bunch, necessarily used to smiling in the face of defeat, as Simon Barnes notes, 'Behind the gallows humour is a hope that, someday, things might be different.' It was fun to see the Australians finally chasing leather and just the beginnings of the self-doubt that was to haunt them for the rest of the summer, The *Daily Telegraph* match report once again linking sporting success with some sense of nostalgic patriotism in the headline AUSTRALIA MEET THEIR AGINCOURT, but this was a punch on the nose, not a fatal beating. It was a one-night party which, although it ended in miraculous victory, was also followed by a few days of anti-climactic hangover once the show reached

Edgbaston the following week. A little like the marriage ceremony that was to follow eight days later, Headingley was a happy and welcome relief – evidenced in Brearley's revelation of the letters he received which he felt showed 'there were hints that the dramatic successes of the national team had some intangible sense of influence on national morale' – but there was scarcely an all-pervading belief that a critical corner had been reached and turned.

So it was too with the continued signs that Thatcher's own performance indicators were beginning to improve – interest rates now substantially lower than in other major industrialised countries and a cease in the fall in industrial production. On 27 July a civil service strike which had been running since March was called off and the return to work was reported as an unequivocal defeat for the unions. After Bernard Ingham's gloomy despatch in the first week of July, his last diary entry of the same month offered a contrast. 'We had emerged from a most difficult month … in far better shape than we might have reasonably expected". Just as Tony Lewis was writing his article suggesting to Botham that, for him, the worst was now over, so the political commentators in his newspaper were writing the same thing of the economic conditions and the tyranny of the unions. 'The worst of the recession is over and looks like being less severe than feared four months ago. However, the future is still deeply uncertain.' And so it was – as with the cricket, not many were convinced of a sustainable recovery, believing the figures offered some light relief rather than concrete evidence of a better future. But with hindsight, what they and Headingley had been was a start.

29 July–31August: Here Comes The Sun

'As the sun shines, we become more optimistic: the number of hours of sunshine predicts scores on ratings of optimism.'

Professor Trevor Harley,
The Psychology of Weather

'A year of disturbing events, 1981 saw recession, violence in Northern Ireland and political turmoil, but Diana was a counterpoint to all that … Even in 1981 when the inner cities were torn apart by riots there was a yearning in society … to muddle along together – the same longing something unifying explains the astonishing popularity of the royal wedding."

Andy McSmith
No Such Thing As Society

'When the players reassembled at Edgbaston, it was clear something had changed.'

Dominic Sandbrook
Who Dares Wins

TREVOR HARLEY'S literally illuminating words above are supplemented in his study by evidence that not only does sunshine often boost levels of serotonin, afford better sleep and improve mood, but that sunny, warm days have more of a beneficial effect on mood when they start occurring again after a period of absence. Perhaps this is why the correlation between the change of both the meteorological and general atmosphere was so marked that July when on its 29th day the weather favoured the royal nuptials with brilliant sunshine. Former Botham team-mate for Somerset and England, Vic Marks, remembered those few weeks after Headingley: 'It was a fairytale match followed by a fairytale wedding and I think people may have been hungry for fairytales around that time.' And if Diana was indeed a counterpoint to disturbing events, she became so in tandem with the nation's now favourite cricketer. Domenghetti recalled that if the Headingley and subsequent Tests gave the country a swashbuckling hero, the royal wedding gave it a virginal princess – and a third cultural icon of the decade came into British life in the very same year, the very same month.

In the aftermath of Headingley came a transformation even more stark and immediate than Botham had instigated. There was in fact a fifth fatality, as pertinent to the story as the four of the winter and spring, before the wedding arrived. On 28 July a disabled man, David Moore, who wasn't a local but happened to be visiting his sister in the area, had been hit by a police vehicle during the Toxteth riots. He died the following morning. It was the first civilian death of the riots, and the last. That news was submerged by another significant event that day – the royal wedding. Of all the remarkable juxtapositions of 1981 here was perhaps the most pronounced and the most gruesome. The darkness of the night in Toxteth which had marked the end of the summer's riots emerged into the glorious sunshine of the day on which the nation intended to rejoice. As Graham Stewart points out, 'Such was the paradox of Britain in the summer of 1981.' Even then, and more so looking back, it felt like a line in the sand – a reversal of direction as, in the words of Stewart, 'a country that was locked in recrimination and shame showed itself no less overcome with celebration and pride'.

The English have a way of approaching, and reporting the approach of, the sort of events we are told will be uplifting and on which the eyes of the world will rest. It is not fashionable to express excited anticipation – far better to profess disinterest and/or make predictions of damp squib anti-climaxes. For evidence see both the Euro '96 football – the first major tournament to be held in England for 30 years – and the London 2012 Olympics which would bring that global fiesta back to the country for the first time in 64 years. I can tell you first-hand from the experience of working for a global sports brand who sponsored both events and therefore had a vested interest in seeing them enrapture the public, that for months in advance the naysayers were the dominant voice. And yet, as a proud nation with a penchant for a bit of flag-waving we can't keep the pretence up forever and when the time comes we put on one hell of a show and hold a communal party which galvanises the nation. Such a process was visible to the letter in advance of the day in the sun at St Paul's Cathedral. The use of the words 'Happy Britain' in the *Daily Express* headline that morning almost needed looking up to check their meaning. Suddenly all the words were optimistic ones, with *The Times* reporting the day as symbolic of the nation's unity and one which would 'lift the spirits of people depressed by consistent economic malfunctioning'. The pride was enhanced by a knowledge that the day of colour was making a statement by being shared with half the globe. An estimated 750 million people worldwide would watch the spectacle of celebration and wonder whether Great Britain might just be making a comeback after all.

Talking of comebacks ... The flag-toting crowds of the wedding were greeted by the sudden arrival of that summer sun which now stayed for the fourth Test which began the morning after. The media were aglow with positivity, reflecting the public's hope that the Ashes might now extend the fun. On the first morning of the Test Botham himself joined the cheerleading in his ghosted column in *The Sun* and urged his team to make it so: 'Prince Charles and Lady Di have set a fine example … now England's cricketers must keep the red, white and blue flying today. Let's put on a royal show.' Meanwhile *The Cricketer* reported 'a large crowd was assembled, drawn partly by the knowledge that the series was suddenly alive again and partly also by the spirit of happy patriotism raised by the royal wedding the day before'. But for a few days England did what they could to give everyone a sober reality check. The evidence was that England were still second best in the contest and that a Coronation or Jubilee-style present of the Ashes remained an odds-against wager. The somewhat underwhelming nature of the series, particularly its batsmanship, had returned. Such was the timidity of both sides' batsmen on a far better surface than that in Leeds, that for the first time in 668 Test Matches not one of them made it to 50, and yet the contest still hobbled into its fourth day. As Australia reached 105-4 heading for 142 to retake the series lead, the air was slowly seeping out of the balloon.

Something was needed. It may have helped England that that fourth day was also only the second Sunday on which Test cricket had been played in England. Even in the summer holidays this bestowed upon the broiling hot day an element of carnival. Now Botham orchestrated not just another spectacular and most un-Australian collapse, but he also conducted one of the loudest and most patriotic crowds the country's cricket grounds had ever seen and what Keating called 'more national delirium all-round'. The atmosphere was more that of Villa Park when the League Championship had arrived just down the road two months before, than what was expected at English cricket. There was more than just celebration here – there was a relief bordering on defiance. Bob Willis saw it first-hand. 'I've never seen such crowds or heard such noise … that roar from the terraces was unforgettable. It has certainly given the citizens of this country something to smile about.' And as large numbers were transfixed by televisions – their own or somebody else's, including those still sat in high street retailers' windows – that sense transmitted itself across the country as sport and society in concert. Dominic Sandbrook was considering the reasons for the huge enthusiasm for the wedding and the royals but could have added in Edgbaston as well when he suggested that the appetite for patriotic escapism was simply much greater in the summer of 1981 because of the shock of the recession and the riots but also because after years of being lectured on how far British morale had sunk, the British people were desperate to feel good about themselves.

This time it felt different. Headingley gave us a moment of fight; now overall victory was suddenly an attainable goal. The Australians' bewilderment was writ large in the glazed eyes of their captain, Kim Hughes, as he tried bravely to negotiate the press conference. The West Midlands-based journalist and Botham biographer Pat Murphy attended that media moment and promptly added another comparison between the year's cricketers and their political counterparts. 'Kim Hughes looked like one of those vapid junior government ministers Margaret Thatcher likes to savage with a curt couple of sentences and a glint of her gamma-ray eyes.' Australia were gone. They were at England's mercy. Now here was a thing. The internal strife of a Labour party conference now began for them, with the old lieutenants Rod Marsh and Dennis Lillee undermining Kim Hughes, the leader they had not wanted and never believed in. It was the Tory Old Etonians and Thatcher all over again. Within days the summer temperatures had reached 30 degrees and the long-awaited warmth pervaded everything. As Murphy saw for himself, 'A British nation already *en fête* for the marriage of the heir to the throne was captivated by the deeds of the England side.' Botham admitted he wasn't oblivious to what it meant to the nation, and what the nation meant to him. 'I loved the support of the crowd that day. Union Jacks flying around. Right up my street.'

But the journey for England and for its cricket team was not to be a serene and linear upward path – such things are noticeably absent in the histories of both. Once again the weather would have its say on the matter. The fifth Test was due to start in Manchester ten days later. What chance the sun would continue to shine as England confirmed their dominance and secured the urn? This is not Manchester's role in life or in cricket. On 6 August the mercurial nature of the weather of 1981 now took the 30 degree-plus temperatures and replaced them with a thunderstorm of epic proportions which handed Manchester its wettest night of the century – and that wasn't an easy distinction to claim. By the time the Test match started a week later, Old Trafford wore its not unfamiliar cloak of grey and the players took to the field in one sweater on top of another. Tom Graveney's review recalled 'The Pennines were invisible all day … and England shed very little light amidst the encircling gloom.' For the cloak of grey had returned to England's batting as well – in truth, aside from Botham's fireworks at Leeds it had never really shifted all summer.

The search for a solid number three in their line-up had evicted David Gower from the side to accommodate Chris Tavaré, which was soon to feel like replacing Mozart with Chopin's *Funeral March* and not conducive to a continuation of the rip-roaring cricket we had been treated to in fleeting moments over the previous few weeks. Tavaré was a talented stroke-player with Kent, but had been brought in to provide stickability and he interpreted the brief to the letter, scoring two of the slowest half-centuries in living memory – in fact beyond that too, as his second effort was the slowest in the history of all English first-class cricket. This is not to denigrate his contribution as wickets fell all around him and

Botham himself would pay huge credit to him, insisting that without this yin to his own yang what was about to transpire could never have happened. It was just the latest contrast in a year that couldn't move for them – the previous day of the series offering sun, heat, flags, raucous celebration and success; the next seeing England crawl to 175/9 at barely two runs-an-over in front of an understandably listless crowd. The day's play also included a classic of a particular type for all England followers. When we do land on a player with the ability to do the extraordinary, we would rather like them to do it every time. Given that statistical history indicates this is unrealistic, there is an anticipation laced with jeopardy whenever they appear in the batting order – will we get one of their special days? We almost find ourselves hoping for wickets which will bring them to the crease so we can get our answer. In years to come it would be Andrew Flintoff, Kevin Pietersen, Ben Stokes. Now it was Botham – the first such player we had had in our midst for decades. His deeds of the last two Tests had scarcely reduced expectation and as England slid to 109/5 that afternoon there was still a tangible sense that it was merely setting us up for 'Beefy to the rescue'. When he left one ball later at 109/6 that numb deflation that comes with such an anti-climax was palpable. Perhaps the last few weeks had been an aberration after all.

Then the summer went preposterous all over again. A rollicking last-wicket stand on the second morning as the sun returned; the lemming-like Australians dismissed in 30 overs and England finishing the day untroubled on 70/1 and suddenly within touching distance of The Ashes. Of course, a twist awaited. Four wickets for 25 runs on the third morning and Lillee and Alderman apparently unplayable once more. This is where Botham arrived on stage with things very much back in the balance to an audience once again riven with angst masquerading as excitement. In his trials and triumphs so far that summer he had both a pair and a blistering hundred to his name. Which he might now reproduce might well decide and define the Ashes summer. And it did. He produced an innings which 'for its ferocious and effortless power and dazzling cleanness of stroke, can surely never have been bettered in a Test match' in the view of *Wisden*. 'Was Botham's Innings The Greatest Ever?' asked *The Times* front page on the Monday morning, eschewing its renowned sober restraint. More hyperbole poured forth from *The Cricketer:* 'From a dreary morning struggle the game was lifted to Olympian heights by the bionic man.' Was it the greatest ever? Perhaps, on reflection, not. Was it one of the most significant ever? For his country, alongside the one from a month before, probably yes. It wasn't just the match-turning runs that mattered but that idea of an Englishman taking on a challenge with ferocious, effortless power – given the times in which it was played it carried no little symbolism. As he swatted Lillee off his eyebrows and far into the crowd time and again, he was swatting away the tribulations of the previous 18 months, for himself and for the rest of us. Frank Keating's recollection of it as 'an innings of unstoppable conviction' was right – the belief which had left him at Lord's was back in spades. His breathtaking 118 was very different to the happy-go-lucky affair at Leeds. It was awash with the confidence of a man who had rediscovered himself and was even serious enough this time to deign to play himself in. He may have been keen on the spectacular, but Botham was also a winner and with this calculated performance he effectively secured not only the Ashes but eternal icon status as a charismatic English hero. Peter Willey doesn't do gushing, but he had no doubts, 'Ian's heroics took the ordinary person's mind off what was going on. They had a hero to look up to.' Job done. David Gower acknowledged that 1981 'was of course the summer of Beefy'. Whilst Gower's rider to this that it is something of a myth that Botham won the Ashes on his own is valid (in a team game there will always be examples of valuable supporting roles in any victory) but the reality is that the summer wouldn't have turned without him and it is no injustice to anyone else that 'Botham's Ashes' is the abiding title for the series. I am always willing to accept John Arlott's word on anything as gospel and he himself was in no doubt. 'It was, though, Botham who lifted the series from the edge of abject slump and the lowest pit of public esteem, to the epic.'

After an inevitably anti-climactic curtain call Test at The Oval, *Wisden* would reflect on the summer we had just lived through with these words:

> 'After several weeks of dreadful weather the sun got the better of the rain and England gained two of the more dramatic victories in the history of the game. In two unforgettable months, English cricket emerged in 1981 from a place of much gloom to a well-being that was reflected even in the enthusiasm with which ordinary men and women set about their labours.'

As the cricket journalist Simon Wilde noted in his history of the England cricket team, those teams have over the years been defined as much by their shortcomings as their triumphs and 'how frequently the grey days outnumber those when the sun shines'. Much the same could be said of the English weather and of the lives in general of the majority of us battling for contentment in a sea of challenges, hence this impact on the enthusiasm and perhaps even the productivity of us all when that sun does come out every now and then. There was a certain irony that 1981 should be the first time in his life, at 67-years-old, that John Arlott had had to watch cricket on the TV from his armchair and get a dose of what the rest of us England cricket followers had been suffering for years. His recollection captured the spirit of the summer and the purgatory of watching such transformations evolve. 'The events were so compelling that, on several occasions, a whole spell of play created such agonising suspense as to be unwatchable, necessitating withdrawal to a distant room with a cool-minded wife to bring news … '

Welcome to our world at last, John.

The Cricketer's September editorial was titled LIFE, COLOUR AND SPIRIT. This is how far the wheel had turned given all three were words which hadn't been employed all year. 'England's victory must have had the same effect on the impressionable young of Britain as that of 1953.' Victory and patriotism all over again. Frank Keating's article HOW IAN AND I WON THE ASHES gave a characteristically humorous sheen to the general mood of satisfaction. 'The truth is, I publicly wrote off the 1981 Test series at around two o'clock on Monday the 20th of July when England were 130-odd for seven. It had been a disastrous summer anyway.'

David Gower put the cricket in its wider context in remembering how 'England dragged itself out of the economic mire and everything was great again thanks to the royal wedding and Botham's heroics.' In truth, not *everything* was great again, but for a time it certainly felt that way. G.K. Chesterton wrote in his critique of Charles Dickens, 'There is a great man who makes every man feel small. But the really great man is the man who makes every man feel great.' This was Botham's gift to the country that summer through his sporting deeds, which is the essence of this story. Something changed and our treasured game of cricket had more than played its part in the remarkable, nation-changing year of 1981. As the shell-shocked Australian captain Kim Hughes would say at the end of the summer, the difference was one man, and one man only. For our wider consideration, it was one man and one woman too. Wilde concluded that what he discovered in researching his England cricket history was 'a tale in which striving and heroism against the odds prominently feature'. If that's the story of England cricket, it is the parallel story of Ian Botham and Margaret Thatcher too.

* * *

That difference in perception and timing which clung to Botham and Thatcher and what precisely their accomplishments might have changed could be seen again in the summer's aftermath. A headline on the front page of *The Times* in September announced that Thatcher was 'The most unpopular prime minister since polls began.' This in a month when Botham had just become possibly the most *popular* cricketer since English cricket began. He would top his country's polls when becoming BBC Sports Personality of the Year three months later and, as Michael Melford wrote in the *Daily Telegraph* at the end of the series, 'It was the abruptness and improbability of the turnaround which made it so memorable.'

Simon Barnes suggests that it is only in sport that you can see the impossible taking place before your eyes. Thatcher did not have that luxury. Economic turnarounds don't tend to happen with the instancy of sporting victories. However, Andy McSmith noted that by the beginning of 1982 there were signs that the worst was over and the medicine was beginning to work, making Howe's 1981 budget look more like a far-sighted act of courage than the destructive folly it at first seemed to be. The reality, and the distinction, was that whilst Botham packed his turnaround moments into just 41 days from his lowest point at Lord's to the winning of the Ashes in August, Thatcher's equivalent moments were spread across two years. The Budget of March 1981 had had the potential to be her Lord's but ended up as her Headingley and the beating of 500-1 odds; victory in the Falklands was her Edgbaston – a second victory against the odds in a maelstrom of flags and patriotic renaissance; but her Old Trafford – her moment of complete victory and passport to future dominance, was the election landslide of June 1983. Botham's medicine had been an instant cure; Thatcher's a longer course of treatment with recovery of a less immediately visible nature. But the figures now bore out the argument. In May 1980 inflation had peaked at 21.9 per cent in her darkest of days; three days after the Ashes were retained it was announced to have fallen to 10.9 per cent; by the end of 1982 it would be down to five per cent. The war against it was all but won.

Thatcher later noted how her policy had begun to succeed. 'The early signs of recovery in the summer of 1981 were confirmed by the statistics of the following quarter which marked the start of a long period of sustained economic growth.' By July 1982 Thatcher's own approval rating had leapt to 52 per cent which is naturally associated with the military success, but historian Mark Garrett believes that 'partly this reflected the government's success in its main objective – the control of inflation'. Political recovery was to follow, slowly, in the wake of those early signs of growth and would culminate in victory in the Falklands, but as she herself insisted, 'We had already won the second Battle of Britain.' Botham had won his own battle too in a summer he summed up as one of discontent and satisfaction, and in similar fashion it would usher him into a long period in the sun. Gower was a first-hand witness as 'Beefy lost the captaincy but found paradise and for a long time after that it seemed to most people, himself included, that there was nothing he couldn't do.' 1981 had made it possible. J.R.R. Tolkien was apparently fond of watching a bit of cricket but didn't live to see that of 1981. Twenty-seven years before, he had published the first book in his fantasy *Lord of the Rings* trilogy, *The Fellowship of the Ring*. Quite how he managed within it to describe so appositely the summer Botham had just lived through is a thing of even greater fantasy, but there it was:

> 'From the ashes a fire shall be woken; A light from the shadows shall spring; Renewed shall be blade that was broken; The crownless again shall be king.'

September – December: Hopes and Fears

IN MID-SEPTEMBER Margaret Thatcher decided the improving conditions and the need for the next stage of the journey to begin meant the time was right for more change and embarked on one of the most significant transformations of her career. That month's cabinet reshuffle was a reflection of her increasing confidence in her overall position, giving her the same air of ascendancy Botham was now enjoying. It was the moment which political commentators had been anticipating since her early days in office. Out went the 'wets' and many of the grandees who had undermined her vision and would now have to do so from the backbenches – their chance of removing her themselves now gone. In their place came ministers who would become synonymous with the Thatcherite decade ahead – Nigel Lawson, Nicholas Ridley, Cecil Parkinson and Norman Tebbit, whose speech at the following month's party conference would go down in legend and confirm that Thatcher now had enough believers alongside her not simply to avoid having to 'turn' but to march forward in a different style to a different place.

She had rid herself finally of the dissension and created a 'squad' full of new blood and on message. *The Times* reported on the reshuffle: 'The final impression is the indelible stamp and style of the PM herself. She has reasserted her dominance. If she succeeds it will be a remarkable personal triumph', and Botham's dominance over English cricket came in the wake of his own comparable personal triumph. Over the next few years both would take that dominance to a global stage. On 3 July 1982 in Cheltenham, Thatcher made a speech in the aftermath of the successful mission in the South Atlantic which included the assertion that, 'we have … a new confidence [as a nation], born in the economic battles at home and, tested and found true 8,000 miles away, Britain found herself again'. It suggested that the rebirth was as much about the external view of Britain and the public's renewed pride in that, than it was about immediate solutions to the ingrained problems at home. Six days later Botham would follow his 128 in the summer's second Test with 208 in the third, an innings characteristic in its power of stroke and its aggression, but one of all-round quality, illustrative of a man totally at peace with himself and his talent once again. From this point on, few would want to take on either of them. The Australians would tend to fall to pieces whenever Botham appeared over the next five years and few opponents of Thatcher would show any greater fortitude.

Before then, however, came more undulations – the reversal in the direction of travel and the last representations of the year of change would now be scattered across its final third, for good and for bad but with an ever-increasing trend of hope. The cricket was done but the transformative moments were not. Now other areas of cultural life made more of their own contributions. For all the happier moments on the way, in the more traditional and escapist elements in the lives of the British people – their love-affairs with their televisions, their sport and their royal family – the first of the seminal happenings was surely the most welcome. On 3 October it was announced that the Maze hunger strike was finally over. The recoveries of those strikers now returned to food felt like another landmark in the recovery of the country. The most horrendous of all the challenges thrown at Thatcher in 1981 and the most difficult and most pressured from all sides in which to maintain the position in which she firmly believed, even when faced with the cold reality of fatalities, had played out. The general reaction was that she had ultimately emerged with a reputation for determination and courage intact.

On the country's televisions a landmark had been reached at the end of August when Moira Stewart, a journalist born in London to Caribbean parents, became the first female black newsreader on the BBC's national news. To today's Britain this might appear to be of no great import but that would be wrong; 1981 had broken another barrier. A new arrival of a more frivolous nature hit the screens a week later, this one to become every bit as synonymous with the decade as Thatcher's new cohorts. On 8 September the first-ever episode of a sitcom called *Only Fools and Horses* aired on BBC One which would run for 22 years and become part of the fabric of British domestic life with its catchphrases and one-liners infiltrating the everyday vernacular. The aspiration of David Jason's perpetually hapless South London trader, Del Boy, to become a 'yuppie' – mobile, Filofax and all – in the final regular series episode of 1989 was a fitting depiction of how the decade had evolved (and the programme with it from its first episode onwards), reflecting the changes in British life. Four days after its first appearance that September, ITV introduced an adaptation of Evelyn Waugh's *Brideshead Revisited*. If *Only Fools* gave a humorous take on modern Britain, this was more of the nostalgia for the happy days of a bygone era that had brought us *Chariots of Fire* earlier in the year. It was, says Andrew Marr, 'an era of nostalgic escapism'. Back in the difficult days of the mid-70s this penchant for looking back could be seen in the success of comedies such as *Dad's Army* and *Whatever Happened to The Likely Lads?* Now, once again the timing was serendipitous as the first shoots of a recovery of national pride were showing. *Brideshead* was more earnest than its comedy partner but filled a need in much the same way – something proven in the huge success of both productions. It gave us a taste of a utopian and rather mythical past; *Only Fools* gave us real life. More than that, in 1981, just as the sun was coming out, it gave the nation a damn good laugh. The relationship between the cultural and the political was to be proven again when the Conservatives adopted Vangelis's *Chariots* theme tune for their 1982 fundraisers, opportunistically linking their own party to a patriotic story of British success.

There was a lot less laughter abroad in the country the night after David Jason had first put a smile on our faces. This was where, in the absence of more cricket and more Botham, sport re-entered the narrative of the year in a manner in complete accordance with all the other mood-influencing contradictory happenings of 1981. The England football team had continued to offer frustration and humiliation all year. Needing a win against the footballing minnow that was Norway at the time, Ron Greenwood's squad travelled to Oslo with the country in full expectation of the comfortable win which would all but confirm their return to a World Cup finals tournament for the first time since the first year of the 70s – a long-term absence which was galling enough for a country which considered itself to be the founder of the game and with every right to contend for its global honours rather than just attend. They were beaten 2-1, sending the Scandinavians into paroxysms of delight and giving the home commentator the opportunity to further acknowledge Thatcher's profile on the world stage by name-checking her along alongside the likes of Beaverbrook, Nelson and Churchill in a joyous final whistle farewell to the vanquished England side and its country which became a much-repeated classic. The highs of the summer's cricket were in danger of disappearing from memory in the footballers' latest cold dose of reality and the further demonstration of the fickleness of sport and the dangers for an Englishman in letting it dictate his or her happiness. Fortunately, that oscillation continued and on the night of 18 November England would crawl to a nervy home victory over Hungary which, as a result of very fortuitous and unexpected results elsewhere, took the country to those finals for the first time in a dozen years. In doing so they gave people another reason to start looking at 1982 with positive anticipation rather than dread.

In that British holy trinity of entertainment, sport and royalty, the latter also stepped up to the plate once more. On 6 November the year's most successful purveyors of true pop, Adam and the Ants, released an album containing two number one singles. It was titled *Prince Charming*. The next day a prince and his new wife charmed the country again with more signs of fresh beginnings. The Palace announced that Princess Diana was expecting her first child and (on birth as a boy) second in line to the throne. The British pored over this news with the happy fascination which only they can muster. And yet the storms were not finished. The 1981 weather had its say again, with 105 tornadoes hitting the country at the end of November. By mid-December heavy snowstorms signalled the start of one of the coldest, most snow-bound winters of the century. As Trevor Harley's work indicates, a 'proper' winter can be just as much of a mood-enhancer as a warm summer and this one was as proper as it gets. Certainly the mood of the country's children was a happy one as days at school were replaced with days sledging down hills and throwing snowballs – no working from home in the 80s. In time, as the weather refused to relent well into February, it would become less of a joy for many, stranded in homes without food or electricity but at the end of 1981 as the festive period approached such a winter wonderland was the perfect tableau.

Whilst Britain battled the cold, England's cricketers were trying to cope with the opposite end of the thermometer and their own storm as their tour to India brought them a taste of reality. After the heady days of the summer, the come down for players and followers alike could not have been more pronounced. Botham's rediscovered ability to do nothing wrong remained in the first Test with nine wickets in searing heat and top score in England's second innings but a defeat by 138 runs had predictable consequences. If there was a place you didn't want to lose the first Test of a series in 1981 it was India. The next four Tests would be excruciatingly tedious slow-scoring draws as the home side protected their lead with little apparent intention of providing any entertainment. The first Test itself was hardly sparkling, with its total of 674 runs taking four days to make. England managed 166 from 100 overs in their first innings. It was a contrasting way to end a memorable year. The storm however, landed four days before the Test when it was announced that 12 England players had signed up to play in South Africa in a series of unofficial 'Tests'. The feelgood factor in the English game had not lasted long and here was another potentially game-threatening divorce to rival Packer. It would not be a happy experience for those who went, and it would deprive the England side and its supporters of the services of several players who undoubtedly would have strengthened the side over the next three years.

Moreover, the announcement early in the tour and the transparency that the side's opening batsman Geoffrey Boycott had been the chief confidant of and recruitment officer for the tour organiser Ali Bacher and the South Africans, inevitability drove a wedge into the tour party from which morale never recovered. Of course Thatcher's government were required to have a view. Whilst her own Sports Minister, Neil MacFarlane, called the manner of its conception a 'deception', he frowned upon it rather than openly castigating the players or entering a debate about its moral rectitude. His prime minister also refused to do so, well aware that as a leader who had maintained links and business ties with the republic she could scarcely now condemn such an enterprise, contenting herself with a line about how the citizens of a free country are at liberty to choose where they travel and that such a liberty was something she held dear and would uphold. Consistent and a potentially defendable argument it might have been, but it was a position which didn't endear her to the majority of the cricket-following public, or indeed, as with the Moscow Olympics the year before, the country at large. The whiff of expediency still circled around her. What Ian Botham's take on the matter was has been the subject of much claim and counter-claim. His professed reason for turning down the tour in the media – that he would not be able to look his mates Viv Richards and Joel Garner in the eye ever again – was scoffed at by Boycott. It is clear there was some discussion in the Botham camp about the pros and cons of joining the tour, however serious or fleeting, and that is hardly surprising. Although Botham's disgust at apartheid was both vehement and genuine and always would be, the assessment of his then agent Reg Hayter that the likely interruption of his England career and the publicity that would go with it would harm both his reputation and his earning potential in such a way as to make the financial upside to the trip less attractive, is likely to have played the decisive role. Much the same would be true when another offer came his way in 1989, which Botham himself admitted was very seriously considered.

One of what became known immediately as 'the dirty dozen' was the former England batsman, Dennis Amiss. He was one who's international career was long over and therefore his own decision may have been more straightforward – financially if not morally – but his words in advance of the tour showed as much naivety as anyone's. 'We don't want to get involved in the political situation, and we don't agree with apartheid. But it's a lovely country in which to come and play cricket. When we get back home I suppose there will be repercussions, but we just hope it will die down, and people will see it as we do.' As with the previous year's Olympics, the debate about whether sport and politics should be kept apart was academic. Here was another example that no such world exists, however much many of its participants and followers might wish that it does.

Even now, the year like no other was not quite done. 1981 departed with a few final shots – the sobering, the portentous and the hopeful. On 8 December Arthur Scargill was elected as the president of the National Union of Mineworkers. Never mind the decisions of Alec Bedser and his cricketing kingmakers, this was one of the most significant selection decisions made during the year and one which was to have even more fateful repercussions than those Amiss had feared. Thatcher would again bide her time. The following January the miners were offered, and accepted, a 9.3 per cent pay rise – something not always remembered in the light of what followed. But Scargill's motivations would be proven to extend further than improving the lot of his members – his was a political battle in which he saw himself as the man who could make or break the governments of the country. As with many who took on Botham in the belief they could best him, for such an end goal he had picked the wrong foe.

The sporting year, meanwhile, finished in a strange mixture of relief and sadness. Three days after Scargill took the stage to take his fight to another level, the century's greatest sporting icon was taking his leave. The defeat of Muhammad Ali by the journeyman Trevor Berbick was a depressingly predictable one. The supposed 'Drama in Bahama' was nothing of the sort as a shambling version of the beautiful athlete of the previous two decades suffered a final humiliation. The fears of many that the retirement had come five years too late were to be tragically borne out. A light had gone out in the sporting world as one of its most transformational years drew to a close. The author of a biography of Ali, David Remnick, felt he had been the pinnacle of boxing, probably of sport, and that era was now at its end. One of Ali's first opponents, Floyd Patterson, understood his rival's significance to sport and to the world. 'With Ali, I came to see that *I* was a fighter, but that *he* was history.' Remnick also mentions something in the delayed retirement which would afflict both Thatcher and Botham before their stories were done. Those who are blessed with such utter conviction in themselves and the role they can play find it hard to accept their own decline and recognise when their moment is past. If the icon's departure was sobering enough for some, the following day's news brought something even more grievous and life-changing. On Saturday 12 December 1981 for the first time in the United Kingdom a diagnosis of a case of AIDS was made.

Amidst the sombre came the hope. Thatcher may have been six months from her vaunted moment of triumph in the Falklands but at the end of 1981 the figures told the story that the change had already begun. A couple of weeks after Ian Botham was presented with his award as the BBC Sports Personality of the Year and as the festive lights went up on trees around the country, most would be paying greater attention to Harry Carpenter, Slade and Morecambe and Wise than to economics, but the numbers were announced nevertheless. Britain's inflation figure was its lowest level since 1973 and across the whole year of 1981 the nation's economy had moved from 4 per cent contraction to 0.8 per cent growth. At last, the uplift in mood was justified not simply by the happy days of Christmas.

Reaction to Thatcher and Howe's next budget in three months' time would be favourable and, in the view of Charles Moore, 'the sting of the controversy which had been so poisonous in 1981 had been drawn … a recovery with Mrs Thatcher in charge had begun *before* the news from the South Atlantic which was to convulse British politics'. In December 1981, at the same time as Britain was being advised by the press that Thatcher was the most unpopular prime minister in history, a coup in Argentina saw the coming to power of General Leopoldo Galtieri and in the words of Andy McSmith 'a year of significant changes closed with one which would ensure the events of the year would indeed have a lasting impact'.

1981 and Ian Botham were a mutually beneficial and unforgettable partnership. The man himself knew it, acknowledging 'the summer of 1981 had changed my life forever'. Such was the explosion of his global profile that he would soon become the first cricketer ever to adorn the front cover of *Sports Illustrated* in the United States. Even across the water it was a sign that Britain might have turned a corner. Something had indeed changed, and the memory didn't fade.

To turn to Frank Keating for a final time: '1981 ensured Ian Botham everlasting greatness for the sporting pantheon, just as Botham himself ensured 1981's greatness for history's.'

PART FIVE:

'The After'
RIDING THE WAVE

1982–1990

'If you throw your heart into a story, you are going to feel a reaction when it is all over.'

Simon Barnes
The Meaning of Sport

TWO THINGS may be said of the years that followed. Firstly, that some of them were almost as tumultuous and were littered with seminal moments for the two lead actors but that this does not diminish the importance of 1981, rather it reinforces it because without it there is every chance things would have happened very differently as the 80s navigated their fascinating path. Secondly, that path continued to be travelled by Ian Botham in the same implausible parallel with Margaret Thatcher and the country she was leading, right to the very end. A brief exploration of this time therefore offers context and should embellish the tale instead of confusing it. 1981 may have been done but its two prime movers were not. Over the next ten years, shaped by the 12 months just gone, they would share a rollercoaster of a decade which reprised how they had just lived their pivotal year, travelling from the heroic, through tribulations and comebacks to their stories' ends.

Their respective positions were assured, unchallenged, their control soon to be absolute. Simon Barnes, not altogether approvingly, saw the England team evolving into one 'based around an inner ring with Botham at its heart'. Thatcher's cabinet, shorn of the old school in favour of a new breed of believers at the end of '81, became very much the same thing – even more so after the landslide victory in the 1983 election. For a time they were at their peaks and they would realise that ambition of restoring national pride, she as Boadicea, he as Sir Galahad.

Heroes

'By 1982, Botham was having the time of his life ... not just as a cricketer – he was famous because he brightened up a drab world.'

Pat Murphy
Botham: A Biography

ON 4 January 1982 another small cultural change touched the nation – or at least those within it with a strange affection for such things. The actor Tom Baker had begun his reign as the longest-serving and most recognisable Dr Who on television at the same time in 1974 as Botham was announcing his own arrival at Taunton. He had become a part of the early Saturday evening furniture for a generation, which I know because I was part of it. But he too picked 1981 as his year of change and on this day he regenerated into Peter Davison as only the Doctor can do. The cultural regeneration wasn't restricted to the TV. The down-at-heel industrial city of Manchester began to hint at a different future after Moss Side and by the time Thatcher departed it had become the heartland of a revival in British musical culture as in the guise of 'Madchester.' That also had its roots in 1982 with the opening of a club called the Haçienda.

In fact, as 1981 slipped into 1982 Ian Botham found himself similarly regenerated – without the Doctor's change of attire but sporting at least a new look, now minus the beard and with the first signs of the mullet which was to become one of the abiding sporting images of the decade. He entered 1982 as the Sports Personality of the Year, the most famous and fêted sportsman in Britain and one of its most recognisable faces full stop. This was to be a launch pad for a year in which he played the role of hero and deliverer of sterling deeds to a tee. The summer would be by some distance his finest calendar year with the bat as he morphed into what he had always had the ability to be – a world-class batsman in his own right, now batting at number five in the order. In the first half of the summer he took India – always a favourite opponent – for successive scores of 67, 128 and a blistering 208 – an innings that Wally Hammond, Garry Sobers or anybody else might have struggled to play. Although things were a little tougher against Pakistan and then at the start of the Ashes tour that winter, across the summer he averaged 62.9. This was a man in his prime. The bowling average may not have matched that of his first three years but he still garnished this sumptuous batting with 27 wickets. And, of course, he rounded off the year on its penultimate day with a moment of pure Botham to win another Ashes Test.

Whilst Botham gave notice of what was to become a year of almost continuous success with a big hundred in India, Margaret Thatcher's year of ultimate victory began more unstably. January was a month of reality checks as first the miners were granted their pay increase and then she had to contend with the announcement that unemployment had reached that once unimaginable figure of three million. The good times were not yet rolling and 'the most unpopular prime minister in history' was to retain her title for a while longer. If January was sobering, March was truly shocking. On the 18th an Argentinian flag had been hoisted on the South Georgia – a faraway land of which we knew nothing – and all hell brook loose at Westminster. Thatcher's decision to push forward with the March 1981 budget had been the most critical of her career and an act of bravery in the face of much dissension and doubt. Now she was faced with another. Should she follow the advice of her Defence Secretary John Nott that once lost, the Falkland Islands territory could not be retaken, or the insistence of the Chief of the Naval Staff, Henry Leach, that not only *could* they be retaken, but they *must* be. It would be a fallacy to suggest Thatcher was never in any doubt and much like the budget almost exactly a year before she knew the implications should a bold decision end in failure. But strength, conviction and a true patriotism which induced a horror that a British sovereign state could be taken by force, won the day. As we know, on 29 March, as *Chariots of Fire* took its Best Picture Oscar, it's writer Colin Welland announced with confidence – possibly over-confidence – and a patriotic pride, 'The British are coming!' And so they were, even if it was hard to consider Port Stanley and the Hollywood Hills as part of the same planet. On 2 April 1982 Britain was at war.

What followed is well-documented history. In our story its relevance is that it was Thatcher's second essential victory – her Edgbaston – following the budget, and it elevated her to the same level of national heroism and symbolic patriotism as Botham. The four weeks from 14 June to 10 July 1982 would provide the zenith of the restoration of national pride. 'The Empire Strikes Back' announced the *New York Times* on its front page. On the 14th, victory in the Falklands was confirmed, Botham celebrating it with his own victory in the first Test of the summer the following day. By the next afternoon, the good news was reaching such dizzying heights that even the England football team joined in. Playing their first World Cup finals match since the first year of the previous decade, they scored the fastest goal in the competition's history on the way to beating a hugely talented French team 3-1. Could this hot early summer get any happier? Yes. Five days on, the heir to the nation's throne was born, the newspaper front pages and television news awash with more images of a country back in the pink. Thatcher was back in the pink herself when two days later a MORI poll gave the Conservatives a 51 per cent public approval rating. Over the next two days Botham, royalist and true blue supporter, topped it all off with his 128 in the second Test. More celebration was to follow at the start of July as both he and his prime minister reached their apotheosis and the country its high point of national rejoicing. Thatcher made her speech at Cheltenham which nailed the Boadicea image for all time. It was Elizabeth I at Tilbury Docks revisited. If this could be considered a 'personal best' Botham followed in the same week with his highest Test score, and for sheer quality perhaps his finest and most assured innings ever. Finally, the morning after Botham was raising his bat for his double hundred at the Oval, the Canberra arrived in Southampton, bringing home troops amidst huge crowds, to loved ones who might never have seen them again, in scenes awash with Union Jacks, brass bands and genuine and understandable emotion. If rightly tinged with sadness that 255 of those troops were not returning, the moment lives in the memory as one of the most indelible of the decade and the Thatcherite age. The process that had begun in the second half of 1981 had reached its summit.

If the rest of 1982 was a less dramatic canvas it was a chance to bask in the renaissance. Once again the weather joined the party, proving again its ability to reflect, influence and enhance mood by offering the revellers a summer of sun. As in 1981 the cultural played its part too in the UK charts. On the day the Canberra returned, the song at number one was the whimsical and optimistic cover by Captain Sensible of 'Happy Talk'. The song came from the musical *South Pacific.* It had the wrong ocean, but other than that it couldn't have been a more perfect soundtrack to a nation in party mode.

Cricket followers were aware that on 12 November the Ashes battle would be rejoined in Australia. Anticipation was at an all-time high after the previous summer's events, not least in Australia where there was an almost pathological need to expunge the humiliation. They duly did so in a series which brough England's supporters back to their more recognised state of anti-climax. Botham himself didn't bestride the winter in the way that had been hoped, or replicate Headingley et al – how could he? With his back now restricting him significantly and his attitude to physical preparation no different than it had been as a 20-year-old, the whispers were of a man carrying too much weight – this time more physically than psychologically. In an unforgiving Australian press looking for revenge they were trumpets, not whispers and, with the subtlety of humour for which Aussie cricket spectators are renowned, the ultimate comment on the matter came at the second Test in Brisbane when a young pig inscribed with the name 'Botham' was released onto the outfield. But Botham, as ever, would have the last laugh and round off his year in inimitable fashion. Already 2-0 down in the series and needing to win to prevent Australia regaining the Ashes, England had given a better account of themselves at Melbourne in the fourth Test. The Melbourne Boxing Day Test is a matter of national significance in that country and the cavernous ground was packed every day with nigh on 100,000 people. This was Botham's sort of stage after a quiet series. Chasing 292 for victory, when Australia's ninth wicket fell at 218 the game was won. Only it wasn't. It is one of the greater and more consistent frustrations of my life that England have had, it seems for my entire cricket-watching existence, a habit of being unable to dismiss bowlers who can barely bat with the same alacrity as they can the rest of the batsmen, especially when it is critical to do so. As a last-wicket partnership of 70 grew, we could see the horror of the Ashes disappearing in almost as fantastical a way as in the Tests of 1981. With three runs required, what do you do? When all hope is gone, chuck the ball to Botham. His innocuous 1-80 to this point was not likely to strike fear into the set batsmen. Except that this was Ian Botham. His good mate Jeff Thomson managed to reach a wide half-volley and nick it to the slips where it was juggled before being taken. In one ball, after 258 of virtually no effect in the match, Botham had written another chapter in his Ashes story and punched Australia in the collective stomach one more time.

1983 was to be a less stellar year although the summer, bar a disappointing World Cup performance, and the early winter were not without their high points with centuries at home and away against New Zealand. In the first week of January, Australia regained the Ashes and it was back to the *Botham's Ashes* VHS for comfort. The year was all about another victory. On 9 June Thatcher led the Conservatives to an election landslide, winning a 144-seat majority in the most decisive result since 1945. Just two years previously such a thing would have been considered preposterous and for some of her own party, including those 'wets' convinced that 1981 would see her off, it was a seismic shock. They had lost, pure and simple. In fact 1981, the budget, the move out of recession and the uplift in national belief – later supplemented by the Falklands, had been the architect of the victory, not of her demise. Where did the 1983 election win really come from? Andrew Marr suggests that the Falklands was 'a popular war. For millions it was a wholly unexpected and almost mythical symbol of national rebirth'. True, but it was really the full stop confirmation of a rebirth which had already begun. The point about the Falklands victory and its role in the coming election was that, in Marr's view, it gave her a strong story to tell about herself and the country that was simple, vivid and made sense to millions. It was certainly an easier, more transparent tale to tell than that of economic recovery and it mattered not only in terms of a reflected glory in victory but in creating an aura and now suggesting that what she had been saying all along about a brighter future might be more plausible – this woman had something about her after all and her claims to the successes of the second half of 1981 were now more likely to be accepted. So success in the South Atlantic may have been a more obvious indicator of revival than the underlying turnaround of '81 but that didn't mean the latter wasn't actually more instrumental – the only difference being that more people believed her now than they did before. What the Falklands did was seal her reputation, but it was far from the sole reason for the landslide vote which would give her the mandate to dictate the decade. The reality was that those two beasts of inflation and the unions had been tamed. Dominic Sandbrook wrote, 'By spring 1982 it was obvious that the unions' glory days belonged to history … and the worst thing was not that Mrs Thatcher was rude to them but that she barely acknowledged them at all.'

Trials, Triumphs and Tribulations

'Over the next couple of years, Ian Botham's press image was to veer from the near-canonisation of 1981 to an opprobrium stemming from a desire to cut him down to size. There was no discernible change in the public's attitude to Botham, other than a heightened expectation that he could work miracles as a matter of course.'

Pat Murphy
Botham: A Biography

1984 WAS to be when the post-81 honeymoon ended. It was a year of trials and tribulations for both and at its heart was something which was to play a central role in both futures, particularly that of Botham, over the next eight years and beyond. The year started with the first overseas tour beset by allegations of wild misbehaviour, ran on through the start of Thatcher's career-defining miners' strike and the horrors of the IRA Brighton bomb and ended with Botham's arrest by Humberside police on drugs charges whilst the first England tour he had missed in seven years was going just swimmingly without him. It was to be only the start. The battle for supremacy in circulation between the country's tabloids was already established but in July 1984 a certain Robert Maxwell finally achieved his ambition of owning one of Britain's major national titles when he purchased Mirror

Group Newspapers and with it the *Daily Mirror*. Maxwell was not only intensely ambitious but gave the impression of being a megalomaniac who would stop at nothing to achieve pre-eminence. His win-at-all-costs approach was more crazed than the more laudable versions displayed by the two people who were about to be caught in his sights. *The Sun* had overtaken *The Mirror*'s circulation in 1978, with those positive consequences for Thatcher's election the following year. It was something Maxwell was determined to reverse. He was also driven to knock off his perch a rival with whom he became obsessed. Rupert Murdoch was the obstacle Maxwell would never surmount. Maxwell's arrival meant an escalation in the tabloid war of epic proportions and, alongside the bingo, battle commenced to find and print the most lurid and sensational stories. Often, stories were precisely what they were. As a national figure whose off-field life was never dull, Botham was a prime candidate to shift papers and win that war. The coming years would see Murdoch's paper, of which Botham was nominally an employee, cut him little slack regardless. Botham himself, and several of his team-mates, would hardly help themselves, railing against press intrusion and fabrications whilst taking their coin for ghosted columns. It was to be an increasingly unhappy marriage.

England's 1983-84 tour to New Zealand and Pakistan has gone down in infamy, supposedly as the 'sex, drugs and rock 'n' roll' trip – in New Zealand at least. In the summer the press had begun to see the value in 'Botham controversy' stories and had started to probe for them with press conference questions to the captain Willis about why he didn't believe Botham should be dropped. By the winter, things had ramped up another level. On the pitch it scarcely helped that England lost both their series (including the first series loss to New Zealand in their history). This included the ignominy of the Christchurch Test in which they began by bowling execrably on a difficult batting pitch and then managed to be dismissed for under 100 twice in a Test for the first time that century. When things run well it is harder for the tabloids to do their thing with any great public support; when they go this badly wrong, press and public alike are looking for reasons and scapegoats. At Christchurch the reasons the *Mail on Sunday* put forward included the team smoking marijuana in the dressing room during the game. It was decried by the whole touring party as nonsense but Botham's journey to trials and bans had been set in motion. 'Booze, birds and pot-smoking' became the media story of the tour. Fortunately for Botham – the principle quarry – his left knee gave in to the need for surgery early in the Pakistan leg and he was flown home, amidst rumours the knee had 'worsened' conveniently at a time when the England management were wondering if concluding the rest of the tour without him might be preferable. It was understandable if that conclusion was being drawn for the first time by some of his fellow players too. He still managed to depart by gifting his pursuers one more story. In a radio interview prior to flying home, he joked about Pakistan being 'the sort of place you would send your mother-in-law all expenses paid'. It was his equivalent of Thatcher's 'no such thing as society' line – taken out of context and deliberately misinterpreted, but it was a full toss for the newspapers nonetheless and caused understandable offence to a proud and sensitive nation which lingers to this day. It was also another example of how cricket could permeate the House of Commons as, ridiculously, questions were asked in parliament. Botham's last on field action of the winter came on 6 March with the end of the first Pakistan Test. At home that very same day, miners walked out at the Cortonwood colliery in Yorkshire and the most infamous strike in British history began, officially announced the following week. The thoroughly unhappy experience of the year ahead was presaged by the death of a picket at Ollerton on 14 March. Over the next 12 months the nation that had come together in 1981 was torn asunder and brought back to bitter division.

The hot summer ahead was another of concurrent battles for Thatcher and Botham, animated with scenes of Caribbean joy on England's cricket grounds and British vitriol and violence in its northern mining towns.

On 18 June England's Test series against the might of the West Indies began and they soon discovered, as would the NUM, that it was a fight they weren't going to win. As England were losing their confrontation in Birmingham, 90 miles away the bloodiest battle of the strike was underway. The 'Battle of Orgreave' was an attempt to blockade a coking plant near Rotherham and the images relayed on the national news that night were every bit as shocking as those from the inner cities three years before. Police horse charges, the wielding of batons, bricks and worse being thrown at the forces of law huddled behind riot shields, fist fights and bloodied faces showed a nation once more temporarily at war with itself. Thatcher had identified it as the moment she had waited for since her party had been brought to its knees in the early 70s and this time there would be no concessions. Steadfastly refusing to be held at the union's mercy, the government prevailed – on 18 June and thereafter. By September a drift back to work had begun and British industry and British society were never quite the same again.

The West Indies series was not the worst for Botham personally, containing as it did at Lord's his best bowling figures and highest-ever score against them. For England it was a different matter, the 5-0 'blackwash' completed on 14 August confirming the relative standings of the teams. Thatcher's own troubles were far from over too. If the unions were in the process of being conquered, another foe was more present than ever. In October at the Conservative Party conference in Brighton an IRA bomb ripped through the Grand Hotel, killing some and seriously injuring others of the Conservative leadership. It was another sliding doors moment for leader and country – Thatcher missed the deadly centre of the blast by a matter of feet and by the following morning was making one of her most defiant speeches ever in the conference hall. The image of a survivor and a leader of strength and conviction was never more apparent. Out of genuine tragedy she became Boadicea once again. Ten days later another tragedy hit the nation's screens as the BBC's Michael Buerk's chilling report from Ethiopia was played on the national news. It put the challenges at home into stark relief and was to instigate the decade's greatest story of direct action and charity – something which would be the narrative of the coming year for both Botham and his country. On 25 November Britain's foremost musical talents, cajoled by the fading pop star Bob Geldof, met in a London studio on a colder winter's morning to record the Band Aid single 'Do They Know It's Christmas?' and an era of celebrity and public philanthropy was underway. Three days later England began their tour of India without their talismanic all-rounder who had wisely decided it was time for a break. As England won a Test series in India against all odds, with many of the younger players coming to the party, inevitably the rumour mill suggested that this was due to the absence of the increasingly dominant, domineering presence of Botham – a narrative the opportunist tabloids were hardly likely to ignore. Though the captain, Gower, always refuted this, there may have been at least some truth to it – compared to the previous winter it was a supremely happy tour – and it gave an indication that Botham's was now a presence which could cower as well as inspire those around him. Thatcher's new young cabinet ministers may have recognised it. If anyone thought the lack of Botham on tour would be a miss for the tabloids and offer him a few months out of the spotlight the last day of 1984 would put an end to that. In the mysterious circumstances of the police turning up on the doorstep of Botham's home that afternoon for no apparent reason, a small amount of cannabis was found in a draw and with his subsequent arrest England's greatest cricketer would again become the country's highest-profile news story. He was to remain so for much of the year ahead – one in which the triumphs for both him and his prime minister would briefly lift the spirits.

Even by Botham's standards 1985 was a memorable year, one which according to Pat Murphy 'contained enough melodrama to satisfy the most demanding of film producers'. He began it under arrest and ended it as the most popular man in the country. Thatcher would not, perhaps, represent the female equivalent but it was a year of significant victory for her too. February had been a month in which both had to defend charges of guilt. Botham accepted his, though he was to be less sanguine about his ultimate punishment. Thatcher, not uncharacteristically, was not ready to admit to hers. Bob Geldof's utterly committed leadership of action to support those suffering in Africa had become the story of the previous two months and had put him in the same national treasure bracket as Botham. As such, when he and Thatcher found themselves in the same place at the same time, in front of the television cameras at the end of the month, public sympathies were always likely to be with him as they crossed swords. Frustrated at what he perceived to be a government response out of step with the strength of public feeling and struggling with an issue of payment of VAT on the funds the charity was raising, he wrongfooted Thatcher who for once didn't have the preparation behind her which she always liked in debate, and he completely argued her under the table. She was presumably empathetic to the plight of the Ethiopians but it sure as hell didn't come across that way. A sense of an unfeeling, dogmatic leader, so convinced that she could not be wrong that her response was more than slightly patronising, again began to take hold. It was to play a large part in her downfall six years hence. Thatcher could, however, happily forget that contest four days later as another reached an altogether more satisfactory conclusion for her. On 3 March the most acrimonious strike in history was called off and rightly reported as an unmitigated Thatcher victory. It was the third battle, after the 1981 budget and the war in the South Atlantic, that she could not have afforded to lose without being forced to leave the scene. If that budget was to prepare the ground for success in core objective number one – the defeat of inflation – then this was the moment which assured the achievement of objective number two – the taming of the unions. The strength of her position was never greater.

It was the taming of the Australians with which Botham was now more concerned and he embarked on a summer of such bravado that his Sir Galahad persona had also never been stronger. The summer of 1985 was to see Botham as the slayer not just of Australia but of bowling attacks everywhere as he broke the record for sixes hit in a single season, smiting them to all parts of the land in the manner of A.G. Macdonnell's blacksmith in *England, Their England*. It was a summer of England, Their England as David Gower's team regained the Ashes with a feast of run-scoring and Botham once again to the fore. For a man who scores 18 in a total of 595/5 declared to be the talk of the innings was Bothamesque in the extreme but was a perfect summation of the summer. Coming to the crease at 572/4 he set about his hijacking of the day, his first and third balls sailing back over the head of the astonished fast bowler, Craig McDermott and into the stands. A fortnight later he sat on the Oval balcony as his captain drenched his locks in what Frank Keating called a 'showdown with a champagne shampoo'. All was right with the world once more and the king was back in his castle.

It wasn't, however, just the role he played in the return of the Ashes which captured the public imagination unlike anything since 1981. He spent the summer engaging the nation as a Richard the Lionheart whose buckle had never had more swash. There was the ill-advised but relatively harmless dalliance with the fake impresario Tim Hudson who promised to make him anything from a Hollywood 'player' to the next James Bond and dressed him in blazers and Panama hats of such colour that his appearance could never be missed. Add in the new bleached mullet and the Rastafarian-coloured wristbands showing his solidarity with his mate Viv, and you have the picture of that summer. So iconic was the tale, so dominant the public image that Keating wrote an entire book on the man and his exploits titled *High, Wide and Handsome – The Story of a Very Special Year.* It was – and it didn't finish with the cricket.

For all the opprobrium of the establishment, the pompous outrage of some of the middle classes and the efforts of the tabloids, Botham remained a man in harmony with and understood by the majority of his public. Many of us like our sportspeople to come with character rather than the deadpan plainness of the post-match platitudes. The disgraces some would like to attach to him were seen by many as nothing of the sort – merely further evidence that here was a man who took life by the throat and lived it in a way we would all love to if only we could. For most, that engendered affection rather than jealousy; for the others … well, that's their problem. But even the latter could not obfuscate the genuinely caring human being who was to show in public for the first time the side of him only friends really knew. The experience of visiting a children's hospital in 1977 and being introduced to a disease called leukaemia made an indelible mark on Botham which has never left him. As he set off on his charity walk the length of Britain at the end of October, appearing on the national news every night as his progress was reported, he began a life of fundraising for his foundation which showed him in an entirely new light. Amidst all the newspaper sensationalism, the stories they loved to report and sometimes embellish, of beauty queens, pot-smoking and fisticuffs, here was a better representation of a man who was determined to enjoy the fruits of his success to the full, but never forgot that he was privileged to be able to do so and that he was luckier than most. Where others talked of giving something back, Botham, completely in character and in much the same way as Geldof the previous winter, got on and did it. It is a part of his story that quite rightly polishes his legacy. By the time he was dipping his feet into the sea at Land's End he was indeed, along with Geldof perhaps, the most popular man in the nation.

Botham's efforts that autumn were an indication that, despite their images as self-improvers and the champions of the individual there was another side to both. Thatcher would conflate the two when referencing the tale of *The Good Samaritan* in defence of policies which sought to encourage individual wealth as well as responsibility and achievement. The point, she said, was that the Samaritan had to have the money to help the poor in the first place. Thatcher recalled the Victorian era as the heyday of free enterprise in Britain but also one which saw the rise of selflessness and benefaction, suggesting this was an important element within of her set of values. The decade's most famous Samaritan Bob Geldof might have struggled to see this whilst involved in his verbal joust with her, and by what appeared to be a rather too ambivalent reaction to one of the decade's most worthy and inspirational days – that of the Geldof-inspired Live Aid concert in the summer of 1985. In another year of coming together, as Botham's triumphant summer played out, on the third day of a Nottingham Test being played in glorious sunshine, that other national (in fact global) shared experience was giving expression to the feelgood factor. The impact of Live Aid on the story of the 80s is well known. Suffice to say it was one of the ultimate illustrations of wider culture on the spirits of the nation and the sense of many who were inspired by it that their prime minister was absent from it in mind as well as body enhanced a somewhat uncaring image. It would be wrong however to consider her Victorian reference as an act. She remained religious all her life after her Methodist upbringing and the values her father and church instilled in her did give her a more empathetic side than might sometimes be visible. Unemployment figures were the stuff of reality but the idea that she didn't care about people's suffering is hard to justify. It wasn't always in the public things that true compassion would be displayed. Her ongoing insistence on writing personal letters of condolence to every family who suffered a loss at the hands of the IRA wasn't something that was trumpeted but was evidence of someone whom the horrors of that conflict hit hard and the wish to offer personal comfort was heartfelt.

If 1985 had been the year of coming together, 1986 would be one of falling apart again as each lived through media storms, bans and resignations, nearly disappeared and finally survived to enable one more victory. England's summer exploits raised genuine hope that on their spring trip to the West Indies they could be truly competitive for the first time in a dozen years. Oh dear. The thrashings on the pitch were accompanied by such media castigation of Botham that his bonhomie finally deserted him. The stories ranged from 'revelations' from a former model of bed-breaking adulterous sex romps with Botham – who happened to be in the company of his father-in-law elsewhere at the time – to more allegations of partying and drug-taking as the ship went down. His form on the pitch improved neither his own humour nor his relationships with the tabloids who had now despatched news, or rather 'investigative' reporters in addition to their cricket correspondents to hide behind hotel pot plants. It was to rival the Caribbean in 1981 as the worst tour of his career. The atmosphere of suspicion had Botham confining himself to his hotel room and presenting a negativity on and off the pitch unknown even in the dark days at the end of his captaincy. This time, team-mates really did wonder about whether his continued presence was more of a hindrance, his vice-captain Gatting finally exploding at him for his dressing room assertions in front of the rest of the squad that the pitches and the fast bowling were completely unplayable. If the team's most talented player was voicing that, what were the rest supposed to think? The whole tour had miserably affected his marriage, his form and his mindset. It was a spring which had undermined him in so many ways and the sense from his own dressing room was that Botham had shunned the collective responsibility of the squad to defend his own personal position. That position even within the team itself was now distinctly precarious.

The same accusation was about to be thrown at Thatcher as she was similarly undermined by the first real internal threat to her leadership. The Westland affair was a convoluted matter in which the main characters portrayed their roles as those of ministers seeking to do the best for Britain in an argument over whether a European or US rescue package was the better solution to the travails of the country's last helicopter manufacturing business. What it actually became was a tale of internecine conflict with all parties leaking against each other and being proven to have been economical with the truth. At its heart sat the ambitious Secretary of Defence, Michael Heseltine, who saw Thatcher's increasingly dictatorial style as something he could turn upon itself to improve his chances of succeeding her sooner rather than later. His ostentatious resignation was explained, he said, by the prime minister's refusal to live by the important principle of cabinet collective responsibility and her increasing belief in her right to dictate government decisions as she saw fit. If, much like when the Soviets handed her the moniker of the Iron Lady, this portrayed her once again as a leader of strength, she was not going to argue. Nevertheless, Thatcher saw the dangers in the fact she now had a talented, ambitious man outside the cabinet as an enemy not a friend. When she lost another cabinet minister to a resignation before the end of the affair amidst accusations of cover-ups and misleading the house, her position, like Botham's, was more precarious than it had been since 1981. Botham came home and Thatcher survived, but more importantly for the long term, reputations had been damaged and in Thatcher's case, having supported the American interests throughout Westland, it made her look significantly anti-European for the first time. Whilst she had no issue with that, others did, and it was to come back to bite her.

If Botham hoped the upcoming summer would give him the chance, against less formidable opposition, to rebuild his own reputation he was shortly to be disabused. After having to discontinue his legal battle with the *Mail on Sunday* regarding their drugs story, he had been forced into an admission that in his youth he had indeed occasionally smoked marijuana. That hardly made him unique as a young man, but it did make him front page news once again. Now, having accepted that his drug admission had not proven he had broken any of its own rules, but hounded by the press and establishment to make an example of him, on 29 May the TCCB promptly banned him for two months. It was, suggests Pat Murphy, a perfect illustration of the confused morality of the age, which seemed to sanction yuppies snorting cocaine overtly whilst pillorying sports people – particularly such an established easy target as Botham – for admitting smoking a joint or two in his youth. As such, once again the public were more forgiving of their player than of the press hypocrisy. Many felt the TCCB ban was more about Botham 'needing his wings clipped', which is probably precisely what Heseltine had aimed to do with Thatcher. Botham was responsible to those above him, Thatcher only to the electorate. If Botham's fate had ultimately been decided by public opinion as hers was to be the following year, he would never have been taken away from us in the first place that summer. Why, through the ups and downs, did he remain so important to and cherished by the majority of that public? Why did he continue to impact their view of their own country? Because he was, at heart, one of them and portrayed an ideal which still mattered. Imran Yusuf alluded to as much. 'Though he played with incredible skill, Botham was a link to cricket's amateur side, as if he took the ethos and hurly burly of English village cricket and applied it to superstardom.'

The Last Hurrah

BOTHAM MAY have been distinctly angry at what he felt was an injustice reeking of double standards, but he then discovered over the following two months that life without cricket and its attendant scrutiny was really rather pleasant. For the first time, he seriously considered packing it all in. Perhaps he should have done, although that would have cost him and us the final two moments of mood-enhancing success which should certainly have been his sign off. Although the press were stoking the debate about whether the dressing room really wanted him back (Gower and Gatting insist it did) for the public, a side and a summer without Botham had been a diminished one – they wanted their spirits lifting again. It was not as if the team had blossomed in his absence. Drab summer weather accompanied home defeats to India and, for the first time ever in England, New Zealand. So when the final Test at The Oval arrived and Botham was back there was a sense of anticipation which had been sadly lacking – a further confirmation that, collective responsibility or not, for many, Botham *was* England.

And why? Because only he could produce the script which now unfolded. His first ball back was a widish half-volley which an apparently transfixed Bruce Edgar nicked to the slips. In his next over Jeff Crowe's lbw made Botham the highest wicket-taker in Test history. As the rain-affected game ground to a draw he embellished it with 59 from 36 balls and the matching of another record – that of the most runs, 24, off a six-ball over in history. As cameo comebacks and demonstrations of what people had been missing go, he had hit his cue in inimitable fashion. He was surely ready for one more crack at the Aussies.

The 27th of October was a day which would come to be seen as one of the emblems of the Thatcherite 80s and another on which something changed. Thatcher was not a huge fan of the Stock Exchange – her Methodist upbringing left her considering it little more than a form of gambling. However, free markets and deregulation were things of which she was more enamoured and, after much planning, this was the day of the 'Big Bang' of deregulation of the Exchange which instantly transported the City of London into the very top tier of international financial market hubs. It was the rubber stamp on the transformation from manufacturing to financial services and a legacy with which Thatcher would forever be associated. There was another big bang coming three weeks later. On 15 November Botham began his last Ashes tour with 138 in the first Test. It was as cavalier and destructive an innings as any before it and set the tone for a series England would dominate from there on. Many Australians were assuming their nemesis's best days were behind him and he was on something of a farewell journey and were mightily shocked to realise the sight of them in front of him had resuscitated the 1981 version. Although his bowling was now in the military medium category and over the next couple of Tests he produced nothing remarkable, Melbourne was once again to prove his type of theatre. England arrived there knowing victory would give them the series. On the first day he rolled back the clock to the days when just the mere sight of him with the ball in his hand turned Australian batsmen into tortured statues and applying no great skill other than his Ashes aura, he proceeded to take five wickets against them for the last time. England duly took home the urn and in an otherwise underwhelming series Botham had managed yet again to be the primary force in two more Ashes Tests. The Melbourne Test concluded three days before the end of the year. Events to come would suggest it really should have been the time to go.

In his rollercoaster year there was one more moment of significance – perhaps one more sign that the end of the year should have been the end of the story. Somerset's committee and their captain had, after weighing the pros and cons, decided to terminate the contracts of Botham's closest friend Viv Richards and valued mate Joel Garner to replace them the following year with the younger New Zealander Martin Crowe. Looking at the detail again it was an understandable decision on purely playing terms, but was handled spectacularly badly by those who made it. It was never going to find favour with Botham who was incensed and immediately gave it the 'if they go, I go' response. His wish was not to leave his county home and his assumption was that his threat that a third star player might leave if the decision was not reversed would win the day. Here was one more connection with the place in which Thatcher found herself at the time. Some team-mates would later say that he had begun to act differently around them – the man who would previously put an arm around the shoulder of the young players was now scaring them half to death with his demeanour and his outbursts. Some felt he had become bigger than the club itself and expected it to dance to his tune. In this he was losing sympathy and affection which would cost him dear. Even his closest friend at the club other than Richards, the more homely and universally popular Trevor Gard, suggested that his mate's miscalculation was in believing he was more popular around the club, even amongst the members and fans, than he actually was by now. Subsequently Botham would lose his battle at a membership vote, the Richards and Garner decisions were ratified by a significant majority and Botham's days at Somerset were over. At the meeting which decided the outcome it was believed those who arrived undecided were swayed by one damning testimony in particular. Nigel Popplewell had been a relatively quiet but intelligent young player on the staff who had grown increasingly disaffected with his chances at the club and recently left to pursue another career. He had always been a Botham man and had no axe to grind but his contribution to the meeting articulated a growing view. The former colleague said he felt that Botham and his close coterie had become self-indulgent and contributed to a deteriorating atmosphere. He saw team-mates being treated with little respect and felt a release in his absence when Botham and the two West Indians were away at the 1983 World Cup. As captain, he felt Botham struggled to get it right with the younger players. After her landslide victory in the election of the following summer, similar things would start to be whispered about Thatcher. Growing bigger than the club; an expectation that their view ought to prevail; an over-estimation of their current popularity within their own circles and an increasing antagonism to a perceived morphing into characters rather too satisfied with their own importance. If it was to do for Botham at Somerset it was, after a last hurrah to match Botham's in Australia, to do for Thatcher as well as the curtain gradually came down.

That last hurrah arrived on 11 June 1987. In recalling Botham's own campaigning in advance of the recent Somerset vote, Pat Murphy drew the political parallel one more time, describing him as 'like a political leader at election time'. Botham's issue was that he wasn't to prove as adept at winning elections as his valued PM. She would now win her third, by another landslide and this time more against the tide of expectation, as if to mirror Botham's unanticipated success in Australia. It was a stunning achievement and confirmed the whole decade would be hers. As with Botham at the start of the year, this was her time to take stock and leave at her peak, knowing that, with inflation at four per cent, the trades unions under control, Britain's global standing reborn and a more positive mindset at home, she had achieved her major objectives. To have mentored a favoured successor and left the scene before the year was out would have saved much heartache.

Treachery With a Smile on its Face

THE ENDS were to come with the same strange synergy which had featured throughout their stories and perhaps three years too late. 1987 might have been the perfect time for both to have taken their leave, when the force was still with them but the first signs were there that it wouldn't always be so. Those characteristics of the most driven self-believers, the insistence they can still make a difference that nobody else can and an inability or unwillingness to accept any evidence which might make a case against this, was to see them exit the stage, not of their own volition but at the hands – in their view, the bloodied hands – of others. That neither was willing to accept that their powers and popularity might soon be waning, that they wouldn't ever have quite the same impact again, or that their country didn't still need them as the only people who knew how to save it, would make for long and bitter ends.

Botham's own Test career can be dissected into four different phases. The 'tyro' honeymoon period from his 1977 Test debut until his appointment as captain; the miserable 14 months and 12 Tests that followed; the superhero era from Headingley until the end of 1986 and his final victorious Ashes Test; and the decline into injury and relative ineffectiveness over the five years from 1987 to 1992. It was this last movement of the symphony, an unnecessarily drawn-out postscript, which his friends and supporters might wish largely to forget. Botham himself to this day doesn't believe in looking back but for those of us who can't help ourselves, to have departed the Test game, perhaps the game full stop, at the start of 1987 having made a significant mark on the Australians for the last time would have been the most deserved and comfortable walk into the sunset. The sight of a sporting and national hero of such stature battling the passage of time without being able to gild his legacy had shades of Muhammad Ali before him, though thankfully without the same tragic physical consequences. Fortunately and rightly, we can remember him as the colossus he was but it is in spite of, rather than partly because of, these last years of un-remarkability. The humdrum did not suit him or sit well with us. The sight before our eyes was proof enough for many but the figures tell the story in black and white [see Appendix 1]. From his 1981 Headingley rebirth to Melbourne five and a half years later he played 51 Tests, scoring 3,040 runs at an average of 41.6 with eight centuries and 15 half-centuries; he took 179 wickets, even if increasingly through the force of his irresistible personality and positivity rather than the classical skills he could employ before his back had its say, at 31.4 and at a rate of three and a half per Test. The accepted measure of the true all-rounder – a batting average in excess of the bowling – was significantly in the black. The next five years, riven with injuries and increasing selectorial ambivalence, produced just 21 Tests and 391 runs at 20.5, with a solitary fifty; his 17 wickets cost 57.5 each and were taken at just 1.2 per Test match. It was an unworthy diminution of an unforgettable career.

The perception of both in these last years was that the quality of self-belief was slipping at times into the dangers of self-delusion. The analysis of Thatcher's third term and her fall in Alwyn W. Turner's political history of the Thatcherite era is titled 'Under The God: 1987– 90'. There was indeed sometimes a sense that both had assumed an air of divine right. This would show itself in Thatcher's increasingly uncompromising management of her team, particularly it's younger members at a time of those accusations from some playing quarters of similar from Botham in his county dressing room. That unsuccessful attempt to win a power struggle against his Somerset committee and members in 1986 amidst allegations from team-mates of a failure to read the room and an over-estimation of his own popularity at Taunton had shades of Thatcher's belief in her own impregnability which would transfer into more entrenched, sometimes almost demonic, attacks on Europe in particular, totally at odds with and in defiance of her senior colleagues. Both miscalculations would end in their departures.

Simon Wilde saw at the close of Botham's career how the regime of the early 90s under Gooch and Micky Stewart did not fit with his own world view, suggesting he didn't bother with fitness to extend his career because he hadn't needed to in his pomp. In leaving Botham out of his tour to the West Indies in 1990 – a place on which Botham would consider rightfully his – Gooch was a good doppelganger for Thatcher's Geoffrey Howe as former loyal lieutenants who did much to support their leaders, turned executioners endowed with a common mixture of the lugubrious and the ruthless. The memorable portrayal of Howe's resignation speech later that same year by Alan Clark as being 'savaged by a dead sheep' might have rung true to Botham. If that's a little harsh on Gooch today, it was the perception of many at the time. If he genuinely wanted to extend his Test playing days then there was fault on Botham's side too. He wasn't going to win the argument this time and he had picked the wrong one in which to mistake strength for self-defeating intransigence. Thatcher would soon make the very same error of judgement and underestimation of its consequences over the European debate. Derek Pringle, once said of his team-mate, 'if it sounds deep, cricket, more than most sports, does lend itself to long periods of reflection and analysis. The other reason to hate Beefy is that he never seemed thus afflicted. Not for him the self-doubt that gnawed away at the rest of us. Even when evidence of his own fallibility sat in his lap he refused to acknowledge its presence. This late-career refusal to listen, even to those closest to them and with their best interests at heart, or to see a benefit in adapting their approach, were traits which had driven their successes but now became instrumental in their downfalls. In a book about change, an unwillingness to do so closes the story. Perhaps, going back to those words of Aldous Huxley that those who have sustained success often tend to be those who believe exclusively that they are right, it was a conscious decision to stay with 'their way' even if it meant goodbye – they had no desire to prolong successful careers on any other terms. Or perhaps there was too great a hubris. Either way, if the 80s were theirs, the 90s decided they could do without them. If Botham's lead to the next generation coming through might, in the eyes of Gooch and Stewart, make it harder for them to create a new culture, so the Conservative Party's most influential decision-makers also felt it was time for a new approach for a new decade.

At the start of the summer of 1987 Botham could point to his exploits in Australia as evidence he could still win Tests for England. However, those Tests were won in ever-less frequent bursts of rolling back the years at the sight of his favourite opposition. A more sober analysis would reveal the wider picture of a fading bowling force against a non-vintage Australian side. The Ashes might carry the greatest cache, but the true benchmark of lasting ability was how you fared against the strongest, as Botham was now to discover. The Pakistan tourists of '87 were an uncompromising bunch sprinkled with exquisite talent. They also had something of a chip on their shoulders and a desire to ram Botham's words about their country, which they saw as an insult rather than a joke, down his throat. It was a fractious series from which the mutual antagonism would stretch long into the future. The likes of Wasim Akram, Javed Miandad and Abdul Qadir on a mission proved too much for England, and Botham had to play second fiddle all summer to their captain Imran Khan in the ongoing rivalry between a glut of world-class all-rounders who dominated the decade. Botham's innate sense of competition made it important to him to sit at the top of that list and to be outshone by one of those players didn't appeal at all. In a dismally wet summer, in eight innings he managed just one half-century, 51 not out to save the last Test manfully in an uncharacteristic and selfless demonstration of skilled defence. It was not to prove his only submission to Imran – a more costly one was to follow in the High Court when the accusations of ball-tampering began to fly.

From here on, there was to be little which could be deemed positive and one more revival, as longed for by the public, never came to pass. Some of what was to hurt him was outside his control; some was not. In this he again had a mirror in Thatcher. Deciding, probably wisely, against a trip to Pakistan, he wintered instead in Australia having signed a contract with Queensland to spend his next three winters there. It seemed the perfect marriage – after all, many Australians grudgingly accepted him as Australian in character. Brisbane's sun, the mates and the wine should have given him the relaxation and chance to play with the joy and freedom he had been missing, but it was an ill-fated affair with Botham suffering the first sacking from a club in his career before the first year was done. Allegations of an over-exuberant lifestyle, boorish behaviour on an aeroplane, fallouts with his captain and with the local police saw him on his way home. Once more it was the establishment that had had enough and sent him packing rather the public or his team-mates, who were enjoying his company. This time even the media, although complicit in the sensationalising of the stories, were on his side and portrayed his dismissal as a heavy-handed overreaction. But it was becoming an increasingly familiar tale.

Back at home, Botham's move to his new county of Worcestershire continued to be a happy one domestically and at the start of 1988 his assumption was that his performances there would soon bring him back into the England fold. But now came the uncontrollable. The back which had meant bowling in pain for many years finally gave up on him and wiped out his season. Since 1984, when Elton John had appeared around the team on the New Zealand tour and Botham had been introduced to Eric Clapton for the first time, his enjoyment of friendships within the world of rock music had blossomed. As Clapton pointed out, that world was one Botham envied – answerable to nobody, the freedom to dress as you wanted, have the time to live your life as you wanted and a playground in which good-hearted misbehaviour was considered essential rather than 'bringing the game into disrepute'.

The sight of Botham at the New Road ground with Clapton, George Harrison and Jeff Lynne became a more familiar one than that of him in whites. They were genuine and lasting friendships – and should perhaps have been another indicaton to him that another world now awaited him outside the game. Clapton saw the attraction of a change of route as well as an admiration for the qualities he felt made Botham what he was: 'He envies my world because rock and roll has always been anti-establishment, which appeals to Beefy. He's a buccaneer, a risk-taker and that's why he's so charismatic – he's come through and beaten the system.' And that's why he was always held in greater affection by his public than by those who ran that system themselves and was therefore treated very differently by each. Nonetheless such high-life connections did little to assuage the feeling that Botham, now moving in very different circles, was getting bigger than, and (possibly unfairly) less committed to the game. It certainly didn't hamper his own self-confidence or change his life view and his disdain of establishment diktats.

This was a point of difference between Botham and Thatcher whilst they both clung on. Whilst the former had plenty of options for a full and fulfilling post-career existence, Thatcher was horrified by the gaping black hole that the loss of her role would create for her. Problems not of her own making were assailing her too, including the terrorist bombing of a packed commercial airliner over Scotland in 1988 and the Hillsborough tragedy of the following year. But also like Botham, she wasn't helping herself and was losing the support of those she felt owed her a great deal. The Poll Tax soon to be introduced was perhaps the ultimate example of her unwillingness to acknowledge danger and adapt, but ultimately the more lethal one was her increasing obsession with Europe and vocal antipathy to the Union's desire for a move to a more federal model. The old patriotic view of her country was brought to the fore as she shouted down such ideas in a way she believed should brook no argument. For both, the time was rapidly approaching when people had had enough.

Back in the saddle at Worcester for 1989 Botham was well aware that the Australians were back in town. After the acrimonious defeats home and away to Pakistan and another thrashing by the West Indians the following summer in Botham's absence, the rare lack of a tour in 1988/89 gave England the chance to trumpet that perennially illusory and unsuccessful concept of a 'new dawn'. The apparently more *laissez faire* combination of Ted Dexter and David Gower were installed and with victories in five of the last six Ashes series behind them there was a feeling at large, players and public alike, that this would be a summer of heroic domination to reprise that of 1985. It wasn't. The weather was gloomy and the Australian captain's new demeanour was gloomier. There was to be none of the bonhomie on and off the field beloved of Gower and Botham and England quite unexpectedly fell apart, going down to their heaviest home Ashes defeat for 41 years. Botham wasn't called upon until the third Test and he could do little to stop the carnage. The series-definer of yore was no more. His last Test against his old enemy would end in an ignominy unworthy of what had gone before. As England went down by an innings and plenty, he broke down with injury, batted at number nine in his last Ashes innings and failed to make it to the crease thereafter. Surely, once again, this was time to step away?

There was another cloud over the summer in the form of the return of the South African rebel tour. Dressing room harmony had been wrecked by a division between those who had decided to forsake their international careers to sign up and those who hadn't. This time, with his career much further down the line, Botham considered it very seriously. He knew he had Viv Richards' support to do what would be best for him financially. He did however value his Test career and legacy and wanted one more crack at writing the wrongs of his record against the West Indies that winter. He insists he took soundings from the new management and that Stewart was hugely pleased when he made himself available for the tour. On this basis Botham rejected South Africa. When, shortly afterwards, the tour party was announced for the Caribbean and he wasn't in it, he considered it an act of treachery. Gooch's stated wish to move in a new direction after the debacle of the summer would last throughout 1990. It was yet another chance to call it a day.

The same autumn there was a cloud gathering over Thatcher too as she suffered what she would perceive as the first act of treachery to rival that inflicted on Botham. Her implacable opposition to a single European currency, despite it not being ruled out by her government's stated policy, meant an argument over conditions for entry into the ERM monetary system which might lead to such integration. Her position was not shared by her long-term chancellor and right-hand man Nigel Lawson, nor her increasingly marginalised former ally Geoffrey Howe. Lawson believed that his remit should allow him the final decision on the matter and he wasn't impressed when belittled by his leader publicly as they each sought to have their view prevail. He would not be the last to feel that way. The old man-management weakness was never more evident and she was then hit by the unexpected and very visible resignation of her chancellor, whose interviews explaining his departure were the first serious challenge to her dictatorial style, Heseltine's previous resignation never being likely to actually topple her. But as with Heseltine, many saw more than a point of principle behind Lawson's action. He was a fiercely intelligent and ambitious man who strongly believed he, more than anyone, had won the 1987 election, and he had been waiting patiently for a long time for his boss to gratefully stand aside. Perhaps it was time to give her a little nudge.

Botham was to appear sporadically in five more Tests across 1991 and 1992, making little impact other than in the irony of his last against the West Indies. In the second innings, the last ball he ever faced from them was hit to the boundary to secure his first win against them in 20 attempts over 11 years. He also came close to finally landing a World Cup, making several impressive contributions before defeat in the final to Imran's Pakistan. But these were oddities and oases in a sea of mediocrity and on 21 June 1992 he left the Test field for the last time just two months after the first general election in 16 years not to feature Thatcher. The real end had, however, come 18 months before in concert with that of his political heroine in the momentous autumn of 1990.

Several of Thatcher's own team, having seen the lead given them by Lawson, sensed their moment as their own divergences from their leader's opinions, horror at her manner and tiring of her hectoring and demeaning of them, followed that of the chancellor. Returning from her latest visit to Europe and a Paris summit where she harangued the top brass of the EU with whom the likes of Geoffrey Howe had been building relationships assiduously, she delivered in the House of Commons a speech of complete intransigence. Listing what she believed were 14 objectives of the Union, and by implication her deputy prime minister, her considered response was to shout 'No! No! No!' For Howe it was the final straw and if Thatcher's speech had been designed to show her strength and conviction, two days later she was going to have to listen in silence to one of far greater significance. At Prime Minister's Questions, Howe rose to give his resignation speech and in front of a stunned House the 'dead sheep' became the spitting cobra. His words not only effectively brought to an end his leader's tenure inviting, as it did obliquely, others to stand against her but it appropriately conflated the worlds of politics and cricket, and confirmed cricket as a reference point for everything British, one final time. Articulating how he felt he had been undermined, he announced, 'I believe that both the chancellor and the governor are cricketing enthusiasts, so I hope that there is no monopoly of cricketing metaphors. It's rather like sending your opening batsmen to the crease only to find, the moment the first balls are bowled, that their bats have been broken before the game by the team captain.' The image of those bats were to be a cricket-loving public's abiding memory of the whole affair. Thatcher still fought, believing she could survive and winning a first ballot in the ensuing leadership contest stiffened that resolve. But as she called in her senior team one by one to gauge their support, the overwhelming response was 'if you stand, I will of course support you, but if you do, I don't think you can win'. It was weak self-preservation and Thatcher, as with Botham before her, saw it as 'treachery with a smile on its face'.

On 22 November 1990 Thatcher tended the resignation that Botham had been forced into ten years before and left Downing Street for the last time. An era of remarkable achievement and unprecedented change was over. Things were not to be the same again, not least for the Conservative Party.

What was the long-term effect of ousting a sitting prime minister with a 100 seat majority and who had never lost an election? Her party chairman of the time, Kenneth Baker was to say in later years that 'there was chaos in the Conservative Party for nearly 20 years'. Now make that 35.

It ties off this narrative neatly that the day after Thatcher left office, England, having once more ignored Botham's keen wish to tour one more time, began their first Ashes series without his presence for 15 years. It was not to be a happy one and it would be perfectly plausible to suggest that in terms of battles against the Australians there also was chaos in the England team for the next 15 years. Andrew Marr's eulogy to Thatcher as a singular personality could have been applied to Botham word for word. 'She had conducted her career with a sense of vivid and immediate self-dramatisation. She had no sense of her own limits.' Such confidence may have inculcated failures to see the signs of trouble ahead and made leaving at the right moment on their own terms as they deserved to impossible, but it had also achieved more in 15 years than would be within the compass of anyone else.

'So ended the most extraordinary and nation-changing premiership in modern British history' concluded Marr. And so ended the most extraordinary, nation-changing career of an English cricketer that anyone can recall.

Epilogue:
What's Left Behind

'If you're going to live, leave a legacy. Make a mark on the world that cannot be erased.'

Maya Angelou

Time For a Change

Assessing legacy is a subjective business. Whether we might have ended up in the same place regardless of the contributions made by certain individuals is an impossible question to answer. But we can consider what facts we know from the past, what we see around us now and offer an opinion, educated or otherwise.

In his conclusion to *Everybody Wants To Rule The World*, Roger Domenghetti suggested: 'there is a lot we can learn if we look at sport closely enough. There is a lot we can learn if we look at the 1980s closely enough. It is vital we don't turn away just because we don't like what we see'. I would add that there is a lot we can learn if we look at 1981 closely enough, not least in the context of 2025's social and political Britain, when many things, some visible and something intangible, changed.

Historians may debate forever the true, lasting impact of 1981 and all that came with it. Andy Beckett takes a balanced view that 'in those years Britain had a burst of energy. Some of its effects are wearing off now … some of them, not always noticed, are still rippling forward'. Beckett claims that it is risky to read too much into a country's direction from its culture, and yet I would argue having explored the story of these years in detail, that at the start of the 80s British culture, including its sport, and how Britons responded to it *was* making a contribution to change. Domenghetti is less equivocal than Beckett: 'We're still living with Thatcher's legacy today, one of the reasons the 1980s still seem so close [is that] it was during that decade that we began to see the outline of what we might call 21st century Britain.'

Developing this further, it is probably easier to draw clear conclusions with regard to what Thatcher left behind than it is with Botham. Sport moves on at a far quicker pace than the country's social and political situation and there is always someone just around the corner waiting to surpass the deeds of those who came before. On the legacy of the Thatcher era, agreement tends to focus on a few broad developments: the move from a manufacturing based economy to one of financial and other services and, more recently, technology; a trend towards greater individualism – some might say self-centredness and greed (although we live in a time of significant philanthropy) – as opposed to the communities of old; a move away (for now) from the consensus politics of the post-war years and from the big state to greater personal freedoms. How much of this was natural, organic evolution? It is true that the core of British industry and manufacturing was in decline well before Thatcher and a belief that she alone was responsible for its demise is a lazy one. A left-wing Labour government in the 70s was no more able to arrest this than the monetarist-based regime which followed it. Indeed in some cases it was the industry itself which played a significant part in its own decay. What Thatcher was the first to do was to see it and tell it as it was. There is little doubt the process of change happened more quickly under her premiership than it might otherwise have done but, though the journey was inevitably rough, it's outcome was also more constructive than it might have been. Bringing facts into the assessment, in terms of the two priorities Thatcher had identified as being critical to Britain's recovery, both were addressed and fundamentally changed. The element she believed was the key to improved economic health and future living standards, the reduction and control of inflation, has to be considered a success. To date we have not returned to the days of 20 per cent and above. Interest rates have continued to fluctuate in tandem with the inevitable ups and downs of the market in a capitalist system and subject to global influences, but the inflation levels of the 70s have become a thing of the past. The releasing of the country and its politics from the control of union bosses was also an achievement which has lasted the test of time. The days of the nation being held to ransom and of such bodies making and breaking governments have passed into history. Hitting both of these targets with a bullseye required an utter conviction and the courage to see the job through in the face of dissension and doubt from all sides. There wasn't another politician in the country in that era it is possible to see doing so.

Finally, Britain's perception abroad in the 1970s was even worse than it was at home with both friends and foes considering its days of influence, even relevance, on the global stage to be at an end. The country was seen as one in the hands of ineffective, grey leaders who had resigned themselves to the management of decline with a consequent loss of pride and patriotism in the British people themselves – one which had previously been seen as a given, regardless of the dire nature of the circumstances of the times. Thatcher undoubtedly turned this on its head – her primary objective and motivation being to win the battle of the soul, change the mindset and mood to one of positivity and hope rather than pessimism and resignation, and to restore the nation to what she considered to be its rightful standing, restoring that national pride in the process. She became a figure of huge influence in the global picture and a 'Boadicea' in defending British interests in both armed conflict and the councils of Brussels. She and Reagan together played the Cold War with enough certainty that, shortly after their tenures ended, the world became a markedly different place. This was change on the largest possible scale.

An assessment of Botham's lasting impact is more nuanced. Before him, English cricket was a fairly run-of-the mill affair. Nobody played the game like him and it had been a long time since an English cricketer, perhaps any English sportsman, had performed in such an un-English and inspirational manner – one that would empty bars and produce immediate spikes in viewing figures. No English cricketer in history had produced the all-round feats he did. What is in little doubt is that he drew more previously disinterested people to the game. How many have stuck with it is impossible to say, but they will be out there. 'There will never be another Botham' would be the conclusion to many a eulogy for his career when it ended. Certainly in terms of his own individual personality this has to be true. Some might argue now that on the pitch English cricket does indeed have one in the form of Ben Stokes. There are plenty of similarities.

As an all-round cricketer, Stokes's batting would probably edge Botham, though it was often felt the latter could have sustained his transitory step up to the level of true world class in that discipline had he given it full focus as happened in 1982 when he averaged close to 50; in bowling, before the hampering problems of Botham's back and Stokes's knee it is no contest, Botham being an opening bowler of significant talents. In almost the same number of innings bowling for England Stokes managed four five-wicket hauls and never took ten in a match; Botham's numbers were 27 and four. Both could catch swallows. Off the pitch, both had their demons and moments which turned some people off them but further drew them to the hearts of most supporters whilst antagonising the authorities – cricketing and otherwise. Both had little time for an establishment they felt at times let them down. It is a matter of fact that Stokes's captaincy has been more successful than Botham's, though it has never prevailed in an Ashes series, and he has proved himself a manager of men and empathic embracer of all characters in a way Botham couldn't. However that captaincy and the philosophy behind it may well owe something to Botham. They share a belief about the way the game should be played and the perspective in which it should be kept. Botham, a generous rather than envious man when he saw a kindred spirit, derived huge pleasure from watching Andrew Flintoff and loves watching Stokes today. But he was playing the Stokes / McCullum way almost 50 years before it was given a title. 'Bazball' might well take Botham's words to Dilley at Headingley in 1981 as its subtitle. 'Let's give it some humpty' was an expression which would fit the brand perfectly. Stokes has the World Cup medal which eluded Botham, winning the final almost on his own but before either he or Shane Warne were there for comparison, Arlott considered Botham 'the greatest matchwinner in Test history' and Pat Murphy wrote in his biography of the man seven years after his career-defining summer, 'No other English cricketer has brought so much unalloyed joy to so many people, many of whom had only the vaguest knowledge of cricket.' Thirty-seven years on, with another nod of acknowledgement to Ben Stokes, that pre-eminence still remains.

Some argue that Botham doesn't deserve to be in the pantheon of the greats because his record against the very best doesn't match the rest of his feats. Set against career averages of 33.5 with the bat and 28.4 with the ball, the equivalent stats versus the West Indies read 21.4 and 35.2. Then again, not many outperformed their career numbers against that lot. His bowling actually stood up reasonably well, with a strike-rate similar to his overall number, although the wickets came at a significantly greater cost. It was the batting which gives the doubters some evidence: only four 50s and no centuries in 38 innings. Stokes did not have a West Indies of the 80s to face, and having missed the Australian sides of Waugh, Warne and McGrath he didn't encounter the other side commonly regarded as one of the strongest in Test history (though Bradman's Australians of 1948 may have a case). Botham rarely played against the strongest Australian sides, though when he did in 1979–80 he proved he could take them on even if the rest of the side couldn't. The respective Ashes records of the two are very similar in batting but worlds apart in bowling. So, you pay your money and you take your choice and bald statistics only tell you so much. What cannot be seriously debated however is the thing that sets Botham apart. Both have won Ashes Tests almost singlehandedly – Stokes's innings in 2019 shading any of Botham's efforts in '81 for its astonishing derring-do and defiance of the odds. But only one has won an Ashes *series* almost by himself – and one which, in the environment and time it was played, was transformational in more than just a cricketing sense. And here is his legacy. Now, in an age when football dwarfs all else, when even a couple of British tennis players found some success, and when fame in many fields has a more manufactured and transient nature, Stokes is rightly seen as a truly great cricketer and one who has both transformed and, to an extent, saved the game. He is not, however a totem of the times. It's therefore hard for people today to appreciate that Botham truly *was*. He helped save not just the game but the country. Roger Domenghetti's words endorse this: 'During the summers of the 1980s, Botham filled a vacuum, showcasing his talents on TV for days at a time when football had barely any live coverage. In the process he transcended both cricket and sport in general to become a cultural icon.'

What Botham did has to be seen in the context of how he did it and when he did it. I hope what has gone before in this book has convinced many that he did indeed play a role in changing the nation and mirroring that objective and motivation of Thatcher's: to win the battle of the soul, change the mindset and mood to one of positivity, pride and hope rather than pessimism, shame and resignation, and to restore the nation to what they considered to be its rightful standing. This is not only his legacy but the thing which ties him, as the biggest British cultural icon of the 80s, to his political twin.

In both cases, in the end and at much the same time, their energy and powers inevitability wore off. But the pride in, and passion for, their country never left them and was there for all to see. Even when his days on the team were over Botham would remind people that he hated to see England lose at anything. Bitter at her treatment or not, the belief in her country and its place in the world was so ingrained in Thatcher that she would share Botham's sentiments when she left centre stage. This is perhaps one of the reasons that they are still so important to a nation which, try as it might to deny it, still has that feeling inherent in it. Even today, every time a new hero is needed on the cricket pitch or a talented all-rounder emerges, and every time the country and the Conservative Party seem rudderless and in need of some radical, committed leadership or some profile on the world stage, the comparisons are made. 'The new Botham', 'The next Thatcher'. It is over 30 years since either plied their trades or had any influence over the country, and still they live on.

Andy McSmith contends that 'more change was crammed into the 1980s, particularly the first half of the decade, than any other decade in the second half of the 20th century'. Out of political chaos, he suggested, Britain arrived at a settlement that lasted, for better or for worse. *Something Changed* is not seeking to convince that this necessarily made everything better, but that McSmith is right that the way we live now follows directly from those turbulent, creative and metamorphic days and that 1981 was undoubtedly the spark. Not all the change was immediate and not all of it unique. But it was when things began to turn. It marked the beginning of the end of the decline in British optimism, in its economy and in English sport since the end of the 60s, and the end of the beginning of Thatcherism.

As noted at the start of this book, change is inevitable and yet sometimes it feels like the wheel has turned full circle. When Labour came to power in 2024, many who voted for them advised that they did so, not through any great support, or even understanding, of what their manifesto might be but because they just felt it was 'time for a change'. Such a motivation for deciding where to put one's cross suggests a vote born of no real conviction or vision and rarely plays out as expected or delivers whatever change the electorate might have had in mind. How many of those who voted on this basis in 2024 now regret it? That will only become apparent next time around. In the 1970s much the same scenario had played out. A left-leaning Labour government replaced a centrist Conservative one which had failed not just the country but the core of its own membership, accused of abandoning key Tory principles in the name of consensus and which had Rishi Sunak in the role of Heath. What happens next in today's Britain will show us how far the comparison runs but it feels eerily familiar. The new government may yet make a success of it. The noises they made from the start, however, sounded suspiciously like those that emanated from Wilson and his cabinet in 1974. Climbing inflation, stagnation of the economy and the paying of the train drivers' union – who of course accepted their inflation-busting pay rise with a 'thank you' in the form of a warning of more trouble to come if they didn't get what they wanted next time – also have a recognisable ring to them. The Conservative Party, licking the wounds of their defeat and fighting internal battles over the direction required to win back their disillusioned vote, have chosen, far from unanimously, a new, female, leader who is undoubtedly a step to the right. Immediately the 'next Thatcher' headlines began. If the public decides the time is right in four years' time for

Kemi Badenoch, they would be unwise to do so in the hope that she can be any such thing. Back in 1979 it truly was 'time for a change' and, for once, that is absolutely what we got.

Ultimately both Thatcher and Botham ended up, and remain, in the words Charles Moore used to portray Thatcher, 'a national archetype around whom argument will forever swirl'. Whichever side of that argument you prefer to be on, they were lodestars of the 80s – guides and often inspirations through the most transformative and volatile of decades. *The Sun's* editorial on Thatcher's departure in November 1990 gave its opinion that 'when the history of the 1980s is written, the name of Margaret Thatcher will be on every page'. Ian Botham won't be far behind her, Keating believing back in 1986 that in amongst all the sermonising hyperbole which gathered around him increasingly as time went by, it was easy to forget that his exploits made him one of the pre-eminent figures in Britain's folklore of the last quarter of a century. What was true 39 years ago remains so today.

Margaret Thatcher's speech at Cheltenham in 1982 was made in the aftermath of the Falklands victory but it was also, obviously, in the aftermath of 1981 and it referenced more than just the battle just won. It contained words which can be used now to summarise both her own legacy and Botham's from that extraordinary year and the journey, in cricket and in politics, in society – its culture and the mindset of the nation – from the self-deprecating days which greeted their arrivals, to the rediscovery of something valuable, though sadly it may no longer be fashionable to say so:

> 'Now that it is all over, things cannot be the same again for we have learned something about ourselves—a lesson which we desperately needed to learn. When we started out, there were the waverers and the fainthearts. The people who thought that Britain could no longer seize the initiative for herself.

> The people who thought we could no longer do the great things which we once did. Those who believed that our decline was irreversible—that we could never again be what we were. There were those who would not admit it—even perhaps some here today—people who would have strenuously denied the suggestion but, in their heart of hearts, they too had their secret fears that it was true: that Britain was no longer the nation that had built an Empire and ruled a quarter of the world. Well they were wrong. The lesson is that this nation still has those sterling qualities which shine through our history … We have ceased to be a nation in retreat … we rejoice that Britain has rekindled that spirit which has fired her for generations past and which today has begun to burn as brightly as before.'

Such a thing mattered deeply to Ian Botham. In 2020 the *Daily Mail* ran a feature on Botham and domesticity: 'On VE Day this year, Ian sat with his family on the lawn of their centuries-old home overlooking a village green in North Yorkshire, with a picnic basket and Dame Vera Lynn belting out *The White Cliffs Of Dover* from the sound system.' And it quoted Botham:

"All the other villagers were on their lawns, too. The picnic baskets had Union Jacks on the lids. It was a great day. I'm very British — very, very British."

He would always be proud that sport, and his sport in particular, had indeed played its significant part in such a national renaissance and had *influenced* this change rather than merely reflecting it.

It is never a bad idea to leave the last words on any subject to John Arlott. As may be apparent by now, I am a fan and a failing student of his. Reflecting on the summer of 1981 he wrote, 'It was moving, historic – above all it lifted cricket in the minds of the ordinary Englishmen to a height many thought it would never attain again.'

As a description of what it did for the country, that is also perfect. 1981 had changed the personal stories of Ian Botham and Margaret Thatcher and the story of the nation, something which would be embellished through the following year. Their achievements were a matter of fact and a matter of pride for many. They may have gone on to divide opinion within British society – loved by some, disparaged by others – and be easy targets for the country's bearers of suspicion against those who succeed, but as Andrew Marr concludes in *A History of Modern Britain*, 'what is not in doubt is that they were the architects of change and true icons of the age'.

The case rests.

Author's Note

'Your matches still light up the sky, and many a tear still lights up in my eye'

Brian May; 'Now I'm Here'

'PLEASE, NOT another "Botham's Ashes" ...' were words that floated regularly through my mind as I set off on the telling of this story. I am fully aware that the 1981 Ashes series and Ian Botham's role within it have been covered extensively over the last 40-plus years, not least because I myself have eagerly consumed most of that content. The objective was, therefore, not a detailed revisiting of the scorecards of that series, but rather an attempt to place it in the context of the world around it – both in the remarkable 12 months that was 1981 and it its prelude and its aftermath. Although 1981 is the central pivot, the narrative became one fascinated by the corollary of its two central characters which expanded the timeframe to take in more than 20 years. From a tale about a year of change in sport and society it became a journey through the careers and fortunes of the two standout political and cultural figures of the age. Context is everything and to assess the seminal nature of 1981, consideration of the years that brought us to it and those that followed, was essential.

In returning to him one last time here, writer Simon Barnes asks whether an (erroneous) notion that sport trivialises all it touches has affected the chroniclers of the ages so deeply as to deny it its proper place in social history. If so, I have attempted here to make my very small contribution to addressing that heresy. Even so, my author inspiration above closed one of his books with the admission that none exist which are perfect and most lack something the author wanted to include but was somehow unable to convey satisfactorily. I am aware of this. He states that, regardless, and like every worthy sportsman, artist, composer and so on, he wears his defeat like a banner of victory. In his case he may protest too much. In mine, I am willing to accept that as my lot.

I perceive sport to be a core component of how we see ourselves as a nation, which says as much about me as an individual as it does about that contention itself. As with any life, I have lived through fascinating times and significant change. I may not have experienced the more serious matter of global conflicts and have consequently been fortunate enough to have lived 58 years free of personal danger, but the world I inhabit now is inevitably utterly different to the one I can first remember. I also had the good fortune to be brought up in the comfort of a loving middle-class family in the leafy suburbs of a predominantly affluent southern city and my life experience was consequently inured to the various hardships bestowed on many by the many tribulations, economic and social, of the two decades covered by this book. Perhaps this is why I can, and frequently do, look back on it through the rose-coloured glasses (actually masquerading as National Health issue with a patch over one eye) I was handed in my youth. I accept at the outset that I don't have direct experience of what befell those impacted by, for example, the privations and emotional scars of the miners' strike of 1984–85, and I have no true concept of what it was to be a black person making a life in inner-city Britain in the early 80s. But the historian and writer cannot draw on every experience first-hand, merely do his or her research as diligently as possible prior to putting down words and opinions.

I am aware that some will have a very different view of particular events and characters that feature in this story and may take issue with my own overall stance, not least in applying, I hope with a degree of balance, a generally positive take on the influence of one Margaret Thatcher on what I consider was a form of recovery within the nation. Hopefully this does not matter or compromise any potential enjoyment in what was written.

In terms of political comment we all have our views but I have tried to avoid making it a personal statement of belief, whilst offering a considered historical analysis which reflects the realities of the time. I accept too the contention of one chronicler of this period that no single narrative can do justice to the complexity of the national experience of the 1980s. But there was an interest in trying.

There are references to England, Britain and the United Kingdom through the course of the book. We live in a diverse and complex set of interconnecting peoples and states and sometimes the strict definition of each of these three 'nations' is hard to apply consistently in all contexts. For example, the England cricket team has been referred to as England although it represents the United Kingdom the majority of the time, and as for the differences between Britain and the UK, rather than going for absolute accuracy I employed what felt like the best fit for the text. United Kingdom can be cumbersome in prose so I therefore seek understanding of any perceived stretching of the boundaries and forgiveness for any offence caused.

The parallel journeys of the nation's political and social fortunes and those of its sporting teams, particularly it's cricketers, were so littered with remarkable synergies that they are the reason the book was written the way it was – with politics and cricket concurrent narratives mirroring each other throughout, whilst the occasional 'as live' recollections and commentaries sought to capture the mood of the times.

Finally, please indulge me. 'The days float through my eyes', wrote David Bowie in his song 'Changes'. This is a book about changes and as someone who turned 14 during the year of 1981 those days still float through my own field of vision. I am possessed of an abiding nostalgia, which is fed in particular by two specific passions – one for sport, evidenced by 50-plus years working in that world and following the teams and individuals to whom I was most attached, and one for the modern political and social history of my country, particularly the era in which I grew up. The Australian cricket writer Gideon Haigh looked back on 1981 and concluded 'there's nothing so fleeting as sporting achievement but nothing so lasting as the recollection of it'. This is what keeps those of us who love sport, and the lift it can give us and those around us, coming back time after time, even when the euphoric moments are few and far between. When they come along in their finest we have them forever. We are all the product of the early years that formed us and the 1970s and early 1980s were the years that formed *me*. Cricket has always played a large part in that. But this book was not driven purely by a desire to rekindle happy personal memories. This was a transformational period in the direction of Britain which affected a change which would dictate its future.

If it is slightly indulgent to have focused on the period of my own upbringing and, additionally so, to intertwine my love of both history and cricket, please forgive me. But it is not contrived. It is a story I believe is worth telling and I have thoroughly enjoyed telling it. To return to one of the quotations at the start of this book, the matches recalled here, those particularly of the 1981 Ashes, still light up the sky for me. And this walk down memory lane has indeed 'brought a delightful bliss'.

Appendix 1

Ian Botham Test Record by Era

	Debut 1977 – Jubilee Test 1980	*Captain 1980 – Lord's, July 1981*	*Headingley 1981 – year end 1986*	*1987–1992*
TESTS	25	12	51	14
Batting				
Innings	35	21	84	21
Runs	1,336	276	3,197	391
Not Outs	2	0	2	2
Average	40.5	13.1	39.0	20.5
100s	6	0	8	0
50s	3	1	17	1
Bowling				
Innings	46	17	88	17
Wickets	139	35	192	17
Runs	2,575	1,158	6,167	978
Average	18.5	33.1	32.1	57.5
Wickets per Test	5.6	2.9	3.8	1.2

Appendix 2

Ian Botham Test Record vs Australia and West Indies

	Tests vs Australia	*Tests vs West Indies*
TESTS	36	20
Wins	16	1
Defeats	11	13
Batting		
Innings	59	38
Runs	1,673	792
Not Outs	2	1
Average	29.4	21.4
100s	4	0
50s	6	4
Bowling		
Innings	66	27
Wickets	148	61
Runs	4,093	2,146
Average	27.6	35.2
Wickets per Test	4.1	3

References

With thanks to The British Library for facilitating access to national newspapers and cricketing periodicals which allowed for extensive research but are too numerous to list individually here.

Moore, Charles, *Margaret Thatcher: The Authorized Biography vol 1-3* (Penguin 2013)

McSmith, Andy, *No Such Thing As Society* (Constable 2010)

Vivien, Richard, *Thatcher's Britain* (Simon & Schuster 2009)

Clarke, Peter, *Hope and Glory* (Penguin 2004)

Sandbrook, Dominic, *Seasons In The Sun: The Battle For Britain 1974-1979* (Penguin 2013)

Sandbrook, Dominic, *Who Dares Wins: Britain 1979-1982* (Penguin Random House 2019)

Turner, Alwyn W., *Rejoice! Rejoice!: Britain In The 1980s* (Aurum Press 2013)

Turner, Alwyn W., *Crisis? What Crisis?: Britain In The 1970s* (Aurum Press 2008)

Beckett, Andy, *When The Lights Went Out* (Faber & Faber 2009)

Garnett, Mark, *From Anger To Apathy* (Vintage 2008)

Marr, Andrew, *A History Of Modern Britain* (Macmillan 2007)

Stewart, Graham, *Bang! A History of Britain In The 1980s* (Atlantic 2013)

Jones, Dylan, *The Eighties* (Preface 2013)

Domeneghetti, Roger, *Everybody Wants To Rule The World: Britain, Sport And The 1980s* (Yellow Jersey 2023)

Thatcher, Margaret, *The Downing Street Years* (Harper Collins 1993)

Wolff, Michael, *The Man Who Owns The News: Inside The Secret World Of Rupert Murdoch* (Vintage 2018)

Coleman, Ray, *Lennon: The Definitive Biography* (Pan Macmillan 1984)

Beckett, Andy, *Promised You A Miracle: UK 80-82* (Random House 2015)

Barnes, Simon, *The Meaning Of Sport* (Short Books 2006)

Smith, Ed, *What Sport Tells Us About Life* (Penguin Viking 2008)

ed. Green, Benny, *Wisden Anthology 1963-1982* (Queen Anne Press 1983)

ed. various, *Wisden Cricketers' Almanack 1975-1994* (John Wisden)

ed. Frindall, Bill, *The Wisden Book Of Test Cricket vol 1 & 2* (John Wisden)

Martin-Jenkins, Christopher, *The Jubilee Tests And The Packer Revolution* (Macdonald & Jane's 1977)

Martin-Jenkins, Christopher, *Twenty Years On: Cricket's Years Of Change 1963-1983* (Harper Collins 1984)

ed. Smith, Peter, *England Versus West Indies 1981* (Pelham Books 1981)

Sydenham, Richard, *Almost Invincible: West Indies In England 1984* (Pitch 1984)

Melford, Michael, *Botham Rekindles The Ashes* (The Daily Telegraph 1981)

Brearley, Mike and Doust, Dudley, *The Ashes Retained* (Hodder & Stoughton 1979)

Botham, Ian, *The Incredible Tests* (Book Club Associates 1982)

Engel, Matthew, *Ashes '85* (Pelham Books 1985)

ed. Rayvern Allen, David, *Arlott On Cricket* (Book Club Associates 1989)

ed. Rayvern Allen, David, *Another Word From Arlott* (Book Club Associates 1985)

Keating, Frank, *High Wide And Handsome* (Willow Books 1986)

Mosey, Don, *Botham* (Methuen 1986)

Botham, Ian, *Head On: The Autobiography* (Ebury Press 2007)
Murphy, Patrick, *Botham: A Biography* (J.M. Dent & Sons 1988)
Gower, David, with Johnson, Martin, *Gower: The Autobiography* (Harper Collins 1992)
Wilde, Simon, *England: The Biography* (Simon and Schuster 2018)
Maconie, Stuart, *The People's Songs: The Story Of Modern Britain In 50 Records* (Ebury Press 2013)
Thatcher, Margaret, *The Downing Street Years* (Harper Collins 1993)
compiled. Levison, Brian, *All In A Day's Cricket* (Constable 2012)
Hayley, Trevor, *The Psychology of Weather* (Routledge 2018)

Fire In Babylon (E&G Productions)
Botham's Ashes (BBC)
From The Ashes (Spectrum)
Margaret Thatcher: The Iron Lady (a2b Media)
Andrew Marr: A History Of Modern Britain (BBC)